NEOLIBERALISM AND EVERYDAY LIFE

Neoliberalism and Everyday Life

Edited by
SUSAN BRAEDLEY AND MEG LUXTON

McGill-Queen's University Press
Montreal & Kingston • London • Ithaca

© McGill-Queen's University Press 2010
ISBN 978-0-7735-3673-9 (cloth)
ISBN 978-0-7735-3692-0 (paper)

Legal deposit second quarter 2010
Bibliothèque nationale du Québec

Printed in Canada on acid-free paper that is 100% ancient forest free
(100% post-consumer recycled), processed chlorine free

This book has been published with the help of a grant from the
Canadian Federation for the Humanities and Social Sciences, through
the Aid to Scholarly Publications Programme, using funds provided
by the Social Sciences and Humanities Research Council of Canada.

McGill-Queen's University Press acknowledges the support of the
Canada Council for the Arts for our publishing program. We also
acknowledge the financial support of the Government of Canada
through the Book Publishing Industry Development Program (BPIDP)
for our publishing activities.

Library and Archives Canada Cataloguing in Publication

Neoliberalism and everyday life / edited by Susan Braedley and Meg
Luxton.

Includes bibliographical references and index.
ISBN 978-0-7735-3673-9 (bnd)
ISBN 978-0-7735-3692-0 (pbk)

1. Neoliberalism – Social aspects. 2. Feminist theory. 3. Political
sociology. I. Braedley, Susan, 1955–   II. Luxton, Meg

JC574.N455 2010   320.51   C2009-906391-3

This book was typeset by Interscript in 10.5/13 Sabon.

Contents

Acknowledgments

This project started with conversations among feminist scholars in the Greater Toronto Area region of Ontario about the theoretical and empirical challenges posed by the way neoliberalism has penetrated so many aspects of everyday life. To provide a forum for such discussions, the Centre for Feminist Research (CFR) at York University organized and supported a conference in September 2007: "Penetrating Neoliberalism: Changing Relations of Gender, Race, Ability, and Class," to investigate the ways in which more than twenty years of neoliberal policies have reconfigured the patterns of daily life. The conference brought together several leading scholars and graduate students doing innovative work on this topic and generated considerable excitement. This book presents the papers from the conference as well as several new papers written for this collection.

We want to thank each of the contributors. We learned a great deal from their work and they were all a pleasure to work with. Philip Cercone and Brenda Prince of McGill-Queen's University Press and two anonymous reviews provided invaluable support. Gillian Faullener compiled the index in a timely and intelligent way. We also acknowledge and appreciate the very welcome financial support from the Aid to Scholarly Publications Program, supported by the Social Sciences and Humanities Research Council (SSHRC). The Centre for Feminist Research (CFR)provides the intellectual community and practical support so essential for feminist scholarship and housed this project from start to finish. We thank Linda Peake, CFR Director 2007–08, Hussan the co-ordinator, and our colleagues at CFR for making this project possible. Finally, we want to acknowledge the pleasure and delight we have had from working and learning together.

Contributors

PAT ARMSTRONG, PhD, is a professor of Sociology and Women's Studies at York University. She is co-author or editor of various books on health care, including *A Place to Call Home: Long-Term Care in Canada* (2009); *They Deserve Better: The Long-Term Care Experience in Canada and Scandinavia* (2009); *Critical to Care: The Invisible Women in Health Services* (2008); *About Canada: Health Care* (2008); *Caring For/Caring About* (2004); *Exposing Privatization: Women and Health Reform in Canada* (2001); and many others. She has also published on a wide variety of issues related to women's work and to social policy. She chairs a working group on health reform that crosses the Centres of Excellence for Women's Health and holds a Canadian Health Services Research Foundation/Canadian Institute for Health Research chair in Health Services and Nursing Research and serves on the board of both the Canadian Health Coalition and the Canadian Centre for Policy Alternatives.

KATE BEZANSON, PhD, is an associate professor of Sociology at Brock University. She also teaches in the graduate program in Social Justice and Equity Studies. She is author of *Gender, the State and Social Reproduction: Household Insecurity in Ontario in the Late 1990s* (2006) and co-editor, with Meg Luxton, of *Social Reproduction: Feminist Political Economy Challenges Neo-Liberalism* (2006). She writes on issues related to gender, welfare states, public policy, and work-life balance. Her most recent research explores the relationship between social class, breastfeeding, and social policy in Canada.

SUSAN BRAEDLEY, MSW, PhD, is a postdoctoral fellow with the CHSRF/CIHR Chair in Health Services and Nursing Research at the York Institute for Health Research at York University. She is the author of "Someone to Watch Over You: Gender, Class and Social Reproduction," published in *Social Reproduction: Feminist Political Economy Challenges Neo-Liberalism* (2006), edited by Kate Bezanson and Meg Luxton, and a number of articles and book chapters that address the intersections of gender, racialization, and class in paid and unpaid work, health and public policy. Her current research on masculinized care provision explores the gendered implications of policy and practice convergences between the domains of public care and public safety.

RAEWYN CONNELL, PhD, holds a University Chair at the University of Sydney and is a senior editor of the journal *Theory and Society*. Raewyn's research and theorizing on the social construction of masculinities has had a major influence on the creation of this international research field: her book *Masculinities* (1995) is the most widely cited research publication in this field. She is the author or co-author of twenty-one scholarly books and more than a hundred and thirty papers in social science journals and edited volumes. Her books and papers have been translated into thirteen languages. Her most recent book, *Southern Theory* (2007), discusses theorists unfamiliar in the European canon of social science and explores the possibility of a genuinely global social science.

KARINE COTE-BOUCHER, MA, is a doctoral candidate in Sociology at York University. Her work on the intersection between inequalities and border regulation includes "The Diffuse Border: Intelligence-Sharing, Control and Confinement along Canada's Smart Border," published in 2008 by *Surveillance and Society*, as well as "Interdictions à la mobilité, identités autorisées et échange de renseignements: La frontière intelligente vue du Canada," forthcoming in *Mobilité(s) sous surveillance. Perspectives croisées EU/Canada*. Her current research investigates the convergence of concerns for border securitization and transnational economic flows in immigration/border security policies and practices.

MEG LUXTON, PhD, is professor of Women's Studies at York University, Toronto. Theoretically and politically she is a socialist feminist whose research interests include the history and politics of the women's movement and the political economy of women's work, especially the interrelations of economics, paid and unpaid work, and state policies. Her publications include More *Than a Labour of Love: Three Generations of Women's Work in the Home* (1980), (with June Corman) *Getting By in Hard Times: Gendered Labour at Home and on the Job* (2001), and (as editor, with Kate Bezanson) *Social Reproduction: Feminist Political Economy Challenges Neo-Liberalism* (2006).

PAULA C. PINTO, PhD in Sociology from York University, has concluded a dissertation on women with disabilities, motherhood, and the policy context in Portugal. Previously, her career in the non-profit sector in Portugal and the European Union addressed issues of poverty, disability, and policy. Pinto's recent publications include "Re-Constituting Care: A Rights-Based Approach to Disability, Motherhood and the Dilemmas of Care," published in the Journal of the Association for Research on Mothering, and a book chapter in Armstrong and Deadman's edited volume Women's Health entitled "Women, Disability and the Right to Health." In addition to her dissertation work, since 2005 she has been involved as research associate in the international project Disability Rights Promotion International (DRPI), funded by the Sweden International Development Agency (SIDA) and Social Sciences and Humanities Research Council of Canada (SSHRC) and codirected by Marcia Rioux and Bengt Lindqvist, the former United Nations Special Rapporteur on Disability.

MARK THOMAS, PhD, is an assistant professor of Sociology at York University. He is the author of *Regulating Flexibility: The Political Economy of Employment Standards* (2009), published by McGill-Queen's University Press, and co-editor, with N. Pupo, of *Interrogating the New Economy: Restructuring Work in the 21ˢᵗ Century*, forthcoming from the University of Toronto Press. His current research examines emerging approaches to the promotion of transnational labour rights, with a focus on the role of transnational labour rights networks.

NEOLIBERALISM AND EVERYDAY LIFE

Competing Philosophies

Neoliberalism and Challenges
of Everyday Life

SUSAN BRAEDLEY AND MEG LUXTON

In the politics of the early twenty-first century, neoliberalism remains a prominent political philosophy for many governments and
international institutions around the world. It is a political force
with which most people in the world must reckon. This relationship
between a political philosophy and people's lives is at the heart of
this book, which we conceived as an exploration of neoliberal policy and its effects on everyday life.

Neoliberal political philosophy aims to unleash and "liberate"
the processes of capital accumulation. Thirty years of neoliberal
policy development in much of the world (see Connell, chapter 2
in this volume) did not rein in capitalism's inherent crisis tendencies. These tendencies were starkly revealed by the economic problems that exploded globally in the fall of 2008. The studies in this
book, completed well before that time, powerfully reveal the logics in economic and social policies that were involved in generat-
ing what the APEC leaders called, "a global financial crisis" (Asia-
Pacific Economic Co-operation [APEC] 2008). At the outset of this
crisis, Warren Buffett, American financial guru and president of
Berkshire-Hathaway, stated:

Unfortunately, the economy is a little like a bathtub. You can't
have cold water in the front and hot water in the back. And what
was happening on Wall Street was going to immerse that bathtub

very, very quickly in terms of business. Look, right now business
is having trouble throughout the economy. But a collapse of the
kind of institutions that were threatened last week, and their in-
ability to fund, would have caused industry and retail and everything else to grind to something close to a halt. It was, and still is,
a very, very dangerous situation.(CNBC 2008)

Buffett's assessment showed insight. In the first half of 2008, the
overextension of credit in the US housing market became obvious as
housing prices declined to levels below their mortgage value. As both
homeowners and lenders went into a spiralling debt crisis, the centrality of financial markets to existing global capital arrangements
became crystal clear. A fifty percent drop in the value of global stock
markets and the demise of all five of Wall Street's investment banks
shook the foundations of the global economy (McNally 2009).
Credit markets tightened dramatically and many businesses failed or
were forced to cut back. Remittances from migrant workers, which
provide substantial portions of GDP in developing countries, plum-
meted (Robert and Servant 2009,16). Unemployment increased in
many countries. In the four months prior to March 2009, 2.6 million
jobs were lost in the United States (Bureau of Labour Statistics 2009)
and 295,000 were lost in Canada (Statistics Canada 2009).

Struggling to understand what was happening, economists and
politicians debated the extent to which the problems were the fault
of bad ethics and greedy people. As then US Democratic presiden-
tial candidate Barack Obama said: "This crisis did not happen
solely by some accident of history or normal turn of the business
cycle ... We arrived at this point due to an era of profound irrespon-
sibility that stretched from corporate board rooms to the halls of
power in Washington, DC ... The result has been a devastating loss
of trust and confidence in our economy, our financial markets and
our government. Now, the very fact that this crisis is largely of our
own making means that it's not beyond our ability to solve"
(Obama 2009). Most stressed that the financial system needed
stabilization, greater regulation, and monitoring. For example, in
November 2008, Portuguese prime minister Sócrates and Brazilian
president Lula da Silva met for a summit to work on "'more just
regulation of globalisation' that would renew international security
and confidence through supervisory institutions and new rules for
financial markets" (Portugal News Online 2008). Virtually absent

from debate and discussions was any critique of the basic principles of neoliberalism or the capitalist system in which neoliberals had such faith.[1] The leaders of APEC (Asia-Pacific Economic Cooperation) expressed the prevailing view: "We reiterate our firm belief that free market principles, and open trade and investment regimes, will continue to drive global growth, employment and poverty reduction" (APEC 2008). Governments responded to this situation in different ways. In the United States and Great Britain – the hothouses of neoliberal policy development since the late 1970s – governments countered with emergency-style interventions, making major financial investments to stabilize markets. Their strategies included nationalizing some British banks and taking over some American lending institutions. Germany, in contrast, rejected government-driven economic stimulus measures. In Italy, where the government was struggling with massive public debt, Prime Minister Sylvio Berlusconi indicated that the Italian people could look after themselves rather than rely on the state (Reguly 2008).

Some of these interventions, such as nationalizing banks, may appear to be at odds with neoliberal policy. Yet there is consistency. These policies were designed to stabilize markets and protect capital interests. The United States government's seven-trillion-dollar bailout package went to the financial sector (McKenna 2008), not to people who had lost their jobs and homes. Although the entire financial system – which is at the core of neoliberal thinking as well as capitalist economies – appeared to be in tatters, and although government responses took a number of trajectories, including more Keynesian directions, the logic of neoliberalism continued to haunt public policies around the globe as governments wrestled with the problems of economic stability. More importantly, neoliberalism continued to be the driving force behind international economic business practices. When meeting in November 2008, the Group of Twenty (G20) – governments who represent sixty-five percent of the world's population – issued a declaration reaffirming their principles: "Our work will be guided by a shared belief that market principles, open trade and investment regimes, and effectively regulated financial markets foster the dynamisms, innovation, and entrepreneurship that are essential for economic growth, employment and poverty reduction ... These principles ... have lifted millions out of poverty and have significantly raised the standard of living" (Group of Twenty 2008).

These "market principles," as expressed in neoliberal policy measures, and their effects on everyday life are explored by the authors of this volume in a number of ways. First, the authors each explore the ways in which neoliberalism has come to penetrate social relations. Like other critical scholars who study neoliberal policy, they examine the ways in which neoliberal perspectives have affected the distribution of social goods and "bads" in ways that reinscribe, intensify, and alter social hierarchies of gender, race and class. But these authors go further. Using specific case studies, they trace the ways in which neoliberal thought has penetrated people, including the ways we understand who we are and how we live our lives.

Second, these authors explore neoliberalism by interrogating the thinking of those who are in positions of power. Their analyses attend to Connell's reminder in chapter 2 that decisions taken by states and international organizations are made by people. These people and the "choices" they make in policy decisions have context, just as all our decisions have context. These choices are both shaped and bounded by history, location and culture, as are all our choices and our life circumstances.

Third, these authors explore neoliberalism by critically examining the paradoxes and tensions that not only emerge from neoliberal policies, as the economic turmoil that emerged in 2008 showed, but seem to characterize them. Within the disparate domains of employment standards, border security, public sector health care provision, childcare, disability policy, and informal caregiving, contradiction and perverse policy outcomes provide clues to uncovering the ways in which neoliberal values, goals, and outcomes diverge and shift. The similarities and contrasts portrayed among examples drawn from the Canadian context (Armstrong, Bezanson, Braedley, Côté-Boucher, Luxton, Thomas) and those from the broader international context (Connell, Pinto)help to build a more complete portrait of the permutations and variations, as well as the continuities, among neoliberal policy development in different contexts.

In penetrating neoliberalism in all these ways, the authors share a critical viewpoint. In often very different ways, and deploying a variety of theoretical and methodological lenses, the authors argue that neoliberalism is not advancing social justice and equality, but is, instead, reinscribing, intensifying, and creating injustices and inequality. The authors' values for social justice and equality are implicit and, occasionally, explicit in their work. Values are at the centre of these analyses, and values of the authors frequently conflict with those that appear to drive neoliberal thought. But social values are not free-floating moral decisions. In the case of neoliberalism and in the cases of the critical perspectives provided in this volume, social values both inform and are predicated on our analyses. Therefore, a brief discussion of the central values inherent in neoliberal thought as it emerged in the mid-twentieth century, and the context and analysis that gave rise to these values, is pertinent here.

NEOLIBERAL THOUGHT: VALUES IN CONTEXT

Some have argued that neoliberalism is morally vacuous, but there is little basis for that claim. Neoliberalism, as elaborated by Hayek and Friedman, and as practised in various forms, has been constructed upon the principles of classical eighteenth- and nineteenth-century liberalism, as developed by De Toqueville, Hume, Locke, and Smith. Liberalism's primary value is individual human freedom from coercion and servitude, which neoliberals believe is inevitably tied to capitalism as a system that promotes expansions of wealth and allows people the freedom to pursue wealth, and therefore to pursue their desires.

Political theorists have asked and addressed the question, "What is neo about neoliberalism?" With its strong roots in classical liberal thought, is neoliberalism really neo at all, or is it just liberalism reprised? Some analysts (Brodie 2007) have pointed to the penetrating aspects of neoliberal policies, which have brought the logic of the market to bear on seemingly every facet of social life, rather than just economic life, as the difference between classical liberalism and neoliberalism. This is certainly a hallmark of neoliberal governance. In addition, the development of neoliberal thought as a counterposition to certain historical developments of the early twentieth century is key, in our view, to an understanding of neoliberal ideas. Neoliberal thought developed as a defence of capitalism and in fierce opposition to socialism. Its proponents believed that socialism had mutated into fascism in Germany and Stalinism in the Soviet Union and argued that socialism promised a false and morally repellent freedom from economic necessity at the cost of limited life choices and an inevitable descent into totalitarianism. (Hayek 1944, 25–6).

Neoliberals have values rooted in this history, and they are strong ones. The opposition to anything that smacks of collectivism or economic redistribution is intense. They believe that individual freedom of choice is maximized through competition. Competition is perceived as a naturally occurring social good, and the best method of social organization, enacted primarily through the mechanisms of price. Indeed, neoliberal thought holds that governments can act to control certain aspects of production (such as methods of production and the use of certain substances) as long as the controls are compatible with competition: they must affect all businesses that compete with one another equally. This logic requires only that the value of the social good achieved is greater than the social costs imposed and insists that policy not restrict competition in any way. Indeed, neoliberal faith in competition makes the maintenance of competitiveness, as the mainspring of capitalism and human freedom, the chief business of government. According to one of its prophets, even democracy as an ideal can be overstated, and only under capitalism is democracy possible (ibid., 69–70).

The centrality of competition, as a neoliberal value necessary to the pursuit of freedom, is difficult to overstate. Competition under a capitalist system is seen to be the least restrictive way of distributing inequality, which is perceived as inevitable. "There will always exist inequalities which will appear unjust to those who suffer them, disappointments which will appear unmerited, and strokes of misfortune which those hit have not deserved ... Inequality is undoubtedly more easily borne, and affects the dignity of the person much less, if it is determined by impersonal forces than when it is due to design" (ibid., 106). Human rights and equality under neoliberalism are the rights and equality to compete, but not the rights to start from the same starting line, with the same equipment, or at the sound of the same gun. It certainly does not include rights to certain outcomes, such as a certain degree of health or education. Competition, because it is portrayed as an "impersonal force" rather than structured by people's decisions, is somehow perceived as fairer than direct government action in the distribution of social goods and risks.

The value of freedom, as conceptualized in relation to competition, is knit together with the belief in a naturally occurring market "order" and a fear of socialism. In 1976, in a comment on the welfare state, Hayek wrote: "The increasing tendency to rely on administrative coercion and discrimination where the rules of law might, perhaps more slowly, achieve the same object, and to resort to state controls or to the creation of monopolistic institutions where the judicious use of financial inducements might evoke spontaneous efforts, is still a powerful legacy of the socialist period which is likely to influence policy for a long time to come" (Hayek 1976, viii).

The notion that financial incentives somehow generate "spontaneous efforts"– which infers that financial incentives and disincentives are *not* a mode of direct control whereas other kinds of governmental instruments are coercive and discriminatory – is key to neoliberal thinking, and although beyond the scope of this introduction, warrants analysis.[2] Hayek shows us that values are not restricted to what we love and want. They are also elicited by what we fear and reject. Neoliberal's values have developed through an adamant rejection of socialism, which they perceive as the precursor of totalitarianism.

This rejection of socialism in neoliberal thought surfaces as an almost complete rejection of collectivism, which, for neoliberals, is defined as planning "against" competition, and therefore against freedom. Neoliberalism, on the other hand, is perceived as planning "for" competition (Hayek 1944, 42). Yet, in the classical version of neoliberalism, if we can call it that, proposed by Hayek, there is a small place for collectivism. Hayek allows that in a wealthy society, such as England at the time he was writing in the early 1940s, a certain degree of economic security from extreme poverty, "sufficient to preserve health and the capacity to work" (ibid.,120) can be provided without undermining freedom. Similarly, a state social insurance program to protect people against illness and accident and programs to deal with disasters is similarly approved, as long as the program does not undermine or reduce competition. Further, Hayek allows for some government interference to modulate economic fluctuation, especially in terms of monetary policy and, to some degree, public works projects.

However, Hayek and the neoliberals who have followed are adamantly against any kind of policy, program, or scheme that interferes with the price/value mechanism of wages. The freedom to choose work and to be paid what that work is found to be worth in competition with others is the basis for all freedom, according to neoliberal analyses. For neoliberals, the social value of work is measured by the wage and restricted only by the wealth available in a given society. They base this assertion on the conviction that if market mechanisms are allowed to operate, what is generally considered work of higher value to society is paid accordingly. Thus the mechanisms of supply and demand are believed to operate in concert with perceptions of value in the labour market. This assertion, which has been demonstrated as false by Ricardo and Marx as well as more recently and convincingly by Picchio (1992), underpins neoliberal belief in competition as the wellspring of freedom.

Individual freedom, in its liberal and neoliberal conceptions, is located in the ability to pursue whatever work one wishes, and to sell one's own labour power for a wage that reflects the social value of one's work to the highest bidder in a free labour market. But what if this analysis contains an incorrect understanding of the wage relation? What if neoliberalism is built upon a hill of incorrect assumptions that has enriched the few at the expense of the many? What if the freedom promised by neoliberalism does not include, for many people, the freedom to be healthy, have meaningful work, have time for leisure, participate in the broader community, or adequately support their children, no matter what they chose? What if poverty is not simply the consequence of making poor choices?

Thirty years after its introduction, neoliberal governments and international institutions were being called to account globally for the growing gap between rich and poor. After the 2008 crisis, the call became much more insistent. Were these dramatic events the result of neoliberal governance, irresponsible business practices, or inevitable crisis tendencies in capitalism or some combination of all three? Neoliberals must answer a number of very tough questions.

CRITICAL THOUGHT: VALUES AND CONTEXT

Representing various critical perspectives on neoliberalism, the authors in this volume write from a different historical moment and different geographic locations than did the founders of neoliberalism. These authors have written while living through neoliberal times. Variously described by these authors as an ideology (Luxton), a project (Connell, Thomas), a logic of governance (Braedley), and a rationality (Côté-Boucher), neoliberalism is no longer an alternative to hegemonic political thought as it was in the mid-twentieth century. It *is* hegemonic political thought. However, it is not the only political thought. These contributions provide not only a critique of neoliberal governance and commitments but they challenge these commitments on normative terms. Just as the founders of neoliberalism countered the development of socialism, these authors counter neoliberalism.

The methods deployed here to critique neoliberalism are unlike those employed by Hayek, Friedman, and other neoliberal theorists, who based their critiques of socialism on macro analyses and broad philosophical and economic arguments. Their methods did not explore "actually existing" socialism's various forms, effects, and permutations, or socialism's effects on differently located people, their motivations and social relations more generally. This absence may be one of neoliberal philosophy's major weaknesses, in that it fails to assess the effects of changing economic and political circumstances in terms of peoples' lived experience. Further, neoliberalism's reliance on the "free self-actualizing individual" as the subject of its philosophy limits its capacity to analyze the social relations within which individuals are born, raised, and live out their lives.

Neoliberal governments have tended to replicate these weaknesses. They have preferred to assess only those policy outcomes that are easily captured in quantitative terms, such as dollars and cents spent or saved, and have neglected to measure the actual success of policy measures in peoples' lives. For example, Armstrong, Braedley, and Luxton (this volume) describe how changes in public health care provision, designed to control costs in the health care portfolio, transfer costs and work to other sectors (including unpaid caregivers) in ways that often increase total real expenditures. Quantitative and financial measures do have a place – and an important one – in policy assessment, and macro analyses are valid. But, we suggest that it is also important to trace the links between people's direct experiences and living conditions, governance and the global economic, social, and political context, in order to adequately understand market and policy regimes. An integrated analysis that takes account of the relations among and between markets, states, families, and communities more effectively captures the full range of regime effects.

Critical analysts start with their concerns for peoples' social participation, well-being, and life chances. While neoliberals stress that individuals make choices, we see that individuals make choices under conditions that are not of their own making. These conditions are frequently shaped by decisions made by the small number of people who hold the reins of power.

In the eyes of many critical analysts, political and economic regimes must be assessed based on the results of their regulation as experienced by those who are regulated (Sen 1993). Neoliberal theory and practice aim to free human beings from excessive state control in order to pursue their own lives through market competition. Most critical positions are not so much concerned with the quantity of governance in people's lives but its quality. What does a particular mode of regulation achieve in terms of shaping people's living conditions, including opportunities for leisure, education, meaningful employment, and social participation? Who benefits and who is left out? Who loses?

These questions allow us to take note of systemic discrimination. For example, an individual prevented from competing in the labour market because of her sex, skin colour, accent, or age may be forced to take employment for which she is "overqualified" or accept lower wages than her peers; she may be prevented from contributing to society to her fullest capacities. When the health care system is in crisis because there are not enough doctors while immigrants qualified as doctors drive taxis or scrub hospital floors, the labour market is not working efficiently and that most precious resource, "human capital," is wasted. The waste of human capacities and the injustice of systemic discrimination also tend to produce social unrest, manifested as alienation or protest. The resulting crime rates and social unrest are costly and threaten social stability (Honneth 1996). At the same time, the existence of systemic discrimination poses a constant challenge to the idea that inequality is "determined by impersonal forces" (Hayek 1944,106), inviting contestations. The authors in this book note that the key arenas of contestation tend to be those relating to gender, race, and class inequalities. Indeed, neoliberalism was developed in part to counter the equality demands of feminist, anti-racist, and anti-imperialist activists, as well as the socialist demands to end class exploitation. In undertaking integrated critical analyses, neoliberalism's unarticulated premises and their consequences become clear. These premises have produced benefits and losses on the basis of gender, race, and class.

Gender Regimes

One of the central distinguishing features of neoliberalism is the gender regime that anchors it. In liberalism and twentieth-century welfare states, it was taken for granted that the self-actualizing individual was a male income earner with a wife who provided unwaged care to a family. Generations of women activists have struggled against the male privilege that this philosophy reflected and endorsed (Rowbotham 1972). Formal discrimination has largely been eliminated in the countries that gave birth to liberalism, significantly freeing women from patriarchal domination (Segal 1999). Globally, women have made significant gains in putting their issues on the political agenda and have developed analyses and ways of organizing to advance their concerns (Mohanty 2003). Unlike liberalism, which rested upon the legal subordination of women, neoliberalism assumes that the individual can be male or female (and perhaps trans). The result is a new gender regime; one that is a consequence of an economy in which men and women are income earners (Fraser 1997). Neither sex nor gender is considered an inevitable block to competing in the market or to aspiring to political power (although the sexism and misogyny revealed in reactions to Hilary Clinton's 2008 unsuccessful campaign for the chance to be the first woman president of the United States indicate that both remain powerful destructive cultural forces in the United States and in global society (Enright 2008)). However, neoliberalism's core theoretical premise and its practice, in conjunction with the prevailing sex/gender divisions of labour in most countries, has resulted in a global decline in women's positions and material well-being (United Nations 1995; Bashevkin 1998).

At least three different, though related, dynamics have played an important part in how the neoliberal project has developed globally in ways that are particularly negative for women. The first is that women's work is so poorly remunerated that women are the majority of poor people in the world and changing economic practices have increased their levels of poverty.[3] In many parts of the world, women are subsistence farmers whose labour is vital for their households' survival. Yet neoliberalism's promotion of international trade agreements and agribusiness investments, to encourage agricultural production for global markets as means of capitalist expansion, undermines these women's efforts and therefore, the survival of their households and communities (Lucas 2007). At the same time, in most labour markets, women have historically been restricted to a limited range of jobs, most of which have been low paid and relatively insecure. Women have typically earned less than their male counterparts and have had access to fewer benefits (International Labour Organization 2004). As governments reduced the controls on private corporations, labour relations and working conditions deteriorated for all workers, leaving the most vulnerable even worse off than previously.

A second dynamic is that women have typically been responsible for most of the unpaid work of social reproduction that gets done in private households. This work has no recognition or value according to the National System of Accounts, the economic system that regulates the world economy (Waring 1988). Reflecting these views, neoliberalism not only assumes that wages reflect the value of the work performed, it also takes for granted the appearance in the labour market of the worker. For the economy to function, employers rely on their workers to show up each day ready and relatively willing to work. For this to happen, workers must be appropriately socialized, educated, and healthy, and new generations of workers must be available to replace those who retire and die. But as Marx pointed out, the capitalist employer can safely leave to workers' own self-interest the day-to-day and generational labour necessary to reproduce workers and their capacity to work. Neoliberals would agree.

However, feminists have shown that social reproduction – the processes necessary to enable workers to show up on the job – involves socially necessary labour, most of which is performed as unpaid domestic labour (Luxton 1980; Seccombe 1992; Luxton and Corman 2001; Bakker and Gill 2003). In most households, women do the bulk of the work required to transform household income (usually subsistence produce or wages) into goods and services that sustain household members. The mundane activities of procuring food and water, cooking, cleaning, and the labours of love involved in making a home and caring for the people who live there, keep people alive on a day-to-day basis and reproduce the population generationally. In so doing, they also ensure the daily and generational reproduction of the labour force (Seccombe 1993). The demands of family responsibilities mean that many women work for long periods of time for no pay, sometimes making them dependent on either their partners or state support and always undermining their capacities to compete equally in the labour market with those unencumbered by family responsibilities or those benefiting from familial support.

Responding to both the demands of the women's movement to address these inequalities and to the need for more workers in the labour force, welfare states introduced a range of social policies throughout the twentieth century. By assuming a (limited) collective responsibility for social reproduction, these policies improved conditions for many women. Policies such as paid maternity and parental leaves, paid family time leaves and childcare services were designed to support women who were juggling paid employment and domestic responsibilities. Some were a partial recognition of the social value of women's unpaid work at home (for example, baby bonuses and pensions for housewives) while a few policies encouraged men's involvement in domestic labour (Baker 2006). Neoliberalism's commitments to reducing state expenditures and supporting private enterprise undermined many of these initiatives. The result was that pressures on individuals and families to juggle the competing demands of paid and unpaid work intensified with a disproportionately negative impact on women (Cohen and Pulkingham 2009; Luxton this volume, chapter 8).

A third dynamic is the vested interest that elite men have in maintaining the sex/gender divisions of labour that sustain their privileges and contribute to their ability to extract wealth. As Connell points out in chapter 2, the leading proponents of neoliberalism are men. They have built into its theory and implementation a specific commitment to maintaining their male privilege. At its core is their insistence that individuals and their families are responsible for social reproduction, and their refusal to acknowledge collective responsibility for the well-being of the population. The more a society accepts collective responsibility for social reproduction, raising taxes to pay for education, health care, childcare, disability support, old age security and a range of other social services, the less wealth is available for private ownership. The more good quality social services are universally available, the less chance there is for private enterprise to make profits in those areas. So neoliberalism allows space for women who are willing or able to live like men, who present themselves as men do and who are able to compete as men do. Margaret Thatcher was a woman who, as British prime minister, was an outstanding promoter of neoliberalism. What neoliberalism resists is any effort to reduce the financial resources available to capital investment, including redistribution of the work of social reproduction to the state or employers.

These three dynamics operate to imbue neoliberalism with sexism. But they reflect only some of neoliberalism's unarticulated premises. Benefits and losses are sustained on the basis of race and class, in ways that further develop these hierarchies of systemic discriminations.

Ethnicity, Racialization, and Racism

As Connell points out in chapter 2, neoliberalism arises out of, and advances, earlier imperialist and colonial domination by the capitalist powers primarily of Europe and later North America over much of the world's population. Central to that project is a racism that insists that white Western European and North American Christians are inherently superior to peoples in the rest of the world. That racism rests on a process of racialization in which subordinated groups of people are designated as "other," based on arbitrary distinctions such as physical appearance, particularly skin colour, and other historically specific traits. The intertwined projects of imperialism, colonialism, and capitalist accumulation and expansion depended on racism and racialization. One the one hand, racist claims of physical, cultural, and religious superiority legitimated, and continue to legitimate, the actions of European/ North American genocide and conquest as European powers seized, and continue to seize, the land, resources and peoples of the places they conquered. On the other hand, as Franz Fanon (1970) portrayed most eloquently, racism also permeated the consciousness and being of subordinated peoples, reducing their capacities to resist or fight back.

The national liberation struggles of the twentieth century largely overthrew direct imperialist rule in most countries. Like feminists, anti-imperialist and anti-racist activists have made important gains, in many places winning formal legal equality for colonized and racialized people. And just as neoliberal theory does not consider sex or gender to be an inevitable block to competing in the market or to aspiring to political power, it does not consider ethnic or racial identity or religious affiliation to be impediments to full competitive participation in the market place. Indeed, in 2008, although the ten most wealthy people were all men, at least half of them were not "white" (Kroll 2008). How these men negotiate the whiteness of hegemonic elite and business cultures remains a question.

However, the fundamental systemic inequalities created by four hundred years of imperial and colonial economic and political domination were exacerbated by neoliberalism. Again, three key dynamics contribute to these conditions. First, maintaining racist regimes privileges elite cultures and peoples. The standard of living for even the white working class of Canada, the United States, and many European countries is enabled by the exploitation of racialized workers throughout the world. Further, processes of racialization permeate everything from the marketized notions of beauty ("white") to ascriptions of athletic prowess ("black") to ideas of predispositions to high tech skills ("Asian") (Gilroy 2000). By assuming that people's opportunities are related solely to their choices, the effects of racialization in producing privilege and discrimination are effaced.

The second dynamic is the ways in which global labour markets and divisions of labour relegate racialized people into work that tends to be more dangerous, more precarious, and poorly paid (see Thomas, chapter 4 in this volume). Further, these workers are not accorded rights to pursue any jobs available. Instead of a free labour market, neoliberal policies exclude workers from many countries, while at the same time ensuring that labour market needs are met with the lowest waged workers possible. For example, temporary migration programs bring foreign workers to countries with particular labour needs without offering them the labour protections or benefits accorded to permanent residents. In Canada, racialized migrant women perform significant care and domestic work for privileged families under exploitative and oppressive conditions. This circumstance not only frees privileged women from this necessary work but undercuts their commitment to struggles for more equitable arrangements (Glenn 1992; Arat-Kroc 2006). At the same time, neoliberal labour markets select workers because they are racialized and therefore exploitable, reinforcing racialization and exploitation in the process (Ong 2007).

The third dynamic is that neoliberalism has increasingly freed up capital to invest wherever labour is cheapest. As a result, jobs flow from place to place as investors locate in places where workers with few alternatives accept work with minimal pay and appalling conditions. This involves exploitation of people already oppressed by imperialism, colonization, and patriarchy. The history of systemic discrimination challenges neoliberalism's claim that free markets regulate wages to the levels appropriate for the work.

Class and the Wage Relation

Neoliberalism is a philosophy that fundamentally deepens class divisions. At its core, it unfetters capital to pursue wealth accumulation through market competition, all in the name of the pursuit of freedom. Neoliberalism celebrates profits as the just rewards for successful competition and honours private wealth as an inalienable right of the individual owner. Its challengers note that the initial accumulations of wealth by individuals and ruling elites of western Europe and later by European settlers in North America were based on imperial conquest, theft, and slaughter (Wolf 1982) and that current accumulations of wealth are based on the exploitation of workers. From this perspective, the idea of a free market is an oxymoron. Those workers, having no other means to make a living, are forced to take whatever jobs they can get and they are paid less than the worth of what their labour actually produces. More importantly, the economic power wielded by those who control resources gives them undue power both to exercise control in their own special interests and to protect their interests and practices from public accountability (Albo 2008).

Neoliberals have argued that wages are the socially ascribed value of work as determined in a competitive market. In examining the actual circumstances involved in the wage relation, critical analysts have argued that this understanding of wages is just plain wrong. As this understanding underpins neoliberal concepts of freedom, neoliberalism's critics have pointed out that this notion of freedom is similarly incorrect. Picchio (1992) provides one of the most effective arguments undermining the neoliberal theory of wages. Returning to earlier classical economic understandings of the wage, she shows that wage rates are shaped by the historically specific costs of daily and generationally reproducing workers.

The neoliberal position that wages are determined by supply and demand and limited only by the amount of wealth in a given society has led neoliberals to deduce that low wages and poverty can only be addressed by measures that do not impinge on wealth creation and accumulation. Therefore, the state can only act in a temporary, limited way to alleviate poverty in exceptional circumstances. Poverty is best attacked through supporting capital accumulation in order to increase standards of living. This perspective has been most nakedly implemented in the "trickle-down" economic policy of the

Reagan administration of the United States during the 1980s but continues to be central to neoliberal policy around the world (Connell, chapter 2 in this volume).

Critical analyses show that wages should be understood as the costs of the social reproduction of labour, based upon the variable living standards of particular classes (Picchio 1992, Seccombe 1993). This understanding makes sense of how the price of labour could remain low, even in a tight labour market, while capital accumulation remained quite unbounded. This situation has occurred in many parts of the world, where real wages have declined, while capital accumulation has proceeded to amass unprecedented wealth (Bakker and Gill 2003). This is the deepening of class divisions.

Understanding wages as the costs of social reproduction of labour means that the supply and demand for labour are linked to social structures, relations, and processes involved in family formation, care work, education, health, and other arenas of social reproduction. These processes are also gendered, raced, and classed. Therefore, from this perspective, state policy makers have much more room to act to ensure the well-being of the population as a whole.[4] Further, states have an obligation to address the systemic discrimination that produces inequality.

This view undoes the dream of a society in which individuals freely make choices in the direction of their desires and take up responsibility for themselves and the outcomes of their choices and chances. The very concept of social reproduction reminds us that people do not live as "individuals" but instead, live in relation to other people. They have babies, raise children, and look after those who cannot care for themselves. They migrate to obtain better living standards, sometimes separating themselves from family members and communities in order to do so. All people have times throughout their life when they depend upon others to look after their basic needs, sometimes because they are incapable of caring for themselves and sometimes because they are able to transfer this work to others. The labour market cannot exist without these processes; indeed these processes constitute the labour market.

This view reveals the ways in which inherited wealth and class, and racialized and gendered privilege act as affirmative action programs. Some individuals may be able to live out the neoliberal ideal. The majority of the world cannot. Neoliberalism can, at least in theory, survive as a political and economic project while acknowledging and reducing sex/gender and racialized discrimination. However, as a project designed to secure the position of capitalist elites, it depends on the exploitation of a global working-class population and has a deeply vested interest in containing any efforts on the part of working-class people to reduce class inequalities. Central to that effort is a commitment to deny the existence of social classes and the possibility of collective action, and to demonize as vehemently as possible the ideals and promises of socialism (Aronowitz 2003; McNally 2005).

CHALLENGING NEOLIBERALISM

Connell has argued that "to understand the world we live in, perhaps our most important task is to understand neoliberalism and trace its consequences" (chapter 2 in this volume). The contributors to this volume offer insights into how neoliberalism works in local situations as their contribution to global efforts to resist and defeat it. Their careful studies are predicated on the understanding that neoliberal policies and practices are not uniform, and their effects are dependent on context. They also acknowledge that neoliberalism's founders were correct in their view that an influential political philosophy can permeate political parties that, on the surface of things, appear to represent a totally different political perspective. Thus mid-twentieth-century "liberal" governments instituted socialist-style policies in some cases, such as socialized medicine in Canada, while in the early twenty-first century, "labour" and "social democratic" governments in many countries have instituted neoliberal policies.[5] After the financial crisis of 2008 became evident, "neoliberal" governments initiated policies that appeared to move in a more Keynesian direction, such as nationalizing banks.

The analyses in this volume suggest that we are all implicated in shaping politics, through day-to-day activities and practices of living. While they point to neoliberalism's most visible traces in government policy, they also draw attention to the practices that support and enable neoliberalism. Côté-Boucher's travellers, Luxton's caregiving family members, neighbours, and friends, Braedley's firefighters, Bezanson's parents, Thomas's migrant and low-wage workers, and Pinto's mothers are individually and collectively engaged in dealing with neoliberalism's consequences. Some, like Luxton's caregivers and some of Bezanson's parents, take in neoliberalism's message, find it bitter, but, unable to imagine that other fare might be theirs, they swallow. Others, like Braedley's firefighters, have a more ambivalent relationship. They both accept and challenge neoliberal restructuring. Some, like Pinto's mothers, continually confront and challenge. These studies suggest that such practices, while sometimes bolstering neoliberalism, could also bring it to its knees. In the context of the global crisis of capitalism that emerged in 2008, these analyses offer, as Armstrong indicates, an argument for an alternative politics that ensures that public money is employed for the public good through democratic processes of governance. With others around the globe, these contributors offer puzzle pieces that help to build a more complete picture of neoliberalism in the early twenty-first century. In doing so, they contribute to a renewed politics that offers an alternative to capitalism.

NOTES

1 McNally's (2009) explicitly socialist critique points out that most examinations of neoliberalism fail to "highlight the systematic failings of capitalism and the need for a radical alternative."
2 See Rose, *Powers of Freedom: Reframing Political Thought* and Ong, *Neoliberalism as Exception* for some analyses that take up neoliberal strategies for governing at a distance.
3 One billion people live in absolute poverty, which means they live on less than one dollar US per day. Seventy percent of them are women. (http://www.un-instraw.org/en/index.php?option=content&task=view&id=894 &Itemid= viewed 8 August 2008)
4 Please refer to Picchio (1992) for a detailed presentation of this argument.
5 For example, the Blair Labour government in England instituted a full range of neoliberal policies under its "Third Way" regime.

Understanding Neoliberalism

RAEWYN CONNELL

Neoliberalism has settled in. The mad heroic phase of the 1980s and 1990s – when Margaret Thatcher in Britain, the kleptocrats in Russia, the technocrats at the International Monetary Fund (IMF), and all their friends and relations fell upon the public sectors of the world and shredded them – is over. The ensuing struggle between left and right neoliberalism – Bill Clinton versus George W. Bush – has been overtaken by global recession. But even as the recession fluctuates, neoliberalism remains the common sense of our era. The debate is about how to get the market working better, not about what should replace the market. Neoliberalism is now the ground from which labour parties, conservative parties, and liberal parties all proceed.

To understand the world we live in now, perhaps our most important task is to understand the market agenda and trace its consequences. For social scientists this is something like the task of understanding fascism in the 1920s and 1930s, which gave rise to Antonio Gramsci's theory of hegemony, Wilhelm Reich's "mass psychology" of fascism, the Frankfurt School's studies of authoritarianism, and Franz Neumann's extraordinary *Behemoth* (1944). We don't have so powerful an analysis of neoliberalism yet. This chapter suggests some directions by which we might arrive at it.

THE CONCEPT

"Neoliberalism" broadly means the agenda of economic and social transformation under the sign of the free market that has come to dominate global politics in the last quarter-century. It also means the institutional arrangements to implement this project that have been installed, step by step, in every society under neoliberal control.

Neoliberalism is most familiar to us as a set of economic policies and their supporting ideas and images. The "free market" is the central image, and the deregulating measures that "freed up" markets, especially capital markets, were among the earliest and most important neoliberal policies. Controls over banking, currency exchange, and capital movement were all loosened or abolished, as one country after another came under neoliberal control from the late 1970s on.

Gradually a fast-moving global arena of financial transactions, consisting of a network of national and international markets in shares, bonds, financial derivatives, and currency, was brought into being. This arena is the core of what corporate executives and financial journalists (as opposed to cultural analysts) mean by "globalization." Through its linkages, the US "subprime mortgage" lending crisis (of which more later) was turned into a global slump.

To unbind existing markets was not enough. Neoliberalism is a missionary faith: it seeks to make existing markets wider and to create new markets where they did not exist before. This impulse has taken neoliberalism far beyond the strategy of deregulation, into a strategy of the endless commodification of services. Needs formerly met by public agencies on the principle of citizen rights, or through personal relationships in communities and families, are now to be met by companies selling services in a market. Whether commodification can become truly universal, or whether there are some social relationships that necessarily resist it, is debatable. We can certainly say that neoliberals have had astonishing success in creating markets for things whose commodification was once almost unimaginable: drinking water, body parts, and social welfare among them.

The most dramatic form of commodification is the privatization of public assets and institutions. In Australia, for instance, over the last twenty years, the national airline, national telecommunications system, national bank, and even the national wheat marketing system have all been turned into companies and sold off by governments. Even in the current recession, privatization is proceeding apace; the Labor party government of New South Wales, the state where I live, is currently moving to privatize some of its prisons. Privatization of public institutions is only the beginning. Neoliberals have been quite inventive in finding ways to commodify services.

Under neoliberal regimes, more and more spheres of social life are colonized by the market. Education, for instance, is commodified by subsidizing private schools to compete with public schools, forcing all schools to compete with each other for students and funds, forcing public universities to charge their students fees, and then forcing the fees up – a history that has been carefully analyzed by Simon Marginson in his *Markets in Education* (1997).

Welfare is commodified by putting the provision of services up for tender and forcing the public agencies that formerly provided them to compete with non-governmental organizations (NGOs), churches, and companies to win the tenders. Many other functions formerly performed as part of the routine division of labour within public sector organizations – such as the printing of official documents – are now "outsourced." They are turned into a commodity, a service bought from companies, while the in-house groups that used to do them are either abolished or turned into small companies to compete for the same contracts.

Housing was already mostly private. Neoliberal governments set about privatizing the public housing schemes that had provided an alternative, however limited, for working-class families; they certainly prevented the growth of new public housing agendas. The result, especially in the United States, was that working-class families that wanted decent housing had no alternative but to resort to high-interest mortgage loans based on shaky security. These were called by the capitalist finance world "subprime mortgages," and their growth eventually provided the trigger for the current recession.

Health services, like education, were partly private even in the postwar welfare states. Under neoliberalism the private, and specifically the corporate, part of the health sector is allowed to grow, fuelled by demand from the affluent, subsidies from government, and the profit logic of insurance firms – which themselves have been transformed from mutuals (a kind of cooperative) into profit-seeking corporations. Under this regime private care becomes normative, and public health care becomes the residual system, the second-best choice for those who can't afford the real thing.

The expansion of market relations allows, at least in principle, a lower level of public spending, and therefore a lower level of taxation. Alongside deregulation, cutting taxes was one of the first neoliberal policies to be put into practice. The passing of Proposition 13 in California in 1978, a referendum to cap property taxes that eventually caused a massive funding crisis in public education, is one of the historic markers of the neoliberal turn. Tax cutting remained, through the presidencies of both George and George W. Bush, a banner cause for neoliberals, and in early 2009 the government of President Barack Obama explored ways to make tax cuts part of its economic stimulus package. In cold fact, the overall tax "take" of the member governments of the Organisation for Economic Co-operation and Development (OECD) has fallen very little. But there has certainly been a shift from direct to indirect taxation, and a marked reduction of taxes on wealth and on high incomes – in other words, a shift to a more regressive tax system.

Neoliberal policies attempted to halt the growth of public sector expenditure, which translated into a real squeeze on public services. This gradual process in the economies of the metropole was packaged in a more drastic form in the International Monetary Fund's "Structural Adjustment Programs" of the 1980s and 1990s. These schemes were imposed by the IMF, World Bank, and transnational finance capital on countries of the global periphery that had got into trouble servicing loans. The price of "rescheduling" loan repayments was the enforcement of neoliberal economic policies, making inflation control and debt servicing the top priorities. The result, in cases like Argentina, was a collapse of economic security and public services.

The commodification of services and the privatization of public sector agencies demand institutional and cultural change. The profit-seeking corporation is promoted as the admired model for the public sector, and for much of civil society too. This affects not only central administration but ground-level urban government, as David McDonald and Laila Smith show in their 2004 study of the relentless privatization of services in post-apartheid Cape Town, South Africa.

With the "new public management," schemes of organization and control are imported from business to public institutions. The discussions in the 1970s about representative bureaucracy and industrial democracy came to a sudden halt, displaced by a new ethos of managerialism. One clear measure of the new scale of managerial power is that managers' salaries and bonuses have risen, in both the private and the public sector, to unprecedented levels. This eventually became a scandal, in the context of the recession, when US finance firms aided by public subsidies continued to pay huge private packages to their apparently inept controllers.

At the same time, an emphasis on labour market "flexibility" produces a growing workforce of part-time, casual, and contract labour at the bottom of an organization. Applying market discipline to the labour force has meant sustaining pressure against unions – from Augusto Pinochet's dismantling of Chilean unions after 1973, to Ronald Reagan's defeat of American air traffic controllers in 1981 and Margaret Thatcher's defeat of British miners in 1984, to John Howard's "WorkChoices" upheaval of Australian industrial relations in 2005. There has been an irregular but insistent rollback of the hard-won entitlements and security of the organized working class.

Thus neoliberalism succeeded in changing the connection between politics and the economy in much of the world. In the metropole, it partially dismantled the Keynesian welfare state, the system of regulated capitalism and state-supplied services that was dominant in the period from 1945 to 1980. In the global periphery, neoliberalism thoroughly dismantled the hybrid social-democratic developmentalist state, with its strategy of import-replacement industrialization, and broke up the social alliances that supported it.

LEGITIMATION AND CULTURAL CHANGE

Such measures are not necessarily popular. There has never been widespread support for cutting social services; polls frequently show greater popular support for maintaining public services than for tax cuts. The startling wealth of the neoliberal new rich attracts popular resentment, which neoliberal journalists call "envy." Popular opposition to the individualizing anti-union "WorkChoices" legislation was a factor in the electoral defeat of the conservative Australian government in 2007.

Neoliberalism, it is clear, has faced a considerable problem of legitimacy. To some extent neoliberals have succeeded in evading this problem. It is common for neoliberals first to gain a position of power (by appointment, by election, or by financial pressure in the case of the IMF) and then to introduce neoliberal policies by a kind of organizational coup. This is called "shock therapy" in neoliberal rhetoric. The Fujimori regime in Peru provides one spectacular example. A political newcomer, Alberto Fujimori won election in 1990 by arguing against neoliberal policies. Before taking office, he was taken in hand by international bankers and promptly turned neoliberal. Another example is the enormous scale of privatization

in the disintegrating Soviet bloc in the early 1990s, the main beneficiaries of which were former Communist officials. Susan Stokes's
book on neoliberal strategy in Latin America is aptly subtitled *Neoliberalism by Surprise* (2001).

But the agenda also needs legitimacy in the long run. Neoliberal
politicians, think-tanks, mass media, and businessmen have therefore made a sustained attempt to promote competition, choice, entrepreneurship, and individualism. These are the intended themes of a
new dominant social ideology that justifies economic inequalities
on the grounds that "winners" should be amply rewarded. José
Luis Alvarez (1996) has shown the sustained international promotion of "entrepreneurship" as an ideology.

In positive imagery, "the market" is represented as a desirable form
of social organization, both fair and efficient. Participation in markets becomes a social good. Negative imagery is also important. Neoliberals continue to attack public enterprise, bureaucrats, red tape,
regulatory agencies, unions, cooperatives, welfare dependency, and
other hangovers from what they present as a discredited past. Jesook
Song (2006), in a study of the effacement of homeless women under
Korean neoliberalism, puts it well by remarking that neoliberalism is
a "sociocultural logic," a social ethos operating through a wide variety of social agents, as well as an economic program.

In this, a deep transformation of culture is at work. Universal commodification is reflexive; it applies to principles and statements as
well as to goods and services. In a neoliberal world, there is no criterion of truth and virtue except what works in the market. The fact
that people buy a product is sufficient proof of its value; the fact that
people vote for a politician is a sufficient test of his or her claims.

So the world is increasingly filled with advertising. The neoliberal city is a jungle of neon signs and billboards, and the country-
side too is increasingly branded. This becomes self-parodying, as
with the proposal to rescue the space shuttle program by sending
up artificial moons on which corporate advertisements could be
projected. But it is not a fantasy that every medium of communication, from the Internet to the hospital wall, is increasingly in-
vaded by commercial marketing messages. Even public schools
are "sponsored" by corporations – the brilliant idea of applying
this across the education system was contributed by the new
Labor government in Australia to the "Ideas Summit" it convened in April 2008.

Politics thus becomes an arena of advertising rather than popular mobilization. The visible part of politics now hardly even pretends to be a public deliberation but is an overt competition between the most effective slogans. The major decisions are made, as Néstor García Canclini (2001) observes for Mexico, in forums that are inaccessible to the public. Mechanisms of representation and collective will-formation are dismantled or allowed to wither. In May 2008 at its state conference in New South Wales, the Labor party voted overwhelmingly against the privatization of electricity; the next morning, the Labor premier of the state announced that privatization would go ahead.

It is difficult to tell how deeply these processes have affected popular consciousness. Claims of a complete cultural shift are certainly exaggerated. Mass opinion polls generally find a majority against privatization, not for it. The election and re-election of social-democratic, radical, or populist governments in recent years in Venezuela, Bolivia, Argentina, and Brazil suggests that there is popular disillusion with neoliberalism in Latin America. In the months following the electricity privatization debacle in New South Wales, a revolt from within the party and the unions resulted in the overthrow of the premier concerned.

Yet conservative neoliberals have been elected leaders of two of the three major European economies, Angela Merkel in Germany and Nicolas Sarkozy in France. The third, Britain, has an entrenched neoliberal regime that will not change much when the government of Prime Minister Gordon Brown is defeated.

As people are obliged to live and work in a marketized world, they find pleasures and possibilities there – which may turn into positive belief in the new system. The appeal to personal "freedom" in the market agenda seems to have a considerable impact on young people, judging from its intensive use in advertising (which we can presume is based on market research). Trade union membership has fallen in many countries, drastically weakening an important cultural base for resistance. Neoliberalism is at least holding its ground in the "culture wars" against radicalism and may still be advancing. Under the regime of George W. Bush and Dick Cheney in the United States, the power of the state was fairly consistently used to promote corporate interests and neoliberal regimes (now called "democracy") throughout the rest of the world. It is not likely that the Obama regime will act very differently in international arenas.

THE SOURCES

Where does neoliberalism come from? The usual account, elaborated in David Harvey's *Brief History of Neoliberalism* (2005) and Barry Smart's "sociological critique" of neoliberalism (2003), is that it was formulated in Europe and the United States by Cold War critics of the welfare state, principally Friedrich Hayek and Milton Friedman. Their ideas were developed into a post-Keynesian economic orthodoxy at the University of Chicago and other centres and applied to the state by "public choice" theorists. The policy implications were worked out by a growing network of right-wing think-tanks, such as the American Enterprise Institute. In the 1970s these ideas penetrated the Conservative party in Britain and the Republican party in the United States and were implemented in the 1980s by the Thatcher and Reagan governments. In the 1990s the Democratic administration in the United States caved in to the neoliberal agenda (most strikingly in then president Bill Clinton's "welfare reform"), and the full package was adopted by regimes such as the Conservative government that came to power in Ontario in 1995, and the Coalition government that came to power in Australia in 1996.

The forces that drove this development are generally understood through a systems model of capitalism. To David Harvey, for instance, neoliberalism is the rationalization of a late stage of capitalism, to be explained through the present need for "flexible accumulation." In Antonio Negri's prophetic 1974 analysis of the "enterprise-state," neoliberalism results from the politicization of the fundamental economic law of value (assumed in classic Marxism to be a matter of iron economic determination), in a system de-structured by working-class struggle.

In the most thoroughly elaborated of these accounts, Gérard Duménil and Dominique Lévy's *Capital Resurgent* (2004), neoliberalism is finance capital's response to a crisis of profitability that emerged in the world's dominant economies in the late 1960s and 1970s. Neoliberalism solved the crisis by clamping down on inflation and the growth of social entitlements; loading negative effects – unemployment, low wage growth, debt crisis in the periphery – onto vulnerable groups; and creating new mechanisms that channelled the benefits of innovation and growth towards share owners and financiers.

The difficulty with all these accounts is the same as the difficulty in most contemporary theories of globalization (Connell 2007). They treat the process as something that arises internally within the global metropole and is then exported to the rest of the world. But the first country to go neoliberal was not in the metropole; it was in Latin America. This was Chile under the Pinochet dictatorship, which replaced the previous agenda of democratization and import-substituting industrialization with a "comparative advantage" strategy based on opening up to the world capitalist economy – a process traced in great detail in Eduardo Silva's *State and Capital in Chile* (1996).

In the 1980s, as neoliberalism advanced in the United States and Europe, it was advancing faster still in the international arena, with the neoliberal takeover of the IMF and World Bank and the creation of the Structural Adjustment Program regime. In the 1990s the great triumph of neoliberalism was in the former Soviet bloc, where a whole new tier of peripheral capitalist economies was created. In the 1980s it was fear about global competitiveness that turned Labor governments in New Zealand and Australia into leaders of neoliberal "reform."

The result of a global shift towards "open markets" and the search for comparative advantage was a huge growth in the volume of international trade. Australian coal headed for Japan and India, Chilean fruit headed for the United States, African flowers headed for Europe, Japanese electronics and Chinese T-shirts headed for everywhere. All of these goods, however, have to be physically transported, the small expensive items by air, the rest in container ships. The consequence is a huge increase in fuel oil consumption: sea transport now rivals the world's airlines as a source of greenhouse gas emissions.

Thus, when looked at on a world scale, neoliberalism seems to have its central dynamic not within the metropole but in the *relation* between metropole and periphery. Samir Amin (1997) is closer to the mark in seeing neoliberalism as the current ideology of capital in dealing with global crisis. The story makes better sense if we understand modern capitalism from the start as having grown up within an imperial economy, and involving an empirical weaving-together of different forms of accumulation – rather than as a tightly adjusted economic machine to which global power was a kind of appendix, an afterthought.

Neoliberalism, then, can be understood as the latest mutation in a sprawling worldwide regime that forged a new settlement between military, political, and business elites in the global periphery and their counterparts in the metropole.

NEOLIBERAL COALITIONS

Neoliberalism cultivates an air of inevitability, but the effectiveness of neoliberal policies is disputed. The raging debates on this question in Latin America alone have been traced by Menno Vellinga (2002). In some countries neoliberal packages have conspicuously failed to gain a local grip.

We need to think, therefore, of the specific configurations of social forces that have allowed neoliberal agendas to gain traction. Vedi Hadiz and Richard Robison (2003) explain the failure of neoliberalism to take hold in Indonesia by the lack of a coalition of social forces capable of installing a neoliberal agenda against popular resistance. The sociologist Michael Pusey (2003), one of the best empirical researchers on neoliberalism, sees the driving force behind the success of neoliberalism in Australia as an alliance of corporate executives, business lobbies, professional politicians, economic-rationalist bureaucrats, and New Right media.

Wherever neoliberalism has gained a grip, corporate managers and large owners of capital form a core element in neoliberal coalitions, always linking neoliberalism to the interests of capital and sometimes taking direct political power. Billionaires in power have included Silvio Berlusconi in Italy and Thaksin Shinawatra in Thailand. The 2009 Labor prime minister of Australia, Kevin Rudd, is not a multi-millionaire corporate entrepreneur in his own right but he is married to one. In the United States, the electoral process gives so much advantage to mass media campaigns that it has been effectively impossible to gain national power without significant funding from business elites. The Obama campaign, however, seems to have had markedly more decentralized fundraising, and this is the strongest indication yet that there has been a shift in the structure of United States politics.

Neoliberalism certainly involves the agency of the rich, but there is something more specific at play. Duménil and Lévy are right in seeing finance capital, rather than industrial or commercial capital, as central to neoliberalism. Global flows of finance have outstripped global flows of goods or people. The neoliberal vision of universal commodification has a deep connection with the extreme abstraction of ownership in contemporary capital markets. One of the most important institutional changes made by neoliberal regimes has been to make central banks "independent" of elected governments. This removes key mechanisms of financial policy – interest rates and money supply

– from any shred of popular control. The central banks are not answerable to an electorate, but they are answerable to finance capital – their boards consist largely of top-level corporate executives. Taxation remains in the hands of elected governments; but under neoliberal regimes this is not a mechanism of social reform.

In other respects, neoliberal coalitions vary. Key roles in installing neoliberal agendas have been played by a military dictatorship in Chile, international bankers in Mexico, Labor party leaderships in New Zealand and Australia, the former *nomenklatura* in Russia, the leadership of the African National Congress resistance movement in South Africa, and the Communist party apparatus in China. Neoliberalism, when seen on a world scale, is not socially homogeneous. As Kevin Hewison and Garry Rodan argue for Southeast Asia (2004), the course of events is regionally specific.

The neoliberal agenda cannot be regarded as a single doctrine or program, or even as a single package of policies. It is, rather, a sprawling family of related policies that get proposed and implemented in different sequences and in a variety of institutional forms. They are linked, however, even if imperfectly, through the mechanisms of global markets, the circulation of neoliberal doctrine (via the economics profession, business media, and institutions such as the OECD and World Bank), and the mutual support of neoliberal states, under the hegemony of the United States.

To emphasize this variability within neoliberalism is not to doubt the importance of economic strategies within this policy family. Nor is it to doubt the active role of the capitalist interest groups identified by Georgina Murray in her study of the Australian and New Zealand ruling classes (2006). Their role is evident in neoliberal think-tanks, which are always supported by corporate money.

THE NEOLIBERAL PROJECT

To see neoliberalism only as a mask for the reassertion of ruling-class interests would miss both the complexity and the dynamism of neoliberal reality. As the Chilean case shows, neoliberalism from the start destroyed old configurations of capital and created new ones, and did so very rapidly. Neoliberalism accompanies and promotes a profound shift in the corporate world from the long-term planning characteristic of an earlier stage of industrial capitalism to a systemic focus on short-term profitability. As shown by the "mark-to-market" accounting in the famous case of Enron Corporation, described by Loren Fox in *Enron: The Rise and Fall* (2003), this even extends to a practice of incorporating profits in the accounts long before they materialize.

To understand neoliberalism we need a different methodological framework from that of systems theory (whether of the left or right). Neoliberalism is best seen as a large-scale historical *project* for the transformation of social structures and practices along market lines. Such a project has to recruit supporters if it is to be successful. It is undertaken by multiple social actors, not just one. It follows complex trajectories through social milieux, which it seeks to change in fine detail. Rudy Dutschke famously advised the New Left of the 1960s to set out on a "Long March through the institutions." Neoliberalism has taken his advice.

This historical project is regionally uneven in its timing and focus. It faces resistance, and its success, though extraordinary, has been incomplete. In the last ten years a notable regional resistance has emerged in Latin America, and there is a constant bubbling of resistance in other parts of the world. It is important to be conscious of the limitations as well as the power of the neoliberal project.

The neoliberal project has multiple sources of energy. The drive for wealth and power of new echelons in business is the most obvious. Less obvious, though in fact mixed with that story, is a gender dynamic.

In the existing feminist literature on the subject, neoliberalism first emerges in the state or economy and then impinges on women, the family, or gender relations. This pictures gender as a realm of effects and women's agency as "resistance." Nancy Naples and Manisha Desai's *Women's Activism and Globalization* (2002) is an admirable collection of studies of this kind. But the analysis, while valuable, does not go far enough. In an interesting paper on urban restructuring, the geographer Phil Hubbard remarks that "neoliberal policies are also about asserting the primacy of virile masculinity" (2004, 682).

He is right: there is an embedded masculinity politics in the neoliberal project. With a few exceptions, neoliberal leadership is composed of men. Its treasured figure, "the entrepreneur," is culturally coded masculine. Its assault on the welfare state redistributes income from women to men and imposes more unpaid work on women as carers for the young, the old, and the sick. Its attack on "political correctness" and its rollback of affirmative action specifically undermine the gains of feminism. In such ways, neoliberalism from the 1980s on offered middle-class men an indirect but effective solution to the delegitimation of patriarchy and the threat of real gender equality. (Note that this concerns neoliberalism in general, not just the specific agenda of anti-feminist, anti-gay neoconservatism.)

Gender change under neoliberal regimes has not been consistently negative. The market theory treats men and women as formally equal market agents, and neoliberal organizations usually have a policy of "equal opportunity." But where women do find benefits, claiming them involves changes in the social construction of femininity. At the very top, this means entering the worlds of management or politics on the terms set by men.

Just as neoliberal theory treats men and women as equivalent market agents, it makes no discrimination on the basis of race. Indeed to the leadership of some oppressed or marginalized groups, neoliberalism can appear to offer a path forward. In north Queensland, for instance, the aboriginal leader Noel Pearson has reproduced neoliberal attacks on welfare dependency and bought in to the idea of aboriginal entrepreneurship. In the United States there are black generals in the military as well as a scattering of female judges and heads of government departments thanks to the equal opportunity policies that neoliberalism selected out from the previous generation's equity initiatives as being compatible with market logic. The widespread acceptance of equal opportunity ideas was manifest in the 2008 election, where the two leading candidates on the Democratic side and the vice-presidential candidate on the Republican side were not rich white men.

The fraught search by neoliberal governments for popular support, however, has made them prone to use racial "wedge" politics, with immigration and refugee issues offering many juicy opportunities – still. Nicolas Sarkozy made effective use of this tested strategy in gaining election as president of France. Neoliberalism's general opposition to public sector expansion and affirmative action measures has created a hostile environment for social justice initiatives of all kinds beyond equal opportunity rules. Neoliberalism is generally hostile to the land rights agenda of indigenous politics, which is of course incompatible with commodification. (That crunch issue is the limit of Noel Pearson's neoliberalism – he remains a land rights advocate.)

That is to say, measures that would give weight and scale to the incremental social changes achieved through equal opportunity measures are largely blocked by neoliberal politics. In that way, neoliberalism has become the main vehicle for contemporary social conservatism.

Some see this connection as arbitrary or accidental. David Harvey, for instance, sees the alliance of neoliberalism with religious fundamentalism in the United States as a matter of political opportunism by the Republican party. I don't think it was so arbitrary. All neoliberal regimes have been created by stitching together a coalition of social forces and finding a locally gripping ideological language.

Neoliberalism is certainly a project of change and transformation, but it is not revolutionary, even in the sense that fascism was fifty years earlier. It involves a reorganization of the mechanisms of social power around existing centres of power: corporate capital, white middle-class men, major professions, managers in state and private sectors. Neoliberalism shifts the balance between dominant groups and lets in new energy and new claimants to power and privilege, without much disturbing the overall systems of inequality or the ideologies that sustain them.

What are the implications of this understanding of neoliberalism for resistance and change? To deal with that question properly would require a whole new essay; here I can simply offer some points to think about. First, neoliberalism as a social project always requires the maintenance of alliances and the temporary solution of cultural tensions. It is therefore vulnerable to changes that unhinge its coalitions or make the cultural problems more difficult to resolve. The growing awareness of environmental problems, for example, seems likely to create serious new difficulties of legitimation for neoliberal regimes. The 2007 defeat of John Howard's government in Australia shows that the pursuit of a radically deregulated labour market can create a backlash from working-class supporters previously tied in to the ruling coalition by a politics of fear.

Second, neoliberalism involves transformation in many different arenas – changes in culture, gender relations, and economic policy regimes, as well as the reworking of relationships inside organizations. The market is certainly the central regulating device in the neoliberal order, but the market is not in itself all-powerful. On the contrary, as the history of neoliberalism very clearly reveals, markets have to be made, nurtured, and sustained. There are therefore many sites from which the neoliberal project can effectively be confronted and perhaps turned back. We do not need to wait for a general crisis of the whole system before effective opposition becomes possible.

Third, neoliberalism draws much of its power from the processes of international economic coordination now commonly called "globalization" – the leverage for neoliberal "shock therapy" has usually come from debt dependency or fear of becoming globally uncompetitive. (The neoliberal treasurer in the Australian Labor party government of the 1980s defended his deregulation policies by insisting that they were necessary to prevent Australia's becoming a "banana republic.") But the world has not become homogeneous; and the tensions that revolve around dependence, inequality, and expropriation are a significant source of large-scale resistance.

Finally, and most speculatively, I return to the thought that there are inherent limits to the process of commodification. The bending of truth cannot go so far as to make economic life itself impossible. The relationships between lovers and between parents and children are penetrated by commodification but they also powerfully resist the alienation that commodification requires. The claims of mutual care and mutual responsibility, and the fundamental requirement of cooperation in human institutions (including, of course, economic production), are perhaps irreducible barriers to the expansion of competitive individualism. The land is the land, not just a factor of production and a source of profit.

There are, it seems, a number of limits that the neoliberal project runs up against. Any and all of them can be sources of resistance and change. But a collective practice is always required to turn this possibility into reality.

3

Risky Business?

Border Preclearance and the Securing of Economic Life in North America

KARINE CÔTÉ-BOUCHER

Cross often? Make it simple, join NEXUS.

The CBSA screens immigrants, refugees and visitors to prevent
inadmissible persons from entering or remaining in Canada.
Canadian Border Security Agency

Leaving Toronto on a plane bound for Quebec City, I sat beside
Louis. This white, middle-aged, skilled worker was returning home
after a week spent in the United States overseeing the IT sections of
plants owned by the company that employed him. Prompted by my
interest (after I revealed that I was doing research on the topic of
border controls), Louis said he sometimes travelled as often as twice
a month and, as evidence, presented his collection of reward cards
for North American hotels and car rental companies. When I asked
whether he adhered to NEXUS – a preclearance program that eases
Canada-United States border crossings for frequent travellers –
Louis replied that he was in the process of applying for a pass in the
hope that it would shorten his travel time.

For Canadian professionals such as Louis, repeated short-term
working trips to the United States and their facilitation by border authorities occur in a context of tighter border controls in North
America. Technological enhancements for passports, visa requirements, fingerprinting and data collection by programs such as US-VISIT

(Amoore 2006), biometric-ready permanent resident cards (Browne 2005), the safe-third-country agreement (Macklin 2005) and other refugee interdiction measures (Crépeau and Nakache 2006) such as detention and deportation (Pratt 2005) have become part of the everyday management of border crossings in the region. Accordingly, analyses of emerging North American security practices have mainly focused on the recent integration of border surveillance measures, the containment of deemed illegitimate migration and anti-terrorism procedures.

Various authors are interested in the ways security in diffuse border spaces constitutes renewed regimes of exception under which the rule of law does not apply, leaving individuals to the unchecked discretionary power of security professionals or to the good or ill will of civilians. These authors underscore that such regimes transform our understandings of sovereignty (Butler 2004; Doty 2007). Others consider the use of intelligence, biometrics, databases, and other security means in the development of an extensive complex of border surveillance (Lyon 2003; van der Ploeg 2006; Salter 2008). While these analyses are useful, they often eclipse any inquiry into the intersection of security developments with other initiatives aimed at the facilitation of economic exchanges and labour mobility as well as the enhancement of market profitability.[1]

In this collection, Connell suggests that neoliberalism has changed the connections between politics and the economy. One particular aspect of this altered relation can be found in the opening of borders by free trade initiatives such as the North American Free Trade Agreement (NAFTA), and their concurrent closing to what is deemed to threaten their smooth operation, such as organized crime, undocumented migration, or terrorism. In fact, it is characteristic of the contemporary neoliberal forms of governing border spaces in North America that the tensions produced by the double imperative of ensuring both security and the continuation of market exchanges are not easily resolved.

Neither focusing on how security measures depend on market logics nor, inversely, on the ways the interests of capital are fashioned by security priorities, this chapter approaches these tensions by examining the articulation of governmental discourses about what constitutes a threat and what contributes to economic prosperity, with recent developments in border risk assessment. As a preliminary investigation into the management of frequent border crossings and of some forms of labour mobility by means of preclearance programs, it specifically pays attention to the consequences of mobilizing different risk rationalities in the facilitation of movement across the Canada-United States border.

What we mean by "risk" is a complex matter that brings together political, technical, as well as moral aspects. Border authorities simultaneously deploy neoliberal forms of risk – stressing effectiveness but also individual responsibility in the management of insecurity – and a precautionary attitude characterized by a refusal to admit any level of threat. This divergence presents a problem for border authorities. On what basis can one decide between the application of the principle of precaution (based on logics of catastrophe) and the neoliberal emphasis on efficiency (especially responsible self-management and risk-taking) in the management of border spaces?

This chapter undertakes an initial exploration of the instruments developed by security professionals responsible for preclearance programs, and their use of these instruments to make security decisions on an everyday basis. In particular, I focus on the treatment of travellers, particularly as it reflects and (re)produces gendered, classed and racialized categorizations as well as the various statuses developed by (inter)national regimes of citizenship – for instance, dual citizen, refugee, irregular migrant, permanent resident, non-status person or citizen. As fundamental categories in the differential use of precautionary and neoliberal approaches to risk management by border authorities, these reconfigured social hierarchies inform us about the contemporary social imaginaries deployed in risk assessments and their boundary-making character for North American societies.[2] The chapter concludes with preliminary remarks about an important trend on which preclearance sheds light, a phenomenon I call the multiplication of authorized identities.

Before I proceed, allow me to introduce a caveat. My work stems from a specific outlook towards global forms of justice that underscores the importance of social positionality. That is, in examining relations of power one must attend to the complex relationships between processes of exclusion and inclusion, as well as operations of privilege (a view shared for example by Braedley in this volume). Certainly, I am conscious of the impact of border security measures upon the most vulnerable, whether refugees, undocumented migrants or racialized travelers, and I have been very critical of public policy on these matters (Côté-Boucher 2008, and forthcoming). But while many asylum seekers are refused visas to Canada and while

intelligence agencies exchange information that leads to the extraordinary rendition of Muslim Canadians or to arbitrary addi-
tions to no-fly lists, the same security and border agencies facilitate
the movement of corporate travellers, the transportation of billions
of dollars in commodities, and the mobility of many "legitimate frequent travellers". I am convinced that numerous projects of social
justice on this subcontinent (whether transnational struggles for labour, migrant, and refugee rights or civil liberties movements) need
to take into account relations of privilege as they are being shaped
along the border. I offer this chapter as a small contribution to the
efforts of many, scholars and activists, in that regard.

SECURING THE FREEDOM OF MOVEMENT:
THE NEOLIBERAL, PRECAUTIONARY,
AND MORAL ASPECTS OF RISK

The relation between market and security, as approached by liberalism, has taken different historical forms. Students of classical liberal
thought are familiar with its concern for the protection of the person,
of property and of market exchanges. Yet liberals not only entrusted
their material and physical safety to a sovereign whose authority is
more or less bound by legal and political limitations, checks and bal-
ances, and constitutional restrictions; they also recognized a time dimension to the sense of security, that is the possibility of having
confidence in what the future may bring.[3] Security provides conditions that are conducive to freedom of commerce, that ensure a sense
of safety against injury, and that allow for the protection of property
against the vagaries of colonial trade and impending uncertainties.
With this in mind, the facilitation, securing and sorting of certain
types of mobility appears as a central focus of early liberal governmental interventions. Since the eighteenth century, growing importance has been given to travel documentation, or what Torpey (2000)
designates as "the monopolization of the means of movement" by
state authorities to control the exits, entries, and displacements of
persons. Intimately connected with a "racial politics of mobility"
(Mongia 2003), this control later prevented the colonized to freely
migrate, yet soon buttressed travel, settlement, and commercial en-
deavour in colonial territory for Europeans by means of identity documents and passports (Salter 2003).

In his study of liberalism, Foucault (2004a) points to the emergence of liberal Europe as a collective subject that, with the help of its intellectual instrument, classical political economy, took the world as the playing field of an unlimited economic progress.[4] The nineteenth-century logic of freedom of movement and commerce thus had its imperialist corollary in a naturalistic and evolutionary appraisal of liberty, emphasizing the possibility of furthering one's own interests anywhere on the globe. The individualistic and egotistic meaning given to liberty also justified the principle of constant self-limitation of governmental action, which Foucault places at the heart of liberalism. This principle is intertwined in complex ways with the previously developed "*dispositif* of security." The latter includes the mechanisms through which phenomena, events, populations, and what later emerged as the social, are apprehended in their probability and on the basis of a logic of costs and effectiveness, both fixing the limits of the acceptable (Foucault 2004b).[5] These define the whole *problématique* of liberalism : "*Liberté et sécurité, c'est cela qui va animer de l'intérieur … les problèmes de ce que j'appellerai l'économie de pouvoir propre au libéralisme*" (Foucault 2004a, 67).[6]

For Foucault, a "political culture of danger," an uneasiness towards present and future events that deploys itself in a multiplicity of realms of everyday life, is characteristic of liberalism. This association of uneasiness towards dangers with the *dispositif* of security has been studied as behind the emergence of "risk," that is, the transformation of uncertainties into probabilities on which one might intervene. Inseparable from an apprehension of the aleatory, mechanisms of security become intertwined with various emerging areas of knowledge – from the calculation of probability through the science of statistics (Hacking 1990) to the assessment of populations (e.g., morbidity and mortality rates), and the likelihood of events according to certain "risk factors"— that become related to an array of preventative initiatives (Castel 1991). Students of Foucault have analyzed within this liberal political culture of danger an interest in the spreading, prevention, and compensation of risk – for instance injuries in the workplace – which emerged together with the social contract instituted by the welfare state (Ewald 1986). Such historical development contributed to what Donzelot calls the "taming of political passions" (1994 [1984]) where leftist revolutionary politics were replaced by reformist redistributive strategies.

Neoliberalism disavows this understanding of security as the diminution and redistribution of the risks encountered within a market economy. Rather than viewing risk negatively, neoliberalism encourages individuals to differentiate between types of risk: some risks are to be taken, while others are to be independently managed or avoided. In this sense, Ong (2006) is correct when she defines neoliberalism as a mode of "political optimization."[7] But what does neoliberalism allege about the social, and how are these claims related to rationalities of risk?

Neoliberalism proposes a radical market agenda that invades all areas of the social. Extending to all social actors and state institutions the values of the market as organizing principle, North American neoliberal thought not only casts *Homo oeconomicus* as its trope but disseminates the logic of the market through all non-economic aspects of human life, from morals to aesthetics, politics to culture (Brown 2005; Lemke 2001). Promoting marketability as its core value and pushing the boundaries of wealth generation by extending commodification to an unprecedented degree, neoliberalism even approaches creative capacities and imagination as capital. In fact, Foucault (2004a) claims that neoliberalism, as promoted by the Chicago school, effects an epistemological mutation that leaves aside traditional economic mechanisms (production, consumption, exchange, etc.) to focus on the development of "human capital."[8]

Consequently, it comes as no surprise that scholars of risk give serious attention to the importance of risk technologies for neoliberal forms of governing. Risk is a clear ally in the production of the enterprising, creative, and mobile subject fundamental to the North American neoliberal world view. Risks are to be embraced (Baker and Simon 2002) and risk taking – whether in financial markets, by insurance companies, or even by extreme-sports enthusiasts – encouraged (Simon 2002). Stressing efficiency and self-reliance in the management of risks, neoliberalism imagines a rational, calculative, and responsible subject who takes into his hands the daily management of the multiple uncertainties he faces. O'Malley (1996) designates this shift in the conceptualization of moral subjectivities as a new prudentialism. Neoliberal thinking about agency emphasizes the autonomy of communities and individuals in making efficient and productive choices about their lives. Disembodied subjects, extracted from their social context, are encouraged to be more self-reliant in their approach to risk, a critical move away from what is seen by the neoliberal doctrine as the dependency formerly fostered by the welfare state. Thus, this process of penetration of the social by neoliberal perceptions of risk ultimately aims at remoralizing individuals through market values.

But an important point remains often overlooked: in stressing agency, neoliberalism obscures social differences of class, gender, and race at the level of discourse, only to maintain and intensify them in practice. In fact, certain types of privileges are necessary in order to constitute oneself as autonomous and productive. Most realms welcoming neoliberal forms of risk are dominated by privileged men, thus actively contributing to the reshaping of contemporary forms of masculine domination. In other domains of social life, empirical sociological research has shown the disastrous everyday consequences of the "neutral" understanding of agency promoted by neoliberal policies. Rather than facilitating empowerment, these policies promote individualism by compelling impoverished women into providing unpaid care (Luxton 2006 and this volume) or more privileged ones into relying on the labour of racialized female domestic migrant workers (Arat-Koç 2006). Furthermore, stepping away from the naturally free subject of liberalism, neoliberalism implements various mechanisms to *cultivate* freedom in individuals, often at the cost of submitting their everyday activities to an increasing scrutiny (Braedley 2006). In other words, as happens with any political rationality aimed at transforming the social, neoliberalism, and the forms of risk that are associated with it, remain "deeply bound up with the sociocultural norms and taken-for-granted assumptions of any given society" (Mitchell 2001, 166).

Yet while embracing risks, or being expected to manage them prudentially, the North American neoliberal subject is pressed to individually search for a heightened sense of security in different aspects of her existence. This phenomenon, which Isin (2004) has aptly designated as the neoliberal production of a "neurotic citizen" governed through her affects, has its corollary in the contemporary sense of having little control over other important processes that shape human existence – this sense of liquidity theorized by Bauman (2006). As a result, current approaches to risk also frequently focus on the global. From epidemics to ecological threats to terrorism, these risks differ from those assessed in most of the past century. Considered to be of rare occurrence but with potentially catastrophic consequences, they appear resistant to measurement, consequently unravelling the previous solidaristic distribution of risks through the welfare state.

In a beautiful essay, Ewald (2002) shows how the emergence of a precautionary principle in the tackling of risks encourages an attitude of doubt, an anticipation of danger focused on the expectation of the worst. While a certain level of risk was formerly considered acceptable, precaution rests upon efforts to reach "zero risk," a risk that is uninsurable, without price. Beck's earlier theories on the risk society shed light on this passage to attitudes of precaution as epitomized by the environmental movement. Accordingly, precaution displaces a fundamental aspect of the historical *dispositif* of security the way Foucault understood it. Averaging is, for global risks, out of the question as we encounter less and less acceptability of certain levels of insecurity.

The relation of precaution to knowledge is thus deeply affected. As Aradau and Van Munster (2007) phrase it, the use of a precautionary attitude in border assessments exposes the contingency of the relation between knowledge and the decisions made by state agents. Similarly, as I have argued elsewhere, the constitution of an intelligence paradigm within border management is replacing exigencies of proof with racialized suspicions (Côté-Boucher 2008). Shying away from traditional requirements of validity, a precautionary politics operates as an epistemological break with rationalized appraisals of risk, leaving more room for anxious evaluations of contemporary objects of unease.

Risk valuations in neoliberal times do not solely reveal the technical nature of risk assessments. The insistence on the technical aspect of neoliberal management of mobility through a focus on mechanisms such as the computerization of travel documents or the use of biometrics overlooks the ways in which risk bears upon an array of subjective perceptions (Haggerty 2003). Approaches to risk are embedded in anxiety, moral panic, and fear; risks are always powerful mediations of moral valuations. This is especially true in situations of high uncertainty: "In less controlled contexts, risk frays into uncertainty, fear, speculation, and unanticipated consequences" (Ericson and Doyle 2004, 6). As argued by Hunt (2003), the problematization of anxiety by invocations of risks constitutes an important tool for the moralization of everyday life. An important social process in the classification of rights and wrongs, but also in the evaluation of degrees of morality in conduct, risk valuations are rarely devoid of social stereotypes.

Consequently, a technical approach to risk can be complemented with a consideration for the various social imaginaries that saturate risk with culturally specific meanings and significations. The same risks bring about different evaluations, are given priority or are ignored, producing diverse "risk portfolios" that depend on the cultural context of their assessment. In a nutshell, risks are selected, ranked, and assessed according to cultural norms (Douglas and Wildavsky 1982). Furthermore, risks are often infused with symbolic content, relating them to forms of thinking that contribute to the creation of social identities by bounding a society against alterities that are seen as endangering its ways of life. A risk, says Hacking (2003, 41), is often constituted as "an assault from across the border on purity." Interested in liberal settler societies (Australia and Canada), Mackey reminds us that notions of risk mobilized in political programs are heavily normative as they are used to "define and maintain conceptual boundaries between self and other" (1999, 111). Shaping exclusions and inclusions through notions of risk, dominant racialized identity narratives give particular insights about the anxieties various groups hold on the perpetuation of their privileged position within specific body politics (Mackey 2002).

It is the task set for the remainder of this chapter to explore these themes as they unfold in the space of the Canada-United States border. Unlike most works on border security, which often equate high risk with exclusion and low risk with inclusion, I examine the tensions created by encounters between different modes of risk valuation along the border. After reviewing the building of a fragmented regime of mobility in the past decades that emphasizes the circulation of skilled labour, business elites, and commodities in North America, I then examine the changes that have occurred in this regime with the introduction of a precautionary logic aimed at tackling terrorism. The reliance on two contradictory approaches to risk management – one stressing efficiency and the other precaution – the multiplication of means of identification, and the reliance on social categorizations and citizenship regimes for the hierarchization of travellers, draw a complex picture of the dynamics unleashed along the Canada-United States border in the bid to protect North American economic life.

TARGETED CROSS-BORDER MOBILITY: FROM NAFTA TO PRECLEARANCE

After the attacks on New York's World Trade Center and the Pentagon on September 11, 2001, a variety of preclearance measures was implemented at border checkpoints in order to ease the mobility of frequent travellers and the traffic of commodities, thus intensifying with political will and resources the timid attempts of the past decade. The liberalization of North American economies has been understood since the 1990s to be partly dependent upon the mobility of business elites. The smoothing of travel opportunities was addressed by NAFTA's chapter 16, which recognizes higher mobility rights for a specific category of *citizen*, that is, business persons. NAFTA's provisions address the facilitation of short sojourns – up to one year – of "Business Visitors," "Professionals," "Intra-company Transferees," as well as "Traders and Investors" in Canada, Mexico, or the United States. Other categories of labour such as agricultural and domestic workers or tradespeople are not covered by NAFTA and require temporary work visas. In short, ever since the beginnings of North American free trade, state authorities have been working towards the constitution of the Canada-United States border as a space of mobility and exchange (Pellerin 2004). These efforts apparently paid off: Canadian authorities estimate that an average of $2 billion in commodities and 400,000 persons move across the Canada-United States border daily (Canada, Embassy to Washington 2008).[9]

Yet the 9/11 attacks produced a turmoil with disrupting effects upon important sectors of the North American economy. Days of paralysis along the "longest undefended border in the world" resulted in significant loss of revenue and the temporary closing of manufacturing plants on both sides of the Canada-United States border (Andreas 2003); the insurance industry was required to pay $55 billion in indemnities, an unprecedented amount in cases of terrorism (Ericson and Doyle 2004). Airlines were also affected, losing hundreds of millions of dollars, some going bankrupt while air traffic diminished by 34 percent (Jorion 2002).[10] Terrorism decisively entered the risk portfolio of the United States, with important consequences for the management of its borders with its economic partners. As with the economic slowdown that began at the end of 2008, Canada's economy was affected by virtue of its entanglement with that of its southern neighbour after more than a decade of free trade between the two countries.

With the aim of preventing further terrorist events, technocrats from Canada and the United States rapidly brought together, in a more or less coherent whole, a disparate set of existing measures (refugee interdiction techniques, methods of intelligence-sharing, immigration legislation, as well as mechanisms to ease cross-border traffic "low-risk" commodities and travellers) with new initiatives that included anti-terror legislative mechanisms, important investments in border infrastructures, the development of surveillance databases, and finally, the new Ministry of Public Safety and the Canadian Border Services Agency.[11] In subsequent years, funding for security increased substantially on both sides of the border, rapidly surpassing the economic costs of 9/11 and transferring significant public funds into the private sector for the purchase of surveillance technologies.[12] The "security-economy nexus" (Coleman 2005) was initially enshrined in the Canada-United States Smart Border Declaration of December 2001, followed by the 2004 North American Security and Prosperity Partnership, in which Mexico also takes part. The first document claimed to work towards the constitution of "a zone of confidence" in North America through risk management: "We will implement systems to collaborate in identifying security risks while expediting the flow of low risk travellers" (Canada, Foreign Affairs and International Trade 2001). The latter text promised to provide "the framework to ensure that North America is the safest and best place to live and do business. It includes ambitious security and prosperity programs to keep our borders closed to terrorism yet open to trade" (Canada, Office of the Prime Minister 2006).

Targeted programs were tested to cope with the consequences of the security measures put in place by United States border authorities after 9/11. Traffic congestion at land and air borders called for resuming the low-risk preclearance experiences of the 1990s, such as the PACE lanes tested on the West Coast (Sparke 2004) and the NEXUS pilot program at the Sarnia-Port Huron border crossing. In conformity with a neoliberal logic of efficiency deemed to focus border agents' work on "high-risk" individuals and commodities, preclearance rapidly became the preferred solution for managing the displacements of individuals "trusted" by intelligence, security, and immigration agencies. Preclearance bestows upon "frequent low-risk travellers," as well as upon companies exporting commodities between Canada and the United States, the privilege of crossing the border without being subjected to lengthy personal identity checks. Those who meet the preclearance criteria are preapproved for all future border crossings, until the privilege comes up for renewal by security services.

There are various preclearance programs in North America. Some are private, but most are governmental. The programs can be national, allowing people to enter one country easily, or bilateral. In the latter case, holders of preclearance passes may cross the Canada-United States border in both directions. Resumed in 2002, NEXUS is a governmental bilateral program that allows easy crossings between the two countries at airports, land border, and marine locations for frequent travellers who are judged to represent a low risk. After submitting an online application detailing address, work, citizenship, and immigration histories, citizens and specific types of non-citizens (see below) considered potentially eligible for preclearance are interviewed at an enrolment centre by officers of Canadian and United States border authorities. If approved by both agencies, the applicant's fingerprints are recorded, a digital photograph of the iris is taken for biometric identification at preclearance airport booths, and the traveller is provided with a card good for a period of five years.

NEXUS cards can be used at sea, air, and land border crossings. At the latter, drivers enter a dedicated lane and point their cards towards a reader. The radio frequency identification technology (RFID) included in the card triggers sensors that send a number to the system, bringing up information about the traveller on the border officer's computer screen located ahead. The agent verifies identity and membership through customs databases. NEXUS members must then show their card to the border agent, proceed through the border, or sometimes submit to a secondary inspection. Government officials claim that cardholders are cleared in nine seconds, while those going through secondary inspection are processed within three minutes on average (Association of Professional Executives of the Public Service of Canada 2006).[13]

A similar process happens at airports, but customs are cleared through the airport's NEXUS booth, which identifies the travellers through iris biometrics. In this case, mobility is made even easier for members: cardholders entering Canada by air, arriving from any world destination (for instance England or China), may use dedicated airport preclearance booths to speed their entry into the country. The equivalent of such privileges in the United States is Global Entry, a pilot program tested in 2008 that allows members to be precleared when flying into the country. Some United States airports also offer preclearance programs such as CLEAR, which is privately run by Verified Identity Pass Inc. Finally, marine preclearance is available through NEXUS-boat, which offers hundreds of telephone reporting sites in Canada and the United States which pass holders can call up to four hours in advance to announce a marine border crossing.

During the summer of 2008, NEXUS was available at fourteen land border locations and eight major Canadian airports. Under the Security and Prosperity Partnership, the three signatory countries have expressed their intention to harmonize existing bilateral pre-clearance programs, NEXUS, Free and Secure Trade (FAST), and Secure Electronic Network for Travellers Rapid Inspection (SENTRI), the equivalent of NEXUS for the United States-Mexico border. In a nutshell, preclearance has been instituted in a few years as *the* solution for the management of trusted travellers in North America.

PRECLEARANCE AND LABOUR MOBILITY

Preclearance programs are publicized by state authorities with an emphasis on the exclusive social status they bestow upon elites. If not directly related to business purposes, the possibility for boat owners of crossing the Great Lakes at their convenience by means of NEXUS-boat nevertheless conveys the image of leisure for the wealthy. Other elements seem to confirm this interpretation. A feature story posted on a government Web page presenting NEXUS cardholders as "enjoying the privileges of membership" insists on this social exclusivity:

> Each time he flies between Canada and the United States, Michael Campbell feels a little special ... Mr Campbell, 65, the co-owner of a hotel in Penticton, BC, is one of a growing number of trusted travelers from Canada and the U.S. who are taking advantage of the expanding NEXUS program to streamline their border crossings. "It gives me express access," says Mr Campbell, who flies to the US about a dozen times a year and has also used his NEXUS card for returning to Canada from abroad. "When you come back after a 15-hour flight, it's special to be whisked through in a matter of minutes." (Canada 2009a)

In return for allowing a high level of scrutiny in their life histories, NEXUS adherents are told they are joining a select club whose members acquire extensive freedom of movement. At the end of 2008, NEXUS counted 250,000 members in the United States and Canada, up from 70,000 in 2004, and the figure is expected to grow to 360,000 adherents by 2010 (Canadian Border Services Agency 2008c).[14] In light of these expanding numbers and elitist governmental discourses, the notion that preclearance represents another contribution to the world of privilege experienced by business classes needs further exploration. It appears important to specify the social groups to which this privilege pertains and to point to the limitations of approaching preclearance in terms of social status and access to wealth.

Preclearance Cards as Tokens of Transnational Privilege for the Business Class?

In an inspired study of securitized economic liberalization in border spaces, Sparke (2006) claims that preclearance programs such as NEXUS introduce new forms of civil citizenship privileges for the business class, extending mobility rights beyond borders while promoting an entrepreneurial selfhood. Certainly, the North American combination of an increased freedom of movement permitted through preclearance programs with the opportunities opened up by NAFTA (such as extended access to property[15] and the possibility of selling one's labour beyond national boundaries for limited periods of time) has pushed the limits of certain liberal rights traditionally confined to the territories of nation-states. According to this view, the privileged status conferred on adherents of preclearance programs is more cosmopolitan than that granted by documents such as citizenship cards or passports, which usually stand for "national symbols of belonging" (Stalder and Lyon 2003).

If we are to take seriously the assertion that preclearance promotes the social status and augments the privileges of the business class, it matters that we explore what is imparted by a notion of preclearance as a program geared to the capitalist elite. A most important aspect to be underscored is the furthering by preclearance cards of the privileges of a *masculinized* business class. The membership of the Canadian Council of Chief Executives (CCCE) illustrates such composition.[16] Not coincidentally, the CCCE has secured the position of the main Canadian private participant to the North American Competitiveness Council (NACC), the business interlocutor of the North American Security and Prosperity Partnership instituted by Canada, Mexico and the United States in 2004.

As mentioned earlier, certain forms of risk, for instance financial risk, that are critical to the neoliberal project are embraced in domains dominated by privileged men. These domains are closely linked to globalization processes, as confirmed by Sklair's (2001) work on the transnational capitalist class. It has been suggested that the contemporary world gender order is intimately connected to patterns of trade and investment, producing an emerging "transnational business masculinity" (Connell 1998; Connell and Wood 2005). I argue that this gendered order also requires high levels of mobility for male business elites that are authorized and supported by state authorities through various measures, such as preclearance in the North American context.

It goes without saying that these greater mobility privileges are likely to contribute to emerging forms of masculinized subjectivation pertaining to transnational spheres. Interestingly, by focusing on an enterprising selfhood, neoliberal policies not only assume but enhance the agency of masculine business elites through border measures designed to facilitate their movement. The sense of freedom and possibility opened up by such programs, together with the insistence by border agencies that the spaces in which these elites meander should be securitized, portray North America as quasi-borderless for the precleared travellers. These policies help further cementing the sense of entitlement, as well as protection of property and self, experienced by masculininized business elites. Preclearance thus plays a part in an extended individualizing experience using borders as tools in capital accumulation or career opportunities. As demonstrated by Luxton in this volume, the shaping of subjectivities achieved by neoliberal interventions in the social is intimately related to an approach to agency that remains grounded in categorizations based on gender and class (and, as demonstrated below, race), while working hard at concealing them. Risk assessment is not foreign to such processes; it obscures the particular gendering of frequent travellers by concealing in technical language the protection offered to transnational masculine business elites.

The expected increase in NEXUS membership in the next few years will not be confined to the masculinized business class. Other groups than those primarily targeted, such as skilled workers, apply to obtain cards. Louis, the air passenger in the introduction, is an IT specialist whose employment requires him to frequently visit different plants in North America and abroad. Such constant *self-"deterritori-alization"* (Deleuze and Guattari 1980) by skilled workers is impor-tant in the maintenance of a competitive position in the global marketplace for workers, the companies that employ them, and the economies they sustain. Since the prosperity of North American economies is deemed to build partly upon the mobility of profession-als, skilled workers, and business persons, preclearance measures sug-gest that the more frequently members of these groups cross the border, the more important it is to decrease hindrances to their trav-els. Low-risk measures further establish and expand the categories of people recognized by NAFTA to be the pillars of the North American economy. The current governing of increased mobility rights is geared towards the surveillance of the smooth circulation of a highly skilled masculinized labour force and entrepreneurial class deemed to be at the basis of the subcontinent's prosperity.

In contrast to NAFTA'S provisions with respect to the mobility of business people, preclearance membership is not restricted to citizens of North American countries. Preclearance cards further complicate the neoliberal reshaping of citizenship by granting extended mobility rights to various categories of non-citizens, permanent residents as well as visitors with student visas, work permits, or "other types of visas."[17] This access to spaces of extended freedom of movement for non-citizens indicates that class-based analyses of the management of elite mobility should be taken up with a consideration for the place of marketable skills in the citizenship rights granted to individuals in-volved in North American migration systems.

Using citizenship and immigration status as assets in global pro-cesses of production, preclearance programs not only expand the civil citizenship rights of masculinized economic elites, professionals, and skilled workers but also increase these rights for specific categories of non-citizens selected for the marketability of their skills or their con-nections with transnational economic networks. A growing literature analyses the ways in which hierarchical relations of gender, race, and class, as well as subjective definitions of nationhood, are intertwined with a differentiated access to citizenship statuses. Sharma (2006) demonstrates that most migrants to Canada are approved for tempo-rary access to the country's labour market through working visas, a tendency on the rise as a record number of migrant workers were granted temporary visas in 2008 (Alboin 2009). Given restricted rights, these migrants are often subjected to poor labour conditions that have been documented for different groups, from farm labourers (Bauder 2006) to domestic workers (Stasiulis and Bakan 2005).

Nevertheless, state authorities have also been concerned with the luring of foreign investors and entrepreneurs in strategic efforts to locate North American economies within transnational production networks. Ong's (1999) influential work has examined patterns of flexibilization of citizenship for Chinese highly skilled workers in Silicon Valley and business migrants to the United States. These immigrants are invited to use their transnational ties and multiple passports in processes of capital accumulation. Similarly, Canadian immigration policies in the 1980s and 1990s attempted to attract Hong Kong investors through expanded business immigration programs (Mitchell 2001). In the same way, provincial nominee programs currently aim at facilitating the hiring of foreign skilled workers for businesses, or attracting multinational investors willing to establish themselves and their employees in Canada. Neoliberal state interventions in market processes thus articulate different mobility regimes, from immigration to frequent travel, actively supporting international masculinized elites and production networks while allegedly positioning North American economies within globalization processes. Global trade and transnational business becomes possible in part when "human capital" is allowed to cross borders frequently.

Security and economic imperatives not only support each other but often erode one another. In particular, security measures have generated anxieties within the corporate sector. In a book on risk management, the New-York-based CEO of Deloitte and Touche stresses that the competitiveness of North American firms is severely undermined by security measures and visa requirements and, as a result, international students are increasingly choosing European countries for their studies, to the detriment of United States universities (Parrett 2007). These students are likely to remain in Europe as professionals, and their loss, in Parrett's view, is an impediment to research and development in the United States and, in the long term, to its global competitiveness. Having to face increased security measures and longer wait-times for visa approvals and renewals, the enterprising subject investing in migration strategies to increase her human capital – in short, the perfect neoliberal subject – may come to envision her future elsewhere.

Between Precaution and Free Trade:
Preclearance and Transportation Workers

Preclearance cards can also be obtained by a group categorized as lower-skilled labour that is often overlooked: commercial freight transportation workers, commonly called truck drivers. In an era of flexible just-in-time production, the transportation of primary resources and the distribution of commodities are vital to the maintenance of transnational trade networks, or as Reifer bluntly puts it: "Without continuous distribution of commodities to consumers, global production and trade would stop" (2004, 17). An important nexus of such distribution, the Canada-United States border is crossed each day by 18,500 trucks (Canada 2009b). Since the 1990s, but especially after 2001, commercial driver designations and customs self-assessment programs have been designed to allow clearance for commodities away from the border for air, marine freight, and highway carriers, thus streamlining commodity transportation through dedicated lanes and allegedly diminishing customs costs for the companies involved. Turning its focus on truck drivers, security has entered the logistics sector and changed workers' lives as well as work processes in other sites of transportation, such as ports (Cowen 2007a).

Free and Secure Trade (FAST) is a preclearance program intended to lower traffic congestion at land border locations. Dedicated FAST lanes are found in twenty high-volume land border crossings, most of which are located along the Ontario border. Participant commercial drivers must present their FAST card to an electronic card reader, if available, and then stop at the inspection booth. As of 2009, it was planned that importing carriers (rail and highway) would soon electronically send their information to a risk management system, eManifest, a few hours before drivers reach the border for the advance processing of their cargo (its equivalent for air shipments is the already implemented Air Commercial Information program).[18] Becoming part of the Partners in Protection (PIP) program (or of its United States counterpart, US Customs Trade Partnership against Terrorism) is now compulsory for carriers who wish to obtain a FAST card. Set up in 1994, PIP "enlists the cooperation" of private carriers in matters of security.

A bilateral preclearance program such as FAST does more than question the assumption that preclearance cards constitute tokens of transnational privilege for the business class – although FAST certainly supports economic exchanges that benefit this class. In the following two cases, the risk management of truck drivers illustrates the ambiguities generated by the meeting of the neoliberal logic of efficiency with a precautionary attitude geared towards the elimination of risk.

The first case concerns the employment by transportation companies of drivers with criminal records. Preclearance cards are now part of the labour process for cross-border transportation workers and are often required by employers. In fact, since the 2006 introduction of the Safe, Accountable, Flexible, Efficient Transportation Equity Act in the United States, a FAST membership – and thus background criminal checks – is compulsory for all drivers carrying "dangerous goods." Consequently, in order to obtain a FAST membership, one needs to be deemed low risk, a possibility technically eliminated for individuals with criminal records.

Citizenship and Immigration Canada has a rehabilitation program for those who may need temporary or permanent admittance to the country. This program is specially advertised to truck drivers (Canadian Border Services Agency 2009b). It may be useful to point out that United States citizens with no criminal record who nevertheless have a record of misdemeanours have been refused access to Canada.[19] It happened in October 2007 to Ann Wright (2007), a former US army colonel and diplomat engaged in war protests in the United States. Why then would Canadian state authorities be *promoting* pardon to transportation workers with criminal backgrounds who wish to enter the country? I suggest that this program hints at the impact that risk management has had on the carrier industry, which is already in dire need of workers. An industry that has greatly expanded since the beginning of the 1990s, the long-distance trucking sector has been claiming more than one hundred percent annual labour turnover and important labour shortages in all of the three NAFTA member countries (Min and Lambert 2002). This does not demonstrate that security concerns are being trumped by economic ones, nor does Ann Wright's case show the opposite. Rather, security services sometimes relinquish a precautionary attitude and accept a certain level of risk in order to protect an industry that is vital to North American economic life. But this form of assessment relies on the self-regulation of a neoliberal subject required to go through a process of moral rehabilitation. Depending on the number and gravity of offences, three to ten years must have passed since a sentence was served, from which point state authorities deem as lowered the risk one is considered to represent.

Nevertheless, not every transportation worker risk assessment by security services presupposes the possibility of remoralization. Another encounter of the precautionary approach with efficiency concerns in risk management is illustrated by the ordeal of a Canadian-Syrian man, which began slightly prior to the introduction of FAST cards. Ahmed El-Maati was a truck driver who frequently travelled between the United States and Canada. In a search of his truck at the Buffalo-Fort Erie crossing in August 2001, an outdated delivery map was found, displaying Ottawa government buildings. Border authorities took El-Maati's picture, fingerprints, and an iris scan. On September 11, 2001, the Canadian Security and Intelligence Services (CSIS) visited El-Maati, who presented them with a letter from his employer confirming that the truck they had searched had previously been driven by another employee living in Ottawa. Less than a month later, CSIS released "information" to the media about a truck driver caught at the border with a "suspicious map". El-Maati hired a lawyer and demanded a meeting with security services. The meeting never happened. CSIS exchanged information with Syrian authorities, where El-Maati later flew in order to get married in November 2001. But Syrian intelligence arrested El-Maati at the airport and tortured him for a year, asking questions seemingly transmitted by Canadian intelligence services. He was later transferred to Egypt, and released in January 2004 after 790 days in prison.[20]

Once security agencies had read into this case the vague possibility of an eventual terrorist plot, the precautionary attitude subsequently adopted by border agents made any legal representation or evidence that might be provided on El-Maati's behalf irrelevant. Thus it would be a mistake to interpret these decisions as misguided individual assessments made by "bad apple" border agents within an otherwise neutral and objective risk management process. Rather these decisions are the result of the embeddedness of the precautionary attitude within border risk management that provides border agents with a significant amount of "discretionary power." More specifically, the authority to make decisions is in these cases not regulated by the rule of law but responsive to the exigencies of another regulatory system, risk management, which is granted legitimacy in the name of national security. The possibility of basing a precautionary reading of travellers on social hierarchies and immigration status is institutionally inscribed in the very logic of border measures; FAST is no exception to this rule. Permanent residents can apply for a FAST card. But they, unlike their NEXUS counterpart, are also officially required to carry immigration and identity documents that might be demanded by border agents (Canadian Border Security Agency 2008a).[21] Non-citizen transportation workers are thus more likely to be subjected to a heightened surveillance by border authorities to complement their pre-approval for accessing preclearance dedicated lanes.

A working-class man and dual citizen, El-Maati corresponded to many contemporary tropes about danger and illegitimate belonging to the polity. When triangulated with a racialized reading of El-Maati's origins in a general climate of heightened anxiety towards Muslims, the questionable evidence provided by the outdated map quickly came to constitute a solid fact that led to the creation of a high-risk profile for the transportation worker. This hardly comes as a surprise. In the past decade, North American Muslims have been targeted through a variety of means. In the United States, interviews and massive deportations of Muslim non-citizens have been accompanied by vigilante denunciations of "suspect Muslims" by ordinary citizens (Volpp 2002; Hagopian 2004). In Canada, the loss of assets because of anti-terrorism laws (Bahdi 2003), indefinite detentions under security certificates (Larsen and Piché 2007; Bell 2006), and extraordinary renditions of dual citizens (Stasiulis and Ross 2006) have been measures primarily implemented against Muslim individuals in Canada. Finally, we also know from anecdotal evidence that since 9/11, Muslim and Arab Canadian men who were required to cross the border for their work have been put on security lists, thus jeopardizing their employment (Canadian Islamic Congress 2006). Interviews with border agents confirm that "driving while Muslim" constitutes an informal basis for racial profiling at the border (Pratt and Thompson 2008).

THE IMAGINARY BOUNDARIES
OF NEOLIBERAL RISK MANAGEMENT

By locating the El-Maati case within post-9/11 islamophobic state practices, I have hinted at the ways in which border risk assessments, which are carried out by security professionals who associate different social categorizations with different levels of threat, are embedded within historically situated social imaginaries through which identities are shifting yet also cemented for a certain period of time. More specifically, social hierarchies in border spaces are

given particular meaning in their relation to contemporary represen-
tations of "dangerous" masculinities, Muslim alterity, and "threatening" foreigners, which compete with moral appreciations of neoliberal
modes of subjectivation – whether efficient, competitive, or prudential.
These meanings emerge from the normative assumptions that define
social relations and legitimate hegemonic understandings of collective life.

Contemporary border risk management cannot be reduced to an
attempt to recast political stakes as problems with technological solutions. In a region where neoliberalism has penetrated social relations through market values, the securing of market exchanges is
also, and simultaneously, a process of creating identity. Given such
centrality of market principles to contemporary definitions of collective life, this process is not devoid of anxiety about the capacity
to maintain the privileged status of North American societies, especially the United States and Canada, in a changing economic environment. With claims to defend North American economic life,
state authorities are thus promising to tame the uncertainties they
consider likely not only to disrupt trade and business but also to
threaten the neoliberal values that sustain the contemporary global
free market economy. This sense of menace, this "existential
threat" (Buzan et al. 1998)[22] to the very permanence of the neoliberal polity, is illustrated by the Smart Border Declaration proposition to develop the region covered by Canada and the United States
into a "zone of confidence" against terrorism: "The terrorist actions of September 11 were an attack on our common commitment
to democracy, the rule of law and a free and open economy. They
highlighted a threat to our public and economic security" (Canada,
Foreign Affairs and International Trade 2001).[23]

In order to fulfil the promise to secure both economic interests
and neoliberal definitions of social relations in North America, intelligence, customs, and immigration agencies translate societal and
economic anxieties into risk valuations. The difficulty in assessing
moral economic subjects, constituted against populations that are
deemed dangerous and unworthy – be they male Muslims, refugees,
or undocumented migrants – rests in the sometimes contradictory
meeting of different risk categories in everyday border management
decisions; one can be considered a potentially productive economic
subject, but nevertheless deemed to be posing a threat. As correctly
underlined by Rygiel (2006, 148), the image of the terrorist as the

uncivilized Muslim man has been transformed in recent years and is now "frequently associated with young, educated, professional men, in the most economically productive age brackets." The securing of economic life in North America stems from, as well as produces, a social imaginary in which those designated as foreigners are considered through a complex dynamic of desire and repulsion, of hospitality and hostility, that is characteristic of racist discursive practices. As illustrated by the various border measures and legal procedures involved in anti-terrorism efforts, the very possibility of differentiating bad from good foreigners or immoral from moral citizens, and everything in between, performs an important legitimating function for border risk management (Engle 2004).

Honig (2001) attributes the complexity of these rapports to what she designates as the play of xenophobia and xenophilia. Suggesting that attitudes of fear towards migrants are often accompanied by high expectations, Honig points to instances where immigrants are anointed with the responsibility of regenerating their host countries through their participation in economic and civic life or the restoration of traditional family arrangements. It is the changing character, the malleability, of this xenophilic/xenophobic dynamic – allowing certain groups to be wished for and later suspiciously regarded – that renders its critique such a delicate task.

Honig's heuristic analysis prevents us from making sweeping generalizations about border risk assessments. The interplay of social hierarchies and hierarchies of citizenship in border spaces does not automatically mean the exclusion or physical endangerment of travellers: assessments grounded in race, class, and gender depend on the location of these travellers within contemporary xenophobic and xenophilic imaginaries. Object of xenophilic desire, the entrepreneurial, hard-working, and eventually successful (European) newcomer has long been the embodiment of the North American migrant. Under neoliberal policies, this figure is transformed into the migrant who can cross borders and use them as resources for production and trade, thus representing an essential asset in maintaining a competitive advantage in the global economy. The longing to maintain a position of supremacy in the world order leads, to paraphrase Ong (2004), to the shaping of an "honorary whiteness" status for non-whites who belong to the various categories of low-risk traveler, skilled worker, or business person. This status is of course extremely vulnerable to historical surges of xenophobia, as illustrated by current precautionary assessments of specific groups of travellers. In short, to expand on Bahdi's words (2003, 295), risk management along the border takes "race as a proxy for risk," but only in its particular intersections with gendered and classed assumptions, as well as citizenship status, as they are informed by the social imaginaries produced amidst the tensions between market and security imperatives.

CONCLUSION: THE MULTIPLICATION OF AUTHORIZED IDENTITIES[24]

I have argued in this chapter that the intersection of market and security imperatives at play in the facilitation of cross-border mobility produces various tensions that represent a challenge to any simple assessment of preclearance programs as a token of privilege. Business classes, professionals, skilled workers, as well as transportation workers make up a variety of groups who are allowed to take advantage of such measures. The meeting in preclearance assessments of the "zero risk" attitude promoted by a precautionary approach with efficient and prudential forms of risk focused on productivity, points to the ways in which hierarchizing readings of articulations of social categorizations and citizenship statuses promote differential types of risk valuations that range from the adoption of a precautionary attitude to the authorization of frequent travel. This boundary-making process is reshaping the moral regulation of travelling individuals in the region but also redefining neoliberal subjectivities along gendered, classed, and racialized lines, therefore relating risk assessment to the shifting social imaginaries that participate in the securing of the neoliberal North American economic life.

At the time of writing, it is too early to speculate on the impact of the economic slowdown upon the implementation of border security measures but the administrations in Washington and Ottawa have not yet given any sign of changing course. I thus wish to bring this chapter to an (unfinished) end by reflecting on the avenues that preclearance has opened up for border security. Similarly to Braedley's review of accidental outcomes of policy implementation in this book, these avenues are lined with paradoxical consequences, that is, with the unintended and unwanted outcomes produced by the meeting of security and market logics along the border. More precisely, the current forms of control designed for border spaces have *increased* the number of ways one can claim a legitimated identity. While multiple security measures have augmented the ways individuals can be stopped at the border through the creation of various categories of risk, the intertwining of neoliberal and precautionary approaches to risk have also led to a burgeoning of the groups of travellers that are recognized by state authorities as having greater rights to cross-border mobility. This trend is epitomized by the broadening of the ways identity can be proven and rights to increased mobility may be exercised for various groups of travellers residing in Western societies.[25] This diversification of means of identification for frequent travellers sheds light on a wider tendency in border risk management, to which I refer as the *multiplication of authorized identities*.

Starting in June 2009, the United States' Western Hemisphere Travel Initiative (WHTI) requires Canadians crossing the land border to present either a passport or a NEXUS card – a measure already in place since January 2007 for air travel. In the wake of WHTI, Canadian provincial governments have attempted to put in place alternative forms of documentation that would lessen their citizens' dependence on the acquisition of a passport and foster their capacity to move back and forth across the border. One of these initiatives concerns the implementation of the enhanced drivers' licence (EDL). These licences are "enhanced" with the same features that are included in NEXUS cards, that is, citizenship information, place of birth, and an RFID chip that allows personal data to be accessible during border inspection. EDLs have been implemented in Quebec, Ontario, British Columbia, and Manitoba in 2009.

A trend is slowly materializing: the preclearance model of authorized identities for facilitated cross-border circulation is currently being expanded to the general population through the addition of securitized features on ID cards that are owned by most adults in both countries. In the wake of the 2004 Real ID Act, which calls for the standardization of driver's licences in the United States, Canadian provincial governments intend to render enhanced driver's licences compatible with those from south of the border. This means including in these cards information that could be exchanged between police and security services of both countries. As a result, some critiques of surveillance practices denounce what could well become a de facto North American ID (Council of Canadians 2008).

Another topic of concern is the readiness of precleared and now voluntary participants in the EDL pilot project to provide important personal information through applications and interviews to state authorities. Prudential individuals willingly enrol in their own safety by adopting securitized forms of identification. Consequently, the neoliberal remoralization necessary for obtaining preclearance cards already shows its potential of spreading beyond the frequent traveller category to other social groups that could increasingly be required to prove their low-risk status in order to qualify for such a *laissez-passer.*

State authorities find themselves under significant pressure to come up with solutions that tackle both security and economic life. In fact, these authorities are now facing difficulties in reorganizing regulation over the dynamics they themselves contributed to unleash in the 1980s and 1990s with the deregulation of market processes and the facilitation of privileged mobilities. North American states are leaking, their cosmopolitan subjects are everywhere: skilled and unskilled workers, finance and business persons, professionals and academics, all move along multiple channels that are accessible to those who have obtained various means of identification.

Let me finish by presenting a hypothetical case that exemplifies the unforeseen consequences brought about by the multiplication of authorized identities. Bhavani was born in India but grew up in England. She is a British citizen (thus holding a European Union passport), and recognized as an "Overseas citizen of India," a program launched in 2006 by the Indian government that amounts to a life visa allowing work, study, and indefinite stay for specific categories of Indian nationals living abroad. Bhavani moves to Canada for her graduate studies, where she is first granted a student visa, then permanent residency after a few years. She soon becomes employed by a company that requires her to travel frequently to the United States. This persuades her to apply for a NEXUS card, which she is granted. Sometimes, Bhavani goes to India to visit her extended family, using her British-EU passport on which is stamped her "Overseas citizen of India" visa. From there, she may travel in Asia using her EU passport; then, she flies back to the UK and spends some time with her parents. When finally returning to Canada, she does not present her passport but instead uses her NEXUS card at Pearson airport, potentially avoiding secondary inspection. Unless the various countries Bhavani has visited during her South Asian stay have agreements to exchange information on travellers (like those between Canada and the United States or the United

States and the European Union), it would be difficult for Canadian state authorities to have precise knowledge regarding Bhavani's whereabouts.

Allowing individuals the use of various types of securitized identification for traveling opens up possibilities for specific groups of people to choose the means of identifying themselves to border authorities. Thus, the multiplication of authorized identities may paradoxically lead to *less* control by state authorities on the mobility of certain travellers. While we pay more attention to surveillance practices aimed at controlling and containing mobilities, the multiplication of authorized identities remains an important feature of the neoliberal re-engineering of social hierarchies and subjectivities in North America.

NOTES

1 This article later refers to notable exceptions in the works of Pellerin (2004) in political economy, and Cowen (2007a, 2007b) in political geography.

2 While my definition of the notion of social imaginaries borrows from Taylor (2004), it differs in an important way. The "shared understandings" of collective life to which Taylor refers are also produced by boundary-making dynamics that enter the production of social imaginaries. As certain groups within a society have privileged access to the resources that enter the production of these shared understandings, they marginalize or exclude other groups from participating in their definition. Furthermore, these hegemonic shared understandings make it difficult to bring about other designations of the collective as well as other expectations and normative notions regarding social relations within that collective.

3 Describing security, this "principal object of the Laws," as that which makes possible the "expectation of the future," Bentham (2008 [1843]) follows his forefathers (quoted in O'Malley 2004). Hobbes (1996 [1651]) claims that "the foresight of [one's] own self-preservation" as well as the possibility of enjoying a "contented life," in short, "safetie," is better ensured by a powerful sovereign located outside the realm of law. To the requirement of physical protection Locke (1988 [1690]) adds the constitution of a durable environment of peace and order for property to beget fruits. Smith (1979 [1776]) joins the special needs of commercial interest for protection against rebellious colonized populations and pirates at sea to a standing army for defence

against "barbarous nations"' and the administration of justice: "The protection of trade in general has always been considered as essential to the defense of the commonwealth, and, upon that account, a necessary part of the duty of the executive power".

4 His opposition of classical political economy to Law, of individual interest to contract, prevents Foucault from considering the centrality of property rights in liberal thought (Grenier and Orléan 2007). His similar inattention to the material consequences of neoliberalism should not prevent us from considering the deepening of relations of dominance and the fostering of inequalities resulting from the emphasis put on market relations in North America.

5 For an understanding of *dispositifs* of security as inscribed in a politics of enunciation and visibility, see Deleuze 1989, as well as my own use of this framework for theorizing border spaces (Côté-Boucher 2008).

6 "Liberty and security, this is what will animate, from the inside, the problems of what I will call the economy of power pertaining to liberalism" (my translation). In an article published in a German newspaper in September 2001 in which he warned that security was becoming the "basic principle of state activity" and "the sole criterion of political legitimation" in the so-called war on terror, Giorgio Agamben (2002) referred to Foucault's work on liberalism: "Since measures of security can only function within a context of freedom of traffic, trade, and individual initiative, Foucault can show that the development of security accompanies the ideas of liberalism."

7 Reviewing Rose's work on "advanced liberalism," Ong claims that former liberal apolitical tendencies are now reproduced within neoliberalism, which promotes "a new relationship between government and knowledge through which governing activities are recast as non-political and non-ideological problems that need technical solutions" (2006, 3). Rather than a novelty, a critique of liberalism as a technicization of the political goes back at least to Carl Schmitt's works. Furthermore, Ong's critique abandons an assessment of the results of a reworking of the social through market values, and an appreciation of neoliberal policies involvement in the constitution of global markets.

8 See especially the works of the winner of the 1992 Nobel Prize for Economics, Gary S. Becker from the University of Chicago, on the notion of human capital.

9 Figures regarding the value of cross-border exchanges in commodities vary and should therefore only be taken as indicative of the interconnectedness of the Canadian and the United States economies. Regardless of the correct numbers, they reportedly decreased significantly in 2008. That year,

cross-border truck traffic decreased by fifteen percent at the Ambassador Bridge linking Windsor to Detroit (Associated Press 2008).

10 Meanwhile, in a public speech made two weeks after the attacks on the World Trade Centre and the Pentagon, George W. Bush, hoping to calm economic anxieties, invited citizens of the United States to keep shopping, travelling, and attending amusement parks as a way to support their economy: "Get on board. Do your business around the country. Fly and enjoy America's great destination spots. Get down to Disney World in Florida. Take your families and enjoy life, the way we want it to be enjoyed" (United States, The White House 2001).

11 For a short genealogy of the management of the Canada-United States border in the 1990s, the different techniques of containment and technologies of surveillance the smart border now relies on, and the constitution of different populations from refugees to migrants and Muslims as terrorists, please refer to Côté-Boucher 2005.

12 For instance, the private company Accenture received US$10 billion to implement the US-VISIT biometric system of fingerprinting and registration of every visitor to the United States coming from countries without visa waivers (Amoore 2006). Created only a few years ago, the 2009 budget for the Department of Homeland Security was anticipated to be $50.5 billion (McIntire Peters 2008). Now under the supervision of the newly created Ministry of Public Safety, Canadian expenses in security are rather smaller: the 2008 budget invests around $150 million in security measures and technologies. Yet since the December 2001 budget, notwithstanding rising military costs in Afghanistan, security and emergency management represent an increasingly important investment in Canada. For a review of the post-9/11 budgetary spending on security until 2004, see the third chapter of the Auditor's General 2004 report, *National Security in Canada: The 2001 Anti-Terrorism Initiative* (Auditor General of Canada 2004).

13 An interesting association between technocrats and business elites, the APEX award, handed in 2006 to the nexus program, is sponsored by Deloitte & Touche LLP. This transnational accounting firm is mentioned later again later in this chapter.

14 In order to attain these numbers, the 2008 Canadian federal budget invests an additional $14 million in the nexus program (Canada, Department of Finance 2008).

15 NAFTA's infamous chapter 11 grants investment rights to corporations.

16 See the CCCE Website at: http://www.ceocouncil.ca/fr/about/members.php (last consulted 13 August 2009).

17 See the online form for a NEXUS application at: http://www.cbsa-asfc. gc.ca/publications/forms-formulaires/bsf658-eng.pdf (last consulted 13 August 2009).

18 The use of Emanifest is voluntary but will be made compulsory in the next few years until its complete implementation in 2014. The federal government invested $430 million in 2007 mainly for this program; a lesser part of that sum is dedicated to planning for the continuation of cross-border business in case of emergency (a likely reaction to the impact of 9/11 on cross-border traffic) and, finally, to the Partners in Protection (PIP) program (Canada, 2009b; Canadian Border Services Agency, 2009a).

19 Misdemeanour is a criminal category for minor (summary) offences in the United States that has no legal value in the Canadian criminal code. Canadian border agents thus have the discretionary power to decide upon what will be disregarded, and what will be interpreted as constituting a criminal record. This latter interpretation was made in the case of Ann Wright.

20 To hear El-Maati tell his story, listen to 27 October 2005 edition of CBC's *The Current*: http://www.cbc.ca/thecurrent/2005/200510/ 20051027.html (last consulted 14 August 2009). The Maher Arar inquiry suggested that further light needed to be shed on this case and that of two other Canadians, Muayyed Nureddin and Abdullah Almalki. Controversial because of its in-camera nature, the Iacobucci inquiry presented its report in September 2008.

21 While some NEXUS pass holders affirm having been required to show supplementary identification along with their preclearance card, it does not constitute an official obligation for this preclearance program.

22 The Copenhagen school in security studies designates the existential threat as the principal object of practices of securitization. While I do not adopt the school's linguistic approach to security – a method that is sometimes forgetful of contexts, power struggles, and social relations – the concept of existential threat remains useful for pointing to notions of belonging and menace that are deployed by security practices.

23 This understanding of a threat to core North American values by the attacks on the World Trade Center and the Pentagon is in line with the actions of the plane hijackers, who targeted, with that very purpose in mind, two power symbols associated with the United States – the stock exchange and the military. Yet when terrorist organizations and states both commit violent acts and agree on the meaning of these actions (as threatening or protecting a way of life), a shadow falls on those who die

and suffer from terrorism and violent state responses. In short, this agreement between terrorist organizations and state authorities on what is threatened obscures the victims of terror for political purposes while silencing those affected by violent counterterror activities.

24 The notion of the multiplication of authorized identities came up when discussing a previous and quite different version of this article with Engin F. Isin. I thank him for his engagement with the present work.

25 The positive designation of trusted traveller accompanies a variety of securitized identity and travel documents where only a passport sufficed before, or nothing at all, which was the case along the Canada-United States border until the end of the 1990s. This is exemplified by the story of Glenn Oswald, from Michigan, who owns a secondary house in Ontario (Vermond 2007). Oswald obtained a NEXUS card for himself and his family in order to facilitate their frequent transits between the two locations. Thus, borderland residents are likely to adopt preclearance cards in greater numbers in the next few years, either for work or simply for shopping and other everyday activities.

4

Neoliberalism, Racialization, and the Regulation of Employment Standards

MARK THOMAS

In the introductory essay to this volume, Susan Braedley and Meg Luxton suggest that two key questions to be asked of neoliberalism are "who benefits" and "who is left out." These questions are particularly pertinent when raised in relation to recent reports on labour market conditions in Canada, which demonstrate that long-standing patterns of racialized inequality have intensified over the course of several decades of neoliberal labour market restructuring (Cheung 2005; Creese 2007; Jackson 2005; Teelucksingh and Galabuzi 2005). Workers from racialized groups continue to experience barriers to secure employment and labour market mobility, and a double-digit income gap when compared across the Canadian labour force overall.[1] When considering the questions posed by Braedley and Luxton, it becomes clear that one of the effects of neoliberalism has been to exacerbate patterns of racialized labour market inequality.

Various labour law and policy studies have identified a correspondence between these conditions of inequality and problems associated with the application of employment standards legislation (Employment Standards Work Group [ESWG] 1996; Saunders 2003; Workers' Action Centre [WAC] 2007). In Canada, employment standards include legislation that regulates minimum wages, maximum hours of work, overtime hours, and paid vacations and holidays.[2] They establish the basic working conditions within a labour market and set a base for collective bargaining (Fudge 2001; Mitchell 2003; Thomas 2009). Moreover, as they constitute minimum standards, they regulate the employment rights of the most vulnerable workers, primarily those engaged in non-unionized jobs in secondary labour markets. Since jobs of this kind are disproportionately held by workers of colour, whether recent immigrants or Canadian-born (Cranford et al. 2003; Galabuzi 2006), it is these workers who are most directly affected by inadequate employment standards.

In this chapter, I explore the relationship between racialized inequality in the labour market and the regulation of minimum employment standards, showing that the two are intricately linked. Furthermore, I situate these processes in the context of a neoliberal re-regulation of Canada's labour market policies. In recent years, employment standards have been profoundly re-regulated through policy reforms based on principles of neoliberalism. As Raewyn Connell indicates in this volume, neoliberal labour market regulation takes the form of policy changes that seek to promote employer-oriented labour "flexibility." I argue that the shift towards the neoliberal model of labour flexibility has weakened an already insufficient system of employment standards by promoting a privatized model of workplace regulation, thereby increasing workers' exposure to market forces. This process has heightened the economic insecurity of those most reliant on the legislated standards.

This chapter contributes to *Neoliberalism and Everyday Life* by examining neoliberalism through the lens of racialization, while simultaneously constructing an intersectional approach that conceptualizes racialization in relation to class and gender dynamics. I develop the analysis through a case study of the regulation of employment standards in Ontario, focusing specifically on neoliberal reforms to Ontario's *Employment Standards Act* undertaken in the late 1990s.[3] I begin by introducing concepts of racialization and labour market segmentation, bringing together research literature on these two themes. Next, I outline the legislative framework that regulates employment standards in Ontario and review the neoliberal reforms to this legislation that culminated in Bill 147 in 2001. It will become clear that the neoliberal reforms to Ontario's Employment Standards Act exacerbated long-standing inadequacies in employment standards legislation and intensified racialized segmentation in the labour market. In the conclusion, I identify several ways in which these conditions may be further entrenched as a result of the financial crisis that began in 2008. My aim is to illustrate the ways in which neoliberalism deepens class divisions and facilitates labour exploitation through the production of a low-wage racialized labour force.

RACIALIZATION AND LABOUR MARKET INEQUALITY

The term racialization refers to the process of attaching social significance or value to perceived biological, phenotypical, or cultural differences between social groups (Creese 2007; Murji and Solomos 2005).[4] This definition is premised on a sociological rather than biological conception of race: it treats race as a socially constructed category in which people are classified on the basis of physical characteristics (Miles 1989). Racialized groups and racial categories are developed through relationships not simply of difference but also power and inequality, in ways that produce hierarchical relationships of privilege and exclusion (Galabuzi 2006).

This sociological understanding of race (and racialization) is based on an intersectional approach to social relations that hinges on the notion that social relationships of race, class, and gender are produced and reproduced through interconnection and interdependence and cannot be treated as separate and essentialist categories (Adib and Guerrier 2003). Racialization must be assessed through an intersectional lens in order to capture the ways in which social relations of class and gender shape, and are themselves shaped through, processes of racialization in the organization of capitalist production and reproduction (Acker 2006). As Mary Hawkesworth explains (2006, 214), "Intersectionality suggests that the processes of racialization and gendering are specific yet interrelated. Racialization may produce marked commonalities of privilege between men and women of the dominant race/ethnic groups. Gendering may produce particular commonalities ... among women across race and ethnic groups and among men across race and ethnic groups."

Racialization is deeply embedded in the social organization of paid and unpaid work and is central in shaping patterns of labour market inequality in capitalist economies. Scholars have looked at racialization from a sociological perspective to explain both the significance and persistence of racial inequality in capitalist labour markets. The "split labour market" theory of Edna Bonacich (1976) provided an early model that identified systemic divisions within capitalist labour markets emerging through wage differentiation along racialized lines. A more complex conceptualization of labour market inequality emerged through several generations of labour market segmentation theory. Beginning with Peter Doeringer and Michael Piore (1971), early segmentation theorists presented a dualistic analysis of the labour market based on a distinction between primary and secondary markets. Primary labour markets were defined by high levels of pay and job security, occupational mobility through internal labour markets, and a high degree of control over work. Secondary labour markets, conversely, were characterized by low wages, poor job security, few formal skill requirements, and little worker autonomy and mobility (see also Wilkinson 1981). Building on this framework, Richard Edwards (1979) identified patterns of racial inequality as endemic in the division between primary and secondary labour markets in contemporary capitalism. He argued that the formation of secondary markets takes place (in part) through patterns of racial discrimination and segregation, leading to a predominance of workers from racialized groups in low-wage and insecure jobs. Emerging out of these early studies, contemporary scholars have developed explanations for segmentation by studying the dynamics of capitalist control, conditions of labour demand, labour supply, and the role of regulatory institutions (Fudge and Tucker 2000; Rubery and Wilkinson 1994).

From this approach, patterns of racialized segmentation may be seen to emerge through the interaction of multiple social and institutional processes. They stem directly from institutional practices that limit the extent to which workers may participate in a labour market and the labour rights they may be accorded. The clearest examples of this are found in temporary foreign worker programs that create a system of "unfree" migrant labour by placing formal restrictions on the ability of participating workers to circulate in the labour market. In Canada there have been a number of these programs, such as the Seasonal Agricultural Workers' Program and the Live-In Caregivers Program (Basok 2002; Sharma 2006; Stasiulis and Bakan 2005). In these cases, the state has created an unfree workforce through labour programs that provide access to racialized foreign workers – agricultural workers from Mexico and the Caribbean and domestic workers from the Philippines and the Caribbean – for limited periods of time. These workers are employed in jobs that are characterized by low wages, long hours of work, and low levels of regulatory protection. Legal restrictions built into the labour programs prohibit workers from seeking alternative forms of employment.[5] Access to citizenship and permanent residency rights are similarly restricted through the labour programs. Denial of citizenship leads to the creation of groups of "highly exploitable and socially excluded workers" whose incorporation into a

secondary labour market is shaped in clearly racialized and gendered ways (Baines and Sharma 2002, 76). Thus, they constitute a
temporary but permanent racialized underclass in Canadian society
– temporary in that the workers' stay in the country is formally limited, and permanent in that the occupational status of the social
group is static.

Labour market divisions have also emerged through racist practices and assumptions that have – in conjunction with the gendered
character of employment – socially organized "undesirable" forms
of work in racialized ways. In her study of divisions of labour in
Canadian auto plants in the years following World War II, Pamela
Sugiman (2001) shows that black men, due to racist assumptions
about their physical capabilities, were most likely to be assigned the
hardest, hottest, and dirtiest jobs. Looking at the formation of the
Seasonal Agricultural Workers' Program, Vic Satzewich (1991) indicates that Mexican and Caribbean men were considered to be
physically well suited to agricultural harvesting, but because of racist conceptions of what constitutes a desirable Canadian citizen,
these same men were deemed"undesirable" as future citizens, a
view that justified the temporary nature of the program's residency
requirements. Through the concept of "gendered racism," Agnes
Calliste (2000) draws parallels between the racialized organization
of employment on the railways and in the health care sector. She
found that in both of these very different occupational sectors,
black workers have been channelled into the lowest-paying, least-
secure jobs. Using the examples of railway car porters and nurses,
Calliste shows how racialized occupational structures formed in
conjunction with notions of femininity and masculinity have the effect of "justifying the restriction of Black women and men to menial and backbreaking jobs" (ibid., 149).

The organization of social reproduction is also shaped through the
intersection of ideologies of race and gender, for example where assumptions about the "natural" abilities of women from racialized
groups have channelled them into reproductive labour (cooking, cleaning, caring) and simultaneously devalued that labour (Acker 2006;
Arat-Koç 2006; Brand 1999). Using an intersectional analytic framework, Evelyn Nakano Glenn (2001) argues that reproductive labour is
racially organized both in private households and the private service
sector. In private households, women from racialized groups have long
been employed as servants to assist upper- and upper middle-class

white women in the completion of household work, thereby absolv-
ing white women of the most onerous aspects of this work. As reproductive labour has been increasingly commodified during the
economic expansion of the service sector, women from racialized groups
have been employed in various "lower-level" forms of reproductive labour as nurses' aides, kitchen workers, maids in hotels, and cleaners in
offices, while white women are more likely to have been employed as
supervisors, professionals, and administrative support staff.

Finally, broad patterns of labour market inequality that have been
present in Canada since the late 1990s have been explained through
the racialization of labour market participation (Cheung 2005; Creese
2007; Galabuzi 2004; Jackson 2005; Krahn *et al.* 2006; Zeitinoglu
and Muteshi 2000).[6] Clear patterns emerge through indicators of overall employment, as well as through occupational breakdowns. While
racialized groups have a labour force participation rate of sixty-six percent, the corresponding rate for the Canadian labour force as a whole
is eighty percent. Further, employment patterns point strongly to racialized labour market segmentation, particularly with respect to recent
immigrants. Approximately one-third of recent immigrants to Canada
are employed in sales and service occupations, as compared to one-
quarter of all Canadians. While comprising approximately thirteen
percent of the Canadian population, they are disproportionately represented in low-income occupations such as sewing, work in the textile
and fabric industries (40 percent), taxi and limo driving (36 percent),
and electronics assembling (42 percent). They are vastly underrepre-
sented in senior positions, comprising only three percent of top executives and 1.7 percent of directors on organizational boards. Finally,
workers from racialized groups have a significantly lower rate of union
representation than other workers (22 percent as compared to 32 percent) despite such benefits of union representation as reduced income
inequalities, improved employment security, and a means to counter
workplace harassment and discrimination. Overall, shifts towards neoliberalism and employer-oriented labour "flexibility" have brought
about increases in labour market insecurity, disproportionately affecting racialized groups.

EMPLOYMENT STANDARDS IN ONTARIO

In this section I outline the legislative framework of Ontario's Employment Standards Act (ESA) and assess the relationship between

neoliberal policy reforms to the ESA and patterns of racialized labour market inequality. This will provide an example of how neoliberalism acts to reinforce long-standing racialized divisions of
labour and intensify class divisions in Canadian society.

Ontario's Employment Standards Act came into effect in 1969. It
combined previously existing minimum standards legislation regulating minimum wages, maximum hours of work, and paid vacations into a comprehensive legislative framework. The original ESA
provided a minimum wage for both men and women and established maximum hours of work at eight per day and forty-eight per
week. An overtime rate of time and a half was set for anything over
forty-eight hours a week and the act established the right to refuse
overtime work. It also provided for time and a half on seven statutory holidays and guaranteed two weeks of paid vacation per year.
The legislation was designed to set minimum standards for Ontario's
labour market and provide legislative protection for those most vulnerable to exploitation.

As a mechanism of social protection, the ESA emerged out of an
approach to labour market regulation that was premised on the gendered norms of the Standard Employment Relationship (SER) (Fudge
1991; Thomas 2004), which was a normative model based on full-
time, year round employment for a single employer (Vosko 2000).
That is, the ESA built upon minimum wage and hours-of-work legislation designed to protect those whose jobs were considered to be
secondary or supplemental to the work of a primary male income
earner. Earlier minimum standards in wages and hours of work were
specifically designated for women workers; low standards were justified in part through the assumption that women's employment was
undertaken to supplement the income of a male earner and was likely
to be temporary. While this explicitly gendered application of minimum standards had been abandoned by the time the ESA was enacted, the legislation was still much more likely to apply to women
workers due to entrenched patterns of occupational segregation created through gendered divisions of labour. Further, the norms of the
ESA remained rooted in the male income earner model, with its assumptions about the secondary and temporary status of women's employment. These relationships contributed to gendered labour market
segmentation by according standards of a secondary status (as compared to those achieved through collective bargaining) for workers
with the least bargaining power.

The core standards of the ESA were altered through minor reforms over the next decade and a half. Termination notice and pregnancy leave provisions were added in the early 1970s and severance pay was added in the 1980s. The minimum wage rose through incremental increases to $6.85 in 1994. Perhaps the most significant addition came through the short-lived Employee Wage Protection Program (EWPP), introduced by Ontario's New Democratic Party (NDP)government in 1991. The EWPP was introduced to provide employees with compensation for unpaid wages, overtime wages, vacation pay, holiday pay, and termination and severance pay (up to a maximum of five thousand dollars) in cases where employers had been found in violation of the ESA (Ontario 1991). Overall, however, while specific standards were improved incrementally during this period, the overall model of regulation – a secondary form of protection for workers outside the standard employment relationship – remained intact (Thomas 2009).

Neoliberalism and the ESA

Neoliberalism as both political philosophy and social policy developed in the context of the capitalist economic downturn that began in the early 1970s. This downturn led to wide-ranging transformations in the social organization of work, labour relations, and labour market policies. Neoliberalism emerged in this conjuncture as a challenge to Keynesianism and as a prescription for a return to capitalist profitability (Harvey 2006; Jessop 1993). Specific neoliberal strategies include the formulation of social policy on the basis of cost-saving measures, a re-orientation of macroeconomic policy to promote flexible innovation, and the skewing of labour relations in favour of individualized and privatized systems. The neoliberal shift across capitalist labour markets brought about, in varying degrees, a transition from "welfare states" – those aimed at the decommodification of labour power through forms of social protection – to "workfare states" geared towards a recommodification of labour power through the elimination of policies that buffer workers' exposure to market forces (Peck 1996; 2001).

Proponents of neoliberalism claim that the model is premised on the idea of reducing the role of the state in regulating the economy. Yet as Karl Polanyi reminds us in *The Great Transformation* (2001), the idea of the self-regulating market in capitalism is a myth: markets are always shaped by and embedded within political processes. Applying Polanyi's insights to the contemporary neoliberal period, Fred Block (2002) points out that despite neoliberal assertions of the need for markets free from government regulation, neoliberalism relies quite clearly on the state to regulate the economy. Drawing attention to the class relations that underpin neoliberalism, David Harvey (2006) highlights the fact that the implementation of the neoliberal model has produced social and economic policies that openly advance the interests of capital (see also Wood 1998). Thus, while in principle neoliberalism identifies the absence of state regulation as a strategy for economic prosperity, in practice it has resulted in the reorientation of social policies in ways that support capitalist profitability.[7]

These neoliberal principles of labour market re-regulation were brought to Ontario's employment standards beginning in 1995, with the election of a Progressive Conservative provincial government under the leadership of Mike Harris. The government pledged to make the province "open for business" by providing employers with greater "flexibility" through a thorough rewriting of the provinces labour laws (PCPO 1995). As Raewyn Connell notes in this volume, neoliberalism emphasizes market-based mechanisms to promote both economic competitiveness and labour discipline. This was the approach taken by the Harris government.

Neoliberal reforms to the ESA took place in several stages. First, in its anti-union labour relations reforms of 1995 (Bill 7),[8] the government terminated the Employee Wage Protection Program and froze the minimum wage at $6.85. This wage freeze remained in effect for nine years. Second, a year later the government introduced Bill 49, which reduced the time in which workers could register formal complaints from two years to six months and placed a $10,000 limit on monetary awards for ESA violations, regardless of the value of lost wages. These first two stages of ESA reform clearly favoured employers over employees and indicated the forms of "labour flexibility" that the government would promote in the interests of creating a competitive economic environment.

The third and final stage of employment standards reform undertaken by the Harris government came through Bill 147, which came into effect in September 2001. These amendments to the Employment Standards Act increased weekly maximum hours of work from forty-eight to sixty and allowed for the calculation of overtime pay to be based on an averaging of overtime hours across a four-week period:

employers could schedule overtime hours without compensation at time and a half provided the total for the four-week period was less than 176 hours. As inferred above, the bill left the minimum wage freeze intact. It also revoked the system of government permits required for excess hours (more than forty-eight per week), introducing instead a requirement for employee "consent" to the new excess hours and overtime averaging provisions.

Despite the claims of the government that it sought to provide fairness and flexibility for both employers and employees, these neoliberal reforms reinforced the already secondary status of employment standards and promoted a model of labour flexibility premised on the enhancement of employer power in the workplace (Fudge 2001; Mitchell 2003; Thomas 2007). Consistent with neoliberal principles, the reforms entrenched a privatized model of regulation for employment standards by removing the requirement for government approval of extra hours and overtime averaging, making such arrangements subject to "employee consent." This shifted the regulation of hours-of-work standards onto the private relationship between employers and employees, thereby enhancing an employer's capacity to exhibit greater control over the scheduling of extra work hours (Thomas 2007). Given the power dynamics of a non-unionized workplace in particular, amendments that were meant to encourage "self-reliance" among employers and employees empowered employers by increasing their control over work time and ensured that the regulation of employment standards was now determined much more directly by market forces (in this case individualized and privatized employer-employee relations). The neoliberal employment standards reforms supported the normalization of non-standard employment relationships, helping employers to maintain leaner staffing levels (supplemented by contract/temporary workers) and flexible work schedules characterized by unstable hours.

RACIALIZATION AND THE REGULATION OF EMPLOYMENT STANDARDS

From its inception, the Employment Standards Act supported patterns of racialized segmentation through its role as a secondary form of labour market protection. The neoliberal reforms of the late 1990s enhanced this dynamic, exacerbating economic insecurity and racialized inequality in the labour market. In this section I explore the racialized dimensions of employment standards, focusing both on long-standing tendencies within the regulation of employment standards and on the impact of neoliberalism.

Low Minimum Wage

The minimum wage freeze at $6.85 from 1995 to 2004 was a key factor in the deepening economic insecurity. As a single individual working full time would need to earn at least ten dollars per hour (2005 dollars, adjusted for inflation)[9] in order to live at subsistence level, the minimum wage freeze created a wage floor that was clearly insufficient to provide an income above the poverty line in the largest Canadian cities for either single workers or those with dependents (Saunders 2003). Yet close to one in five Canadian workers earns less than ten dollars per hour. Of those workers, one-third are the sole income earners in their family, almost half are over thirty-five, and one-third have a postsecondary degree or diploma.[10] As with other aspects of labour market inequality, there is a racialized dimension to these figures: racialized families are two to four times more likely to fall below low-income cutoff measures.[11] As members of racialized groups are more likely to be employed in low-wage employment, they are most directly affected by the low minimum wage.

This segmentation is reflected in overall employment earnings for members of racialized group that are below the Canadian average, indicating the connection between low-income employment and a broader racialization of poverty (Galabuzi 2006; Jackson 2005; Teelucksingh and Galabuzi 2005). There is a persistent double-digit earnings differential, where the average earnings of workers of colour are approximately 85 percent of the average for all Canadians. Racialized groups constitute 21.6 percent of the urban population but 33 percent of the urban poor. A year after arriving, new male immigrants earn 63 percent of what their Canadian-born counterparts earn; the figure rises to 80 percent for those who have been in the country for ten years. While the gap closes somewhat over time, it does not disappear. Further, new immigrants are more than twice as likely as people born in Canada to experience chronic low incomes. These employment and earning differentials have contributed to a broader racialization of poverty, where racialized groups are more likely than non-racialized groups to have overall earnings below the poverty line.[12] While a low minimum wage cannot be viewed as the sole cause of these patterns, a minimum wage that clearly falls below the level of a living wage is a key contributing factor.

Insufficient Coverage

The Employment Standards Act was intended to provide a minimum standard for the labour market and legislative protection for workers deemed most vulnerable to employer exploitation. Yet despite these very general aims, coverage by the ESA has always been circumscribed by exemptions designed to ensure that there was some "flexibility" in the application of legislated standards (Kinley 1987; Thomas 2009). In industry-specific terms policy makers attribute the need for exemptions to "variations in terms of employment, types of work, and characteristics of certain industries."[13] Taking the examples of paid domestic work and home working in the garment industry, it becomes clear that the application of exemptions is connected to the racialization of particular forms of employment.

When the ESA was originally enacted, live-in domestic workers who were employed by a householder were exempt from coverage because of the "special relationship" created through employment in a private household and the perceived difficulty of measuring and enforcing hours of work and overtime.[14] The exemption of domestic work reflects long-standing patriarchal tendencies to undervalue reproductive labour by characterizing it as work that is "naturally" women's work, and treating it as a private household matter and thus outside the acceptable realm of state regulation (Macklin 1994). According to the Ontario Labour Ministry's Women's Bureau, "these attitudes toward domestic work have, in turn, led to an exclusion of such workers when labour legislation has been passed in almost all jurisdictions."[15] Moreover, the gendered processes that lead to the devaluation of reproductive labour in private households intersect with racist ideologies that deem work of personal servitude suitable "only for those disadvantaged in the labour force" and justify the employment of racialized women in the most physically demanding forms of this type of labour (Adib and Guerrier 2003, 429; see also Acker 2006; Brand 1999; Glenn 2001). In the case of paid domestic work in Canada's Live-In Caregiver Program, racialized ideologies of femininity contribute to the commodification of reproductive labour by naturalizing the employment of migrant women from the Philippines and the Caribbean in a form of work that is "invisible" to the regulatory processes of the state. Exemptions from legislated standards based on the invisibility of privatized reproductive labour must be understood in relation to the "gendered racism" that underpins paid domestic work (Calliste 2000, 143).

Through the 1980s and 1990s, coverage by key standards of the ESA was extended to domestic workers in response to continued pressure from community groups representing immigrant women working in domestic employment. Minimum wage, weekly rest periods, overtime pay, vacation pay, and public holiday provisions were extended in the early 1980s.[16] Live-in domestic workers were also included under the maximum-hours-of-work provisions in Bill 147 (Ontario 2001). While this trend towards legislative inclusion may seem to contradict the neoliberal project, the expanded coverage was hardly a breakthrough for domestic workers when considered in relation to the other aspects of the bill, particularly those that undermined standards concerned with excess hours and overtime averaging. In other words, the broadening of employment standards protections for live-in domestic workers was countered with neoliberal policy reforms that reinforced employer-oriented flexibility through the privatized model of labour regulation. This will be illuminated further in the section on enforcement and complaints processes, below.

The details of ESA coverage of home workers in the garment industry are somewhat different, though the patterns of racialization are nonetheless evident, particularly in the "invisibility" of the work due to its gendered and home-based character. Home workers in the garment industry, most often women who are recent immigrants, generally work through subcontracted employment relationships and on a piecework basis (Gabriel 1999; Ng et al. 1999; Yanz et al. 1999). When the ESA was enacted in 1969, home workers were covered by minimum wage, vacation pay, and wage-collection provisions but excluded from maximum hours of work, overtime pay, and statutory holidays.[17] With sustained pressure from garment worker unions, along with growing awareness of widespread employer abuse,[18] momentum to improve minimum standards for these workers grew through the 1980s (INTERCEDE 1993). The provincial NDP government of the early 1990s significantly improved protections for homeworkers under the ESA by legislating coverage for maximum hours of work, overtime pay, and holiday pay, and by adding a ten percent premium to the minimum wage in order to cover overhead costs such as heating, electricity, and machinery. The new legislation also required employers of homeworkers to provide a written summary of employment conditions and to pay a fee to obtain homework permits. The funds collected through the permit fees were to be used to finance the costs of additional enforcement.[19]

The social democratic reforms of the early 1990s significantly advanced coverage of home workers under the ESA. Once again, however, the potential effects of these reform processes were quickly undermined by the neoliberal project that reshaped the regulation of employment standards, beginning with the minimum wage freeze in 1995 and culminating in the enhanced mechanisms of employer-oriented flexibility in Bill 147. As in the case of live-in domestic workers, the effects of extended coverage under hours-of-work and overtime provisions were countered by these reforms, which together kept wages low, made the complaints process more difficult, and ensured greater employer control over the regulation of key standards.

A third example of insufficient coverage by the ESA relates to the growth of temporary employment relationships. Employment rights such as statutory employment standards typically apply only to those in traditional employment relationships, such as when there is a single employer. There are types of work that fall outside this legal category and thus outside the scope of the ESA. Companies that hire workers through temporary agencies, for example, are not considered to be the direct employer of these workers and therefore avoid legal responsibility for employment standards violations they may commit. Yet while the temporary agency is the legally recognized employer, the subcontracted arrangement with the client company distances the agency from the actual regulation of working conditions, such as hours of work, overtime, and time off through breaks and leaves (WAC and PCLS 2008). In these situations the "invisibility" of the employer makes it difficult for workers to seek legal redress for employment standards violations. With temporary employment arrangements, employees whose work situations are already precarious may be reluctant to complain to either the client company or the temporary agency for fear of losing their jobs. Another related practice that is becoming more common is for temporary agencies to misclassify employees as "independent contractors," characterizing them as technically self-employed and therefore exempt from employment standards legislation, though in fact their job retains all of the key characteristics of the employment relationship (WAC 2007).[20] The transitory nature of contracting operations, the lack of responsibility of the client company, and the invisibility of employment through independent contracting arrangements, effectively exclude these workers from ESA coverage. Meanwhile, non-standard and precarious forms of employment are increasing.[21]

In the case of domestic and home workers, determination of exemptions from the legislated standards cannot be separated from the invisibility of the work (which is done in private homes), or from its highly gendered and racialized character. Where people are defined as self-employed or employed through temporary employment agencies, it is the character of the employment relationship itself that becomes invisible, as we have seen, through subcontracting arrangements. The various forms of invisibility contribute to exemption from employment standards coverage. Further, they are connected to sites of employment that are occupied predominantly by workers from racialized groups, constituting an implicitly racialized dimension of ESA coverage.

Ineffective Enforcement

While the ESA generally provides broad coverage of minimum standards, the application of those standards is widely uneven. In other words, formal coverage by employment standards does not necessarily ensure effective workplace protection. Violations of minimum standards – through unpaid wages and vacation pay, late and irregular pay, wages that fall below minimum wage, unpaid overtime, lay-offs without notice, hours of work in excess of the allowable maximum, and work without scheduled breaks – are frequently reported by those working in precarious non-unionized forms of employment. The systemic nature of employment standards violations is evident across a wide range of occupations and industries, including garment production, construction, retail, cleaning services, personal services, and food and beverage services (de Wolff 2000; ESWG 1996; WAC 2007).

There are clear relationships between ESA violations and processes of racialization. As discussed above, many workers reliant upon the ESA are members of racialized groups, including recent immigrants.[22] In commenting on this tendency, the Employment Standards Work Group (ESWG), a coalition of community legal workers who assist workers with employment standards complaints, noted that "women,

men and women who are immigrant workers, and visible minority workers face the greatest exploitation" (1996, 1). The long-standing nature of these general findings is illustrated by a study of job conditions for Chinese restaurant workers in Toronto, undertaken by the Chinese Restaurant Workers Advisory Committee.[23] The report documented long and highly irregular hours (averaging more than fifty per week), a lack clarity regarding overtime pay, and employee reluctance to complain about working conditions. The situation was described as a "cycle of vulnerability" in which workers "remain locked in a job ghetto; trapped by their long hours, and afraid to rock the boat about their working conditions."[24] Workers also had inadequate access to information about employment standards, meaning that they had little knowledge of existing standards and complaints procedures.

Similar problems have been documented for home workers in the garment industry and live-in domestic workers. Homeworkers experience highly variable wage rates and many earn below the minimum wage. Other employment standards violations include not receiving vacation pay, hours of work that exceed the legal maximum, unpaid overtime, and payment for less than a negotiated piece rate (Intercede 1993; Ng et al. 1999; Yanz et al. 1999). In the case of live-in domestic workers, major problems include excessively long hours and underpayment of wages. While they may be paid the legal minimum wage, their employers often fail to recognize that they are putting in large amounts of overtime, which thus goes unpaid.[25]

The primary enforcement mechanism for employment standards legislation lies in an individualized complaints-based process. The Ministry of Labour maintains a workplace inspections process, but fewer than one percent of Ontario workplaces are targeted for random inspection (WAC and PCLS 2008). Without a comprehensive proactive enforcement process, the onus of reporting employment standards violations lies with individual employees. Fear of job loss or other employer reprisals ensures that approximately ninety percent of complaints are filed by employees who no longer work for the employer in question (ESWG 1996; Kinley 1987).[26]

These problems are exacerbated by power imbalances in the workplace created through processes of racialization. Such imbalances are particularly pronounced in workplaces that employ recent immigrants, as these workers face additional disadvantages due to language barriers, immigration status, and economic insecurity. This dynamic is prevalent amongst live-in domestic workers, whose fear of deportation often prevents them from complaining about employment abuses. This was confirmed by a representative from INTERCEDE, an organization that assists domestic workers with employment standards complaints: "The fact that they are on temporary status really lessens their capacity to enforce legal rights that are already existing."[27] A community legal worker who assists immigrant workers in downtown Toronto attributes employment standards violations to the intersection between immigration status and economic insecurity: "About eighty percent of the ones that I work with, do not have permanent status in Canada. These are people who are extremely vulnerable. They need that work ... A permanent job, and having a letter of reference from your boss, is crucial."[28] Overall, the individualized disputes resolution process, like the neoliberal reforms to the ESA, privatizes the regulation of employment standards and makes workers – particularly racialized workers and those who do not have permanent residency status – highly susceptible to the profoundly unequal power relationships that characterize many employer-employee relationships.

Again, the neoliberal reforms of the Harris government magnified these tendencies, specifically by making the complaints process less accessible and elevating employer power over workers through the emphasis on "self reliance" in dispute resolution: in effect, supporting employer non-compliance with employment standards legislation. As discussed earlier, Bill 49 directly reduced the capacity for workers to file a complaint by reducing the time limit on filing from two years to six months. Given that workers, especially those in precarious forms of employment, may be reluctant to file a complaint, a six-month window is insufficient. As for those without permanent residency status, one person I interviewed put it thus: "If you had a longer time within which to file a claim, then someone who feels she really had a claim to make, but didn't want to do that to jeopardize her landed immigrant status, once she had that, she could very well do that."[29]

As we have seen, the provisions of Bill 147 directly enhanced employer power in the workplace. The pretence of "consent" was built on the theory that the relationship between employers and employees is one of equals; that "there is no power imbalance in the workplace and that workers are free agents."[30] In an employment relationship defined by economic insecurity, however, as it is for those who are most reliant on the ESA, "you cannot say that you don't want to work this long, these kind of hours ... The employer will say 'you can stay, or you can go.'"[31] This situation is exacerbated where workers are not permanent residents of Canada: "There is a qualitative change in terms of how people assert their rights when they don't have any status in the country, and when they do ... The last thing they would like to have is bad relations with their employer, who they want to work with for 24 months so that they can smoothly go through the 24 month requirement."[32]

The neoliberal emphasis on self-reliance as a primary enforcement mechanism places the burden of enforcement on individual employees, who may themselves be in a very vulnerable position vis-à-vis their employer. The result is a "flexible" workplace in which power relations are adjusted in favour of employers. Workers from racialized groups are further marginalized by an employment standards regulatory framework that implicitly enhances, rather than counteracts, employer power.

CONCLUSION

This chapter points to a central contradiction in Canadian society. In recent decades Canada has become increasingly multicultural and multiethnic. The percentage of members of racialized groups in Canadian society increased from four percent in 1971 to 13.4 percent in 2001. By 2011 immigration will account for virtually all labour force growth. Yet despite commitments to government policies of multiculturalism, this growth in cultural diversity has been accompanied by the entrenchment of pronounced patterns of racialized inequality in Canadian society, particularly in the labour market. Clear patterns of labour market inequality take several key forms that are connected to the inadequacies of employment standards legislation. As we have seen, these patterns are reflected in the impacts of an inadequate minimum wage, exemptions from legislative coverage, and ineffective enforcement mechanisms.

The neoliberal policy reforms to employment standards legislation emphasized a privatized model of labour regulation that enhanced employer control over working time and ensured that the legislated minimum wage fell far below the standard of a living wage. The reforms promoted a version of "labour flexibility" in which flexibility furthered the commodification of labour power – the enhanced role for market forces envisioned by proponents of the neoliberal project. As this analysis has shown, the reforms have also deepened class divisions and facilitated labour exploitation through the production of a low-wage racialized labour force.

The financial crisis of 2008 created conditions that further intensify these patterns of labour exploitation and racialized inequality. With a social security net already eroded by several decades of neoliberalism, workers have been left without the kind of social and economic policies that might buffer the effects of market forces (CLC 2009; Monsebraaten 2009). As unemployment levels increase, racialized groups – having unemployment rates already well above the Canadian average (Statistics Canada 2008) – are particularly hard hit. Those already in precarious employment relationships experience further insecurity as the crisis unfolds and class polarization intensifies (Winsa 2009). Governments seeking remedies to the crisis have been under pressure to develop labour market policies that promote competitiveness by deepening employer-oriented "flexibility."[33]

To counter the current dimensions of economic insecurity and polarization, an alternative direction is needed. With respect to employment standards, this means implementing progressive reforms that create a living wage rather than a minimum wage, extend legislative coverage to broader categories of employment, and facilitate effective enforcement practices. Such reforms would mark the starting point for broader efforts to challenge the multifaceted conditions of racialized inequality in the labour market, thereby constituting a first step in real movement towards workplace equity.

NOTES

1 In this chapter, I use the definition of "racialized groups" as developed by Teelucksingh and Galabuzi (2005), which refers to persons other than aboriginal peoples who are non-Caucasian. This definition is also based on the Federal Employment Equity Act definition of Visible Minorities.

2 Employment standards for most workers are regulated by the provinces, although some employees fall under the jurisdiction of the federal Canada Labour Code.

3 Key informant interviews undertaken for this research were conducted between August 2001 and May 2004, and during June and July 2007. Interviews were conducted with the following: representatives from

labour organizations (provincial, national); representatives from community organizations engaged in employment standards reform; community legal workers who provide assistance to, and work with, non-unionized workers who experience employment standards violations; and officials from the Ontario Ministry of Labour. Interviews referenced in the notes are coded as follows: ER – representatives from non-unionized employee organizations; CL – community legal workers; U – union representatives; G – representatives from the Ontario Ministry of Labour.

4 See Murji and Solomos (2005) for a detailed examination of the development of this concept, as well as debates regarding is application and interpretation.

5 The Live-In Caregiver Program permits workers to apply for citizenship after two years of continuous employment. This is not an option in the Seasonal Agricultural Workers' Program.

6 See also "Understanding the Racialization of Poverty in Ontario" Fact Sheets. Accessed September 2007 at http://www.colourofpoverty.ca

7 In addition to the class dynamics of neoliberalism indicated above, feminist scholars have clearly identified the gendered dimensions of neoliberal policies (Bezanson and Luxton 2006; McKeen and Porter 2003; Jenson et al. 2003). For example, neoliberal policies have promoted the privatization of social services and the lack of support for childcare, which, in the context of persisting gendered divisions of labour, have increased the demands on women's responsibilities in the home. Neoliberal policies have also reproduced patterns of gendered labour market inequality through transformations in income security policies (for example, Employment Insurance) that are premised on the male income earner model of paid employment.

8 For a discussion of Bill 7, see Schenk (1995) and Jain and Muthu (1996).

9 This figure is based on the 2005 before-tax low-income cut-off of $20,778 (Murray and Mackenzie 2007).

10 Judith Maxwell, "No Way up the Pay Scale." Toronto, *Globe and Mail,* Tuesday, 8 October 2002, A21.

11 "Understanding the Racialization of Poverty in Ontario" Fact Sheets. Accessed September 2007 at http://www.colourofpoverty.ca

12 "Understanding the Racialization of Poverty in Ontario" Fact Sheets. Accessed September 2007 at http://www.colourofpoverty.ca

13 Archives of Ontario (AO), Record Group (RG) 7–78, Memorandum, Re: Ontario Federation of Labour, 6 April 1976.

14 In the mid-1970s, they were given coverage under the following: the collection of wages, equal pay for equal work, equal benefits, pregnancy leave and notice of termination provisions. They remained exempt from most of

the key standards regulated by the act, such as minimum wages, maximum
hours of work, overtime pay, public holidays, and vacation pay. AO RG 7–
168, Policy Subject Files, Memorandum, Employment Standards Branch,
17 May 1985, p. 6.

15 AO RG 7–78, Overview of Domestic Workers in Ontario, Women's Bureau,
Ontario Ministry of Labour, November, 1976, p. 25.

16 AO RG 7–78, Program, Statistics, and Current Legislation, 1982; AO RG 7–
186, Policy and Program Development, News Releases, New Provisions
Relating to Terms and Conditions of Employment Applicable to Domestic
Workers in Ontario, 20 December 1980. AO RG 7–168, Memorandum
(Untitled), To John R. Scott, Director, Employment Standards Branch, 12
April 1985; AO RG 7-168, Memorandum (Untitled), 17 May 1985.

17 AO RG 7–78, Current Issue, From W.B. Cook, Administrator, Industrial
Standards, Re: Homeworkers – Garment Industry, 17 September 1982.

18 AO RG 7–78, Current Issue, From W.B. Cook, Administrator, Industrial
Standards, Re: Homeworkers – Garment Industry, 17 September 1982.

19 AO RG 7–186, Policy and Program Development, News Releases, Homeworkers to Get Improved Working Conditions, 16 December 1993.

20 Interviews, U1, August 2001; ER2, November 2001.

21 The legislative rights of workers employed through temporary agencies
was undergoing changes at the time of writing. In May 2009, the Ontario
Government passed Bill 139, *The Employment Standards Amendment Act
(Temporary Help Agencies), 2009*. The Bill contained provisions to: reduce
barriers to permanent work for temporary agency workers; prohibit fees
charged to workers by temporary assignment agencies for finding employment and for services such as resume writing and interview preparation;
ensure that employees have information about their assignment such as
pay schedule and job description; and require agencies to give workers information about their rights under the ESA. The government also enacted a
regulation to ensure that temporary agency workers have equal rights to
holiday pay, effective to January 2, 2009. The legislation is scheduled to
come into effect six months after Royal Assent.

22 Interview, CL2, September 2001.

23 AO RG 7–78, Letter, Gary C. Yee, Metro Toronto Chinese and Southeast
Asian Legal Clinic, to Penny Dutton, Director, Employment Standards
Branch.

24 AO RG 7–78, Report of the Chinese Restaurant Workers Advisory Committee, June, 1987.

25 Interview, ER1, September 2001.

26 Interview, CL2, September 2001; Interview, U2, August 2001.

27 Interview, ER1, September 2001.
28 Interview, CL1, September 2001.
29 Interview, ER1, September 2001.
30 Interview, CL2, September 2001.
31 Interview, ER2, November, 2001.
32 Interview, ER1, September 2001.
33 At the time of writing, the Ontario Liberal government was threatening to cancel a minimum wage increase scheduled for 2010 (Campion-Smith 2009).

5

"Child Care Delivered through the Mailbox"

Social Reproduction, Choice, and Neoliberalism in a Theo-Conservative Canada[1]

INTRODUCTION

There was a brief window, early in the first decade of the 2000s, when the era of neoliberal spending cuts and rescaling of the Canadian welfare state slowed and even reversed course. The federal Liberal government, in power for thirteen years, rode a wave of economic growth and budget surpluses. By the middle of the decade policy thinking about demographic change, poverty, and gender seemed to indicate that important elements of the Canadian welfare state were poised for a new progressive gender-aware expansion. The hodge-podge system of tax credits for children was reorganized and was delivering money directly to households, based on income, in recognition of the high costs of caring for and raising children (see Battle 2008). Maternity and parental leaves were extended to almost a year, and although eligibility for and remuneration under the Employment Insurance system remained relatively low, the change was an important recognition of the work of social reproduction (Bezanson 2006; Cameron 2006). Most significantly, the federal Liberals negotiated the legal framework with the provinces and territories for what was to become a national childcare system, emphasizing non-profit, high-quality, centre-based, affordable childcare. Even the contentious topics in the leaders' debate that followed the dissolution of Parliament and the election of 2006 headlined key equality and income security issues: childcare, abortion (not usually on the Canadian menu), poverty, charter rights, and same-sex marriage, to name but a few. On the way to the ballot box, Canadians waffled. In January 2006, a minority Conservative government was elected, under Stephen Harper. In virtually all respects, but especially with regard to social spending, the environment, and family policy, the policies and ideological positions of this leader and this party departed dramatically from the route Canada was on. Exit the post-neoliberal Liberals, enter the libertarian-leaning neoliberal theo-Cons.

The Conservatives, under Stephen Harper, held together a government until the fall of 2008, when an election was called. In the November 2008 election, they retained a minority government due in large measure to the unpopularity of Liberal leader Stéphane Dion and to public consternation about the Conservatives' underreaction to the sudden economic collapse of major international companies and banks (Leblanc 2009). The fall of 2008 turned into the early twenty-first century's equivalent of October 1929 and brought the near-hegemonic acceptance of neoliberal orthodoxy to its knees. The Harper government weathered the storm, but barely. Yet despite a grudging budget in January 2009 that placed Canada in a deficit, the blend of conservative orthodoxy and neoliberal ideology remained intact and in many ways deepened in the new post-September 2008 Canada, threatening to prolong and worsen the financial crisis. With Keynesian approaches gaining ascendancy worldwide, Canada was out of step with its peers in the Organisation for Economic Co-operation and Development (OECD), cleaving to an increasingly discredited approach that favoured a disembedded market economy built upon a nostalgic vision of family life.

This chapter explores the particular blend of classical neoliberal economic thought that informed the Conservative party's vision for Canada and twins it with the exceedingly socially conservative moral character of the policy aims of the governing Conservatives. Focusing on the Universal Child Care Benefit (UCCB), introduced in 2006 as a *replacement* for a national childcare strategy, I provide evidence about childcare from a case study of members of thirty households in Ontario who had children under six years of age and explore their experiences of cash in lieu of services. These micro-level experiences of a classically neoconservative policy choice show that the ways in which neoliberal practices are *lived* limit people's options. Direct income transfers to mothers are good public policy, but they do not constitute or create childcare and cannot redress major conflicts between the labour market and family life. I look at this version of childcare policy through the lens of feminist political economy and argue that atavistic approaches to familial life ignore the increasingly precarious income and social realities of Canadians – particularly women – with children. More ominously, I find that the economic and social vision that the Harper minority was rehearsing – and, with a majority, would immediately stage – fosters the steep social and specifically gender stratification that is the legacy of neoliberal experiments worldwide.

THE POWER AND THE TORY: STEPHEN HARPER AND THEO-CON NEOLIBERALISM IN CANADA[3]

Political commentators have suggested that Canadians did not have a real sense of what the Harper Conservatives were really about (see for example Laxer 2006). The central beliefs of the Conservatives were utterly at odds with what Canadians claimed to be their core values, particularly concerning publicly funded health care and environmental protection.[4] The Conservatives, thanks to Harper's firm grasp on the party's "message" in his minority government, managed to keep a Potemkin veneer of similarity with past Tory approaches of a redder hue. The Conservatives in Ottawa were, however, very far from the Tories of John Diefenbaker or Brian Mulroney, and their leader came from the right wing of the populist and religiously based Reform and Canadian Alliance parties. Many Members of Parliament – notably the former leader of the Canadian Alliance and cabinet minister Stockwell Day – had deep ties to anti-choice, homophobic, pro-gun and pro-"traditional" family religious and lobby organizations.[5] The name Conservative itself is misleading as the prime minister was an enormous critic of the Progressive Conservative party, a Member of Parliament for the Reform party of Canada, then head of the ultra-right-wing National Citizens' Coalition (founded to fight *against* public health care), then leader of the Canadian Alliance party. The name "Conservative" reflects a compromise with the former Progressive Conservative party when it and the Alliance merged in 2003.[6]

Stephen Harper's political career hinged on deeply regional issues, particularly "western alienation" and the need to keep the urban central-Canadian political and public sector "elite" at bay (see Flanagan 1995). In 2000 Harper codrafted the Alberta Agenda, a five-point near-secessionist plan for the province. He claimed to want to build a "a stronger and much more autonomous Alberta. It is time," he said, "to look at Quebec and to learn. What Albertans should take from this example is to become 'maîtres chez nous'" (Harper 2000, A18). The ideas in Harper et. al's Alberta Agenda declaration are, as columnist Jeffrey Simpson has noted, "unworthy of someone seeking high national office" (Simpson 2001, A13).

Prime Minister Harper and his party were nested in what is sometimes called the "Calgary School," a version of Burkean (and, some argue, Straussian)[7] conservative political thought, and a classical Hayekian approach to fiscal and social conservatism embraced with all the zeal of George W. Bush, Margaret Thatcher, and Ronald Reagan. In short, the Conservative philosophy was avidly pro-decentralization and pro-privatization; it espoused the dramatic reduction or abolition of the welfare state and held that a Conservative morality should be brought to bear in areas such as the courts, charter rights, crime, private property, family, the military, and immigration. Harper surrounded himself with friends and advisors whose views were far from those of the Canadian mainstream; they included right-wing evangelical minister Charles McVety (president of the Canadian Christian College and of various lobbies including the Defend Marriage Coalition[8]), author William Gairdner who espouses traditional family values, and conservative academic Tom Flanagan, who among other things argues against aboriginal land rights and refers to the environmental movement as a "radical left-wing ideolog(y)" (Flanagan 2007, 18). The Conservatives espoused a slow-and-steady approach, masking their populist theo-conservative roots with a focus on neoliberal economics. Flanagan (2007) even published a playbook of sorts outlining how to turn the country "blue."

Stephen Harper is a well-read economist (he holds a master's degree in economics from the University of Calgary) and consummate policy thinker and strategist. His intellectual approach to governance, taken from his own writings, political biographies, and from the work of his close advisors, is that of a true believer in Friedrich von Hayek's and Milton Friedman's neoliberalism stressing free trade, free markets, limited regulation of industry, and limited government

spending other than on defence and the promotion of commerce. Indeed, his is an exceedingly purist approach to sections 91 and 92 of
the constitution in terms of federal and provincial jurisdictions, viewing all matters of social reproduction as provincial and local (see
Cameron 2006 for an excellent review)[9]. Harper has repeatedly
called for a return to Edmund Burke's classical social conservatism
(Harper and Flanagan 1998; Harper 2003), which tempers some of
the elements of populism he was so uncomfortable with in Preston
Manning's vision of the Reform party.[10] He summarized his own vision in a speech to the very conservative Civitas organization:

> Its [Burkean Conservatism] primary value is social order. It
> stresses respect for customs and traditions (religious traditions
> above all), voluntary association, and personal self-restraint
> reinforced by moral and legal sanctions on behaviour ... We
> [Canadians] need to rediscover Burkean or social conservatism
> because a growing body of evidence points to the damage the
> welfare state is having on our most important institutions, par-
> ticularly the family ... [C]onservatives have an obligation to
> speak forcefully ... [on] a range of issues involving the family
> ... such as banning child pornography, raising the age of sexual
> consent, providing choice in education and strengthening the
> key institution of marriage.

Harper argued that in addition to significant neoliberal economic efforts, such as "deeper and broader tax cuts, further reductions in
debt, further deregulation and privatization" (2003,8), conservatives
must focus on moral issues. He lashed out at the liberal moral "nihil-
ism" of the modern left (particularly the Liberal party) and its puta-
tive supporters in the media and universities. He further suggested
that emerging debates "in foreign affairs should be fought on moral
grounds" (ibid.,9). He concluded that "the rediscovery of the conservative agenda requires us to maintain the coalition of ideas that is the
heritage of enlightenment liberalism and Burkean Conservatism ...
while retaining a focus on economic issues, we must give greater place
to social values and social conservatism" (ibid.,11). This vision was
summarized by Gairdner (1998,5) in his introduction to an edited collection that features a prominent article by Harper and Flanagan:

> He [sic] [a true Conservative] is also prepared to defend the full
> range of natural differences that arise from the free expression of

talent and effort in each human being, and thus will refuse in principle to forcibly equalize society. He generally seeks local solutions to human problems rather than any homogenizing state action. He is naturally anti-egalitarian, and finds poisoning and immoral the idea of forcibly leveling society, of trying to raise the weak by weakening the strong. He believes that the only truly equal societies are to be found in prisons, and that levelers who gain sufficient power will always turn the whole of society into a prison. He is not surprised to find that freedom sprouts social and economic inequality, nor is he worried about it as long as all are governed under the same rule of law, and decency and charitable instincts are encouraged everywhere, especially at home and in local communities.

Harper's notorious characterization of Canada in his 1997 speech to the United States Council for National Policy as "a Northern European welfare state in the worst sense of the term, and very proud of it" (2008,1) summarizes his views concisely. In public, however, Harper has been for the most part careful to stick to a message of free markets *über alles*, and he has trodden a careful path to avoid being associated with the more virulent reactionary Christian right approaches of his home parties. Indeed, he argued that the Third Way parties of former British prime minister Tony Blair and, indeed, former Canadian prime minister Jean Chrétien had essentially made hegemonic the key ideas of neoliberalism (Harper 2003). Hence the real fights had to be fought along moral lines; but the package of ideas would be more palatable to the electorate if delivered in the form of an economic rather than a moral pill. Despite his distancing himself from the hot-button issues (abortion, same-sex marriage, gun registries, euthanasia, immigration, and so on) that in the public view had branded the Reform and Alliance parties as fringe regional parties, Harper is himself a born-again Christian evangelical and he created a coalition in the Conservative party that is reminiscent of the process by which the Christian Right gained prominence and power in the Republican party in the United States. He referred to the American conservative movement as "a light and an inspiration to the people in this country [Canada]" (1997,1). Harper consistently claimed that for a political party to be taken seriously on a national stage, issues of personal conscience and morality should not be included on party platforms but should be subject to free vote in the House of Commons. Stories have circulated in the media, for example a long in-depth article in the respected Canadian magazine *The Walrus* (MacDonald 2008) about the ties between the Conservatives in Ottawa and various branches of the American Christian Right that are moving into Canada. While the suspicions of a hidden agenda persisted, Harper himself maintained a bland and neutral exterior, an image he was able to preserve thanks to his office's direct control over the content of most communication between MPs and the public.

In 1998 Harper and Flanagan coauthored a paper outlining how social conservatives and fiscal conservatives (they referred to them as theo-cons and neo-cons) could come together in Canada, a task Harper ultimately accomplished with the merger of his Alliance party with the Progressive Conservatives. "There are far too many organizations and groups," they lamented, "with vested interests in big government and redistributive politics, and dedicated to propagating and legitimizing collectivist values" (1998,177). They praised Britain under Margaret Thatcher and John Major, the United States under Ronald Reagan and George Bush Sr., and the provincial Conservative parties in Alberta (under Klein) and Ontario (under Mike Harris) for "doing yeoman's service in trimming back the excesses of the welfare state" (1998,177).

The brand of neoliberalism he espoused is deeply familiar to anyone who has witnessed the devastating effects of International Monetary Fund (IMF) loans on developing countries since the 1980s and to those who watched its trickle-up effects on the distribution of wealth in Britain under Thatcher and the United States under Reagan. As I have argued elsewhere (Bezanson 2006), this kind of neoliberalism has insidious gender effects and vastly increases social inequality. Conservative neoliberal theo-conservatism poses even clearer threats to income and social equity in Canada: women, the poor, families (their definitions and rights), and indeed the institutions of the welfare state that foster greater equality of opportunity, all stand to be straitjacketed into atavistic ideas of community and regional life. Moreover, the profound anti-federalism of this party with its implacable anti-government stance ensures that the Quebec question becomes the trump card for massive provincialization. Instead of being actively gutted, social spending is being regionalized and privatized. At a period in Canadian history when women's employment was at an all time high (almost seventy percent of women with children under the age of six were employed full time),[11] and when more women than men were completing university, same sex-marriage was recognized as legal, and women had access to safe and free abortion, the Conservatives threatened to return Canada to the pre-war, pre-Marsh Report period of massive class, income, gender, race, and sexual-orientation inequality, achieved though economic (tax cuts and credits and no meaningful investments in social infrastructure) and constitutional (decentralization) means[12].

The 2008 federal budget reflected deft political and economic strategy, even as it massaged a there-is-no-alternative-to-neoliberalism message in the face of the then *potential* economic slowdown. In the two years between 2006 and 2008 the Conservatives spent almost all of the enormous accumulated surplus left by the Liberals (Chase 2008; Canada 2008). In the style of American Republicans they donned the cloak of tax cuts and, in a period of brewing economic calamity, left the country with a precarious safety net. They also left little money for opposition parties to make promises with when an election was called in the fall of 2008.

The 2008 budget was the culmination of two years of policy reversals in a host of areas. Defence spending was up nine percent over 2006–07 and a whopping thirty-seven percent over 2000–01 (Staples and Robinson 2007)[13]; various environmental commitments, both national and international, were being abandoned; and funding for equality-seeking organizations such as Status of Women Canada and the court challenges programs were all but axed. The Conservatives required the removal of any and all references to the word *equality* from the mandate of the only institutional voice for women within the Canadian government (CRIAW 2006).

The 2009 federal budget represented a reluctant nod to global opinion about the need for a renewed Keynesianism in the face of global economic catastrophe. Harper and his party were so deeply rooted in neoliberal ideology that the economic statement they issued in the fall of 2008 responding to the economic meltdown in Europe and the United States and its encroachment on Canada proposed a tax-cutting approach to governance and no stimulus. This prompted the hasty formation of a coalition of Liberals, New Democrats, and Bloc Quebecois with the aim of ejecting the Conservatives and taking office by defeating their economic update in a vote of non-confidence. Prime Minister Harper went to the Governor General and asked that Parliament be prorogued less than a month into the new session. The January 2009 budget, ostensibly a stimulus budget, was mostly strategic neoliberalist, featuring tax cuts with some loath spending on roads and other physical infrastructure. It contained virtually no money for human infrastructure and absolutely nothing for childcare. Critics charged that even the investments in physical infrastructure were dependent on matching funds from provinces and municipalities, which were already cash strapped, thus inevitably delaying or cancelling the effects of any stimulus (Battle et al. 2009; CCPA 2009). This kind of spending, moreover, stimulated mostly male employment in the construction business, while female jobs in the public and parapublic sectors, especially in care work, were cut in the name of economic exigency. The opposition Liberals, under their new leader Michael Ignatieff, reluctantly supported a slightly modified budget.

Despite global questioning of the Washington-consensus version of neoliberalism, the Harper government gave its economic fundamentalism a thin patina of appeasement spending and tax cuts. From 2006 the Conservatives, making the most of their minority position, have drawn on classical neoliberalism to move the country stealthily down a fiscally and socially conservative path that is largely made in Alberta: to fight, as Flanagan eloquently put it, the "common enemy – the hypertrophic welfare state, dominated by a soi-disant progressive élite, that wishes to remake society according to its own rationalistic vision" (2007,13). Childcare was a central stage on which this "common enemy" was fought. Using that classical neoliberal trope of "choice" and adding to it a soupçon of a critical feminist catchphrase, they lulled an electorate in need of economic support for the raising of children into a quiet complacency. The fiscal crisis provided the Conservatives with an opportunistic rationale for failing to invest meaningfully in children and families. It also smoothed the path to creating a post-welfare state Canada.

THE UNIVERSAL CHILD CARE BENEFIT

The 2006 federal election campaign was a sight to see. Canada genuinely seemed poised to begin remaking itself in its own best former image as a generous, intelligent, peacekeeping world citizen; a forward-thinking redistributionist country run on the understanding that we are only as strong as our weakest link. The leaders pounded at one another over key feminist issues, even when the organized feminist movement in Canada had in fact been trampled by the previous decade's massive gutting of social spending and shredded support for equality-seeking organizations. Three of the four parties – the Bloc Quebecois, the leftist New Democratic Party, and the *now* relatively left leaning Liberal Party – highlighted the importance of funding public health care adequately, banning handguns, creating a national system of not-for-profit centre-based daycare, and building on human and charter rights for Canadians. The Conservatives did not rail openly against these popular issues, yet their actual beliefs were not brought clearly to light. They relied on a five-point plan, which they repeated non-stop. It was not really a plan for governance, but it was an acceptable tool with which to reprimand the Liberals for their thirteen-year ruling streak and the recent scandal over their sponsorship of ad agencies in Quebec. The five-point Conservative plan was woefully simplistic and in many ways easy to pitch. The key features included cutting the federal goods and services tax, thereby significantly reducing federal incomes, and eliminating the Liberals' childcare agreements with the provinces, replacing them with a *taxable* cash transfer to parents of children under the age of six. They proposed that parents should receive one hundred dollars per month per child, ensuring "choice" in childcare. They also promised incentives for businesses to create childcare spaces, a strategy that had failed abjectly in Ontario where it had been tried in the 1990s.

Canadians have long needed affordable high-quality childcare and it has been on the national agenda since at least 1993, though at the federal level little was done to address the problem systematically until the early 2000s. As the table below illustrates, in Canada a dual-earner/female carer is the norm (see Lewis and Giullari 2005; Bezanson 2006), yet before Harper, supports for the work of social reproduction were negligible.

The Conservative "born again baby bonus" (Battle 2006, 49) has little to do with childcare. Like the name Conservative, the title "Choice in Childcare Allowance" (later renamed the Universal Child Care Allowance) was more bait-and-switch tactic than substantive policy. While Canada had a reasonable Child Tax Benefit that contributed to the cost of raising children on the basis of income, there was a substantial need for meaningful policies to assist with the costs of childcare. The Conservatives, deeply decentralist as they were, tried to appear equitable in their approach to childcare even as they

Table 1
Childcare in Canada at a Glance, 2004

- Percentage of children aged 3 to 5 whose mothers work in the paid labour force: more than 70 percent
- Number of licensed childcare spaces available for every 100 Canadian children: 12
- Number of licensed childcare spaces available for every 100 Canadian children, excluding Quebec: 8

Adapted from Canadian Council on Social Development 2004.

argued against federal involvement in any and all social spending.[14] Consistent with their family values approach – and with their trumpeted warnings about the perils of "institutional" or "state-run" childcare – they offered cash to families, ostensibly in recognition of the best judgment of struggling families about how that money should be spent. As Prime Minister Harper himself said: "Paul Martin [the former leader of the Liberal party] has said that child care money shouldn't go to parents. He says it should go to experts 'who know what's best' for children. Well I believe that there are already millions of child care experts in this country, and their names are 'mom' and 'dad'" (cited in Johnson 2006, 448).

The nascent system of Early Childhood Education and Care was demolished shortly after the Conservatives took office in January 2006. The UCCB was soon put into effect. The money was, as predicted, nowhere near enough to cover full-time childcare which costs between $6,000–$12,000 per child per annum (Battle et al. 2007,8) or to allow a parent to stay home. The incentives for businesses to create childcare simply did not work, as the Conservatives own $120,000-plus task force study showed (Galloway 2007). The UCCB money (after taxes) was not only unequally distributed across income and family groups but it was funded by *removing* the young child supplement money ($249 annually for low- and modest-income families) from the geared-to-income Canada Child Tax Benefit. For the most part, those with money got more money under the UCCB, while those with less got less. An analysis by the Caledon Institute of Social Policy (2006) laid bare the refamilialization and anti-collectivism of the Conservatives. As Table 2 shows, the allowance significantly favoured *one-earner* couples over single parents and two-earner couples. Modest-income families were especially penalized. One-earner families tend not to have significant childcare expenses; thus such a

Table 2
Net Value of the UCCB, Families in Ontario, 2006

Earnings	One-Earner Couples	Two-Earner Couples	One-Parent Families
$0	$0 to 1,200	$0 to 1,200	$0 to 1,200
$10,000	$1,176	$1,176	$1,176
$30,000	$673	$460	$607
$50,000	$1,049	$827	$802
$100,000	$1,032	$778	$655

Adapted from Battle, Torjman, and Mendelson 2006, 2.

structure was consistent with Prime Minister Harper's conservative family values morality, if not entirely consistent with an approach favouring smaller decentralized government.

Taking into account the loss of the young child benefit supplement and income taxes paid on the $1,200.00, *no* family ended up with the full amount. Thus, welfare families netted $951.00 while working poor and modest-income families were in the $600.00 to $800.00 range (Battle et al. 2006,2).

The UCCB came as a monthly cheque, usually in the mother's name, and so Prime Minister Harper made good on his promise to deliver "a Choice in Child Care Allowance parents can see. A monthly payment parents can count on. A new Allowance that no politician will ever be able to take away without you noticing" (CPC 2005).

HOUSEHOLD EXPERIENCES OF THE UCCB:
NOT UNIVERSAL AND NOT CHILDCARE

We now turn to some reflections on the effects and limits of the UCCB based on the first of two rounds of interviews with members of households in a longitudinal study tracking the impacts and gaps in policies addressing the work/life balance. How did families with young children experience the new UCCB? For most, it meant extra cash – which they needed – but it did not even begin to help resolve the dilemma of being employed and having young children to care for, a dilemma that only increases as the economy worsens. A universal benefit delivered in a mother's name is a good policy tool. The one hundred dollars was a gesture, however, not a solution to structural problems facing families. For those with low incomes, one hundred dollars could steady some of the teetering but it could not pull a family back from the precipice created by the combination of precarious work, low income, and an absence of childcare. Worse, having opted for a hollow, nostalgic glorification of family life, the government eliminated the *hope* that a comprehensive high-quality system of childcare might be put in place.

The longitudinal study was designed to track people with significant paid work and caregiving responsibilities. The interviews captured the experiences of families in which there were elders or young children to care for; families in which a baby was expected (allowing for assessment of the leave provision); and families in which a baby had recently been born. Some of those with young children were on maternity or parental leaves. All eligible families began receiving the UCCB in the summer of 2006, when the first round of interviews began. The second round, conducted with the same people an average of twelve to eighteen months after the first round, reported in greater detail on the impact of the UCCB and various other federal, provincial, and workplace policies over time. Of forty-eight families in the study, thirty-three had children under the age of six when interviewed in 2006–07. They reflect various levels of household income, household composition, and ethnic heritage.[15] Members of thirty households with young children were interviewed in three different parts of Ontario: twelve in the Greater Toronto Area, eleven on the Niagara peninsula, and five in central-north Ontario. Table 3 shows the income spread of the families in the study.

Household configurations varied: among the thirty households with young children, six were single-parent families; one consisted of two parents, their kids, and a close friend who assisted with childcare and household maintenance; and the others consisted of spouses or partners and their children.[16] The ethnic origin of members of the different households varied. Data were collected from the primary respondent. Among those with children under six, primary respondents identified themselves as being primarily or secondarily related to the following cultural/ethnic groups:

2 First Nations
3 First Nations and European
1 African Canadian

Table 3
Income Ranges

Income Range[i]	Percentage of Families*
$0–24,999	13%
$25,000–49,999	23%
$50,000–74,999	26%
$75,000–$99,999	13%
Over $100,000	16%

i. Members of households were reluctant in the first round of interviews to divulge precise total household income and opted for income ranges. The second round yields more precise categorizations. Twinning households with LICOS (Low Income Cut-Offs) or LIMS (Low Income Measures) is challenging for round-one data and thus ranges are presented here, with the recognition that such ranges translate differently when household size and geography are taken into consideration.
*The numbers have been rounded.

2   French Canadian
1   Jewish Canadian
2   mixed European
3   East Asian
3   Eastern European
1   Mediterranean
4   unspecified other European
7   "Canadian"
1   Anglican

Most of the parents in the study noted that while every little bit of money helps, the UCCB money itself could not pay for childcare. A single mother living in central-north Ontario lamented that the one hundred dollars "pays for maybe half a week. It's six hundred bucks a month for daycare if you work all the time." Wanda, her spouse, and their four kids (two of whom were under six) found the two hundred dollars they received "handy" but said they spent it on taxes and diapers. "But, if you're thinking of it for childcare," Wanda added, "… the cheapest we found is thirty-five dollars a day plus you have to take your lunch for each [child]. So that doesn't cover it." Cindy and her spouse have two children under the age of six. She explained that she received the two hundred dollars in July

2006 but that it was not helpful because her child tax credit went down: "The child tax credit went down $150 so I don't know if that's because of our tax year or whether the taxes have changed with the government or what. But I'm not seeing a real benefit ... now I'm getting this $200 ... that $200 is taxable [where the child tax benefit is not] so I'm not too impressed." Oksana and her partner, who had two children, were also worried about the implications of the UCCB for their child tax benefit when they first got the monthly cheque. They felt that the money was "a waste of time ... if it's going to cost our daycare that hundred dollars a month. For every person that gets that hundred-dollar cheque, is that hundred dollars going to come out of a daycare somewhere? If it is, it is a waste of money." Others echoed Oksana's sentiment. Ava, a full-time student with a part-time job and a single mother of a toddler, said that it made a difference to have one hundred dollars in her pocket, but that in the long run "having universal [government-funded] daycare would be more beneficial. Because daycare costs what? Thirty dollars a day, so thirty dollars times thirty days is like nine hundred dollars, compared to a hundred dollars."

Some of the people who were interviewed put the money towards household expenses; others put it towards the costs of daycare; still others put it in an account for their children. Indeed, the targeting of mothers as recipients of moneys for children (the cheques usually come in the mother's name) means that the money ends up paying for items related to the needs of the child (McKeen 2004). No one in the study suggested that the amount was sufficient to change their labour market attachments or to make their childcare costs significantly more manageable. Cindy, whose two children were both under six, said that she just didn't understand how the UCCB could be considered universal childcare. "I don't understand the universal childcare [allowance] I guess. Because two hundred dollars a month if I was working at home or working out of the home ... it isn't enough for two children ... it's not significant. I'm still thankful to have it, but I don't see it as significant."

Some respondents were supportive of the UCCB. Rebecca, a mother of one who lives in the Niagara region with her partner, said: "Regardless of whatever [Stephen] Harper's agenda is, childcare was on his agenda. Hello, when has that been on a federal platform for election, ever? What he was saying [was] that he wants to make life easy for the parents, right? He's got his own world view on how that's gonna work. [It's] warped ... [but] that fact of the matter is, it's on the radar screen now." Similarly, Joanne, a single mother of one who also lives in the Niagara region, applauded Prime Minister Harper's decisiveness:

> I think, you know, as much as everybody thinks Stephen Harper is an idiot, he's done more for daycare, like he said, "okay, yeah, we need spots, so let's find a way to actually do it without just talking about it" ... [I have received] the hundred dollars a month. I have mixed feelings. I mean you're not gonna turn away a hundred dollars a month. There are side effects, there are ramifications to taking the hundred dollars a month ... It's taxable, so the problem is, it gets added to your taxable income.

She added that if someone is bumped into a higher income tax bracket because of the money, there are additional implications: "For some people who are really close to that tax bracket, you just bumped them into the next tax bracket, which changes everything. Which now they're paying more income tax, not just tax on the hundred dollars a month. Not just that, but your child tax credit goes down because you're making more money ... that hundred dollars is a huge help throughout the year though ... it's more than the Liberal government did."

Some mothers, on the other hand, were utterly outraged at what felt like an election bribe. Heidi, a mother of one child under six who lived with her spouse and older child in the Niagara region, said scornfully, "I just Blackberried my mother yesterday and I said: 'That goddamned Stephen Harper! He's sending me a hundred dollars a month!?' It's an insult. It's a bloody insult ... I feel like it is the biggest shame, the biggest setback for women ... twenty-five dollars a week ... it's a joke." Marissa also called the UCCB "a joke":

> The whole promise that they made was that the government was going to be giving families with children under the age of six a supplement every month to help offset the cost of different funds, different fees that you have. So everybody thinks this is such a great idea, but yet come income tax time you turn around and they're taking three-quarters of it back from you. So how is that helping? It is not beneficial, it is not help ... you're doing a disservice to everyone. And it's a real slap in

the face because nobody publishes it. Nobody told anyone that, "Hey, guess what? It's a *taxable* income."

Felice, a mother of two children under six living with her spouse in the Greater Toronto Area, was self-employed on a full-time basis. She scoffed:

> It's taxable, ha ha ha, and they call it a universal childcare bene-fit. It's not universal and it's not childcare. It buys me no child-care. If you actually work it out dollars and cents, by the time taxes are taken off it *might* get me two days a month ... And that's useless to me if I can't find [any childcare spaces] ... to put them [my kids] ... I don't need a tax break, I need childcare and I can't get it, and I certainly can't get [any childcare providers] that I have any confidence in at this point [because there are no spaces].

The model of childcare available in Quebec was mentioned in most interviews. Many wondered out loud why that model, in which childcare is available at a cost to parents of seven dollars a day at daycare centres and at private homes that were regulated – could not be replicated. Nishka, a mother of three who lived with her spouse and a family friend, stated: "A national childcare program could be the most beneficial program going ... [Let's] take Quebec as a model. And what's the problem? [We have to] get with the pro-gram." Yolanda concluded that even though families need extra cash, they also need a real universal childcare plan. Erasing the sup-plement and putting it towards a universal childcare plan, she said,

> would be more beneficial, not only to me, but to a lot of other families. You're taking a hundred dollars away ... Break it down to twenty-five dollars a week, go even further it's ... five dollars a day. Five dollars a day does not make any substantial difference to any one person in this city, in Ontario, in Canada ... Put it to-wards a universal childcare plan. *Fund* daycare centres. *Fund* pre-school centres. Make the rates reasonable, you will have a higher employment rate, thus making a lower unemployment rate, you will have a happier household across the board because people are getting out. You're not getting that cabin fever syndrome that

a lot of stay-at-home moms suffer from. You're getting better-educated children, better well-rounded children, you're benefiting the economy ...

CONCLUSION: SOCIAL REPRODUCTION, GENDER, AND THE NEW CANADA

The work that is involved in the daily and generational reproduction of the population is referred to by feminist political economists as the work of social reproduction. As I have argued elsewhere (Bezanson 2006; Bezanson and Luxton 2006), social reproduction is concerned with the dynamics that produce and reproduce people in material, social, and cultural ways. It speaks to the ways in which states act to mediate and stabilize social relations in particular historical periods in order to ensure economic and social stability (Cossman and Fudge 2002; Bakker and Gill 2004). The aim in liberal welfare states in the postwar period has been to mix the contributors to this necessary work. In different periods, the state has taken on greater portions of the responsibility along with the financial and affective costs; in others it has shifted the work onto households (and women's labour within them), to the market to provide for a price, or to the third, or voluntary, sector (Ursel 1992). The state thus plays a central role in structuring the *inputs* into, and *conditions* of, social reproduction in its approach to regulating the labour market, by providing income support and by underwriting child, elder, and dependent care (see Bezanson 2006).

For the Harper government, the issues surrounding social reproduction were at once plain and fraught. In many ways, they were caught in the dilemma posed by neoconservative social values and neoliberal economic beliefs, which often contradict one another when it comes to issues of gender, family life, and caregiving (see Brown 2006). The former is misogynist, traditional, and anti-egalitarian; the latter is less concerned with who does what work and more concerned that it be done cheaply, taking advantage of existing circuits of inequality in any society. Moreover, the libertarian leanings of Prime Minister Harper himself made him suspicious of federal constitutional encroachment on provincial rights, a position that has the potential to redraw the constitutional allocation of spending on social services and thus the kind of gender order of this new neoliberal era in Canada.

The brand of neoliberalism that the Harper Conservatives espoused did not differ dramatically from the model deployed by the federal Liberals under Chrétien, except in zeal and fidelity to its philosophical origins. Indeed, the federal Liberals (like other "third way" parties such as Blair's Labour party or Clinton's Democrats) laid the foundation for a "purer" neoliberalism with their actions throughout the 1990s, which they only began to reverse after 2000.[17] While the shift from a relatively universalist (rights-based) to a residualist (needs-based) welfare state began in Canada, as in most other advanced industrial welfare states, in the late 1970s and escalated through the 1990s (Pierson 2001; Rice 1995; Pierson 1996; Myles and Pierson 1997; Prince 1999; McKeen and Porter 2003), the federal Liberals under Chrétien oversaw an intensification of the process of retrenchment and saw a massive realignment in federal-provincial relations, in social spending, and in philosophical commitment to the goals of the Keynesian welfare state (Bashevkin 2000; Bashevkin 2002). They made virtually hegemonic an approach to governance based on debt and deficit reduction, the devolution of responsibility for program and service delivery, and a "remixing" of responsibility for social welfare among the state, families and households, the third sector, and the private sector (for a good overview see Myles and Pierson 1997; Bezanson 2006). Further, federal and provincial governments weakened the policy-making process by drastically reducing funding to third-sector organizations, especially lobby organizations advocating for vulnerable groups, by altering parliamentary and regulatory processes and by concentrating policy- and decision-making power in ministries of finance (Bezanson 2006; Rice 1995; Rice and Prince 2000).[18] Federal neoliberal policies in the 1990s, with their emphasis on free markets and less state intervention, and an approach that blamed the individual rather than the market for poverty and unemployment, created fertile ground for the success of the federal Conservatives.

The Harper version of neoliberalism promised a vision of constitutionalism and social policy reminiscent of the American Republican Right. While Prime Minister Harper himself had advocated the marriage of theo-conservative and neoconservative (or, more accurately, neoliberal) approaches, the theo-conservative view of personal life and the "family" rests on a far more interventionist and surveillance-oriented state (see Luxton, this volume). Most studies of the effects of neoliberal structural adjustment policies (see Elson 1995 for example) find that the process bears with particular severity on the poor, and poor women in particular. The addition of retrograde views of women's equality translates into a de facto policy position that women should rely on male incomes for their sustenance and access to entitlements. Public policies such as childcare play an enormous role in enhancing or making more challenging the conditions under which paid work, care of others, and care of self takes place. The gender order in Canada in 2009 was one in which men and women were primarily adult workers, and in which women undertook the bulk of the work of caregiving.[19] Policies such as the UCCB were insidious in that they offered cash in lieu of services: they recognized that caring for kids is costly, they recognized that the work should be supported, and they offered the illusion of "choice." Yet they occluded, by presenting their brand of childcare as childcare *sui generis,* the reality that children *require* quality care and that women and men are workers in the much-praised neoliberal economy, even when it falters. Those interviewed about the UCCB needed *services* and *adequate funding* for childcare – in short, a childcare strategy that is mixed and responsive to the needs of a variety of family forms, not a small, taxable, and unevenly targeted payment.

NOTES

1 The phrase "childcare delivered through the mailbox" comes from Liberal leader Stephane Dion's speech at the Liberal leadership convention in December 2006 (see politicsblog.ctv.ca). He was describing the Harper government's approach to early learning and childcare in Canada.

2 The author wishes to thank Renee McKinley for her excellent research assistance, and Sarah Bezanson and Jan Campbell-Luxton for their insightful comments and suggestions.

3 The term "theo-con" is taken from Marci MacDonald's essay *Stephen Harper and the Theo-Cons,* published in *The Walrus,* 12 February 2008.

4 For example, a recent poll found that Canadians overwhelmingly support slower economic growth in an effort to avert global warming (Curry 2007). Removing Canada from the Kyoto accord was part of the Conservatives' campaign platform and they have rescinded significant environmental commitments.

5 According to Flanagan (2007) and Johnson (2006), Campaign Life, the organized political wing of the anti-choice movement in Canada, sold Alliance memberships in 2002 for Stockwell Day.

6 In 2000 a convention was held to explore the creation of a united social conservative party by bringing together the Progressive Conservatives (PCS) and
   the Reform party. They sought a name with more appeal than "the United
   Alternative" and thus briefly and tragically called themselves the Canadian
   Conservative Reform Alliance Party, or CCRAP. The party later became the
   Canadian Alliance party, and the PCS remained their own separate party
   until their eventual merger in 2003 (see Johnson 2006; Flanagan 2007).

7 See Drury 2004, for example.

8 In their 2008 budget, the Conservatives introduced changes to the Income
   Tax Act that would deny tax credits to TV and film productions with "of-
   fensive" content. Charles McVety, a well-known evangelical activist,
   claimed that his organization's lobbying efforts are to be credited for the
   initiative (El Akkad 2008). Such public eruptions of Christian influence on
   the Conservatives are quickly quelled by the party, but the fissures in "message" and the undertones of fundamentalism continue to surface.

9 Cameron (2006:50–51) summarizes the rationale behind the 1867 division
   of powers. She notes that "activities thought to be essential to continent-
   wide expansion, as well as those thought to be inherently national, were assigned to the central state" (Section 91 of the BNA Act 1867), while "those
   thought to be important to the survival of French Catholic culture or that
   were of a 'merely local or private nature' were given to the provincial governments" (Section 92). Thus Section 91 gave the central government power
   over trade, commerce, banking and so on, while "hospitals, asylums, charities; 'property and civil right'" among others were left to section 92.

10 He noted in 1998: "Modern conservatives, beginning with Edmund Burke,
   have been leery of radical political change and have put emphasis on incre-
   mentalism and on traditional institutions as safeguards of order and freedom ... Conservatism in this sense ... [is] bereft of the zealous tinge that
   has been attached to populism" (Harper and Flanagan 1998, 177).

11 Indeed, in 2003 66 percent of mothers whose youngest child was three or
   less were in the paid labour force, 75 percent whose youngest was between
   three and five were, and a whopping 82 percent of those with a child of six
   to fifteen years were employed (Friendly and Beach 2005).

12 The Marsh report was published in 1943 (entitled *Report on Social Security for Canada*) and served as an important basis for the modern system of
   Canadian social welfare.

13 Harper supports the American war in Iraq and denounced former prime minister Jean Chrétien for not sending Canadian troops. From a foreign policy
   perspective, he has actively supported Israel and was the first world leader to
   cut off funding for Hamas when it took over the Palestinian Authority.

14 As noted in Bezanson and Carter 2006, 58:

> One of the challenges of developing federal social policy in Canada is the
> division of constitutional responsibilities for social programs, which results
> in a lack of uniformity in service provision nationally. With few exceptions,
> provincial and territorial governments are responsible for funding and deliv-
> ering Early Childhood Education and Care (ECEC). ECEC services targeted
> to First Nations peoples, military families and new Canadians are provided
> federally (Friendly and Beach 2005). There is tremendous variation across
> provinces in the accessibility and cost of regulated child care and some varia-
> tion in the provision and age limits for kindergarten. Translated into prac-
> tice, there were spaces in regulated child care for fewer than 20 per cent of
> Canadian children aged six and under in 2001. This compares to 60 per cent
> in the United Kingdom. An estimated 62 per cent of Canadian children are
> in unregulated care (Friendly and Beach 2005). Incomes for child care work-
> ers in formal and home based care outside of Quebec are extremely low, the
> work is almost exclusively done by women, and staff turnover rates are high.

15 Due to data gaps regarding income for three of the households in round
    one of the interviews, they are not included in the analysis presented here.

16 Some families had stepchildren and foster children as well. Because those
    we interviewed had children under the age of six years, they tended to be
    relatively young. Given an average age of first marriage in Canada of 28.5
    and 30.6 for women and men respectively (Statistics Canada 2007) rates of
    divorce or separation were likely lower for the interviewed group.

17 A craven reading of their political strategy would suggest that they weak-
    ened advocacy and interest groups when it suited their ends and then re-
    named themselves as defenders of minority rights and opinions when their
    grip on power was weakened.

18 I outline the Liberal role in creating the conditions for a Harper-style gov-
    ernment in my 2006 book. I noted then (p. 8) that

> many of the federal policy initiatives undertaken in the 1990s in an effort
> to reduce the scope and size of the Canadian welfare state were swift and
> far-reaching. In the very early part of the 1990s, the Canada Assistance
> Plan (CAP) was dismantled and replaced with the Canada Health and So-
> cial Transfer (CHST). The CHST effectively eliminated federal-provincial
> cost sharing for social assistance and social services. It eradicated national
> standards related to the social rights of poor Canadians associated with
> social transfers.
>
> In addition to further cutting and decreasing eligibility for Employ-
> ment Insurance, the federal government cut the total cash transfers to
> the provinces by a third in 1995 (Rice and Prince 2000). Although the

2000 and 2003 health care meetings between the First Ministers and the federal government promised to restore transfers for health care, federal cuts have had a significant effect on the provinces' ability to deliver health care services (Prince 1999). The emphasis at the federal level rested on active social policies which fostered incentives for labour market participation. The lumping of federal funding for social assistance, health, and post-secondary education into the CHST block transfer, in combination with an employability model of social policy delivery, permitted the introduction of punitive workfare-styled policies at the provincial levels and increased targeting for other social programs. Moreover, a preference for negative income tax policies (tax credits rather than service provision) altered the capacities of Canadians to access public services.

19 See Adkin and Abu-Laban 2008 for a good Canadian analysis of Nancy Fraser's Universal Breadwinner model.

6

Beyond the State

The Making of Disability and Gender under Neoliberalism in Portugal[1]

PAULA C. PINTO

INTRODUCTION

Since the 1980s the global turn towards neoliberalism has placed the welfare state under attack. Worldwide there has been a discernible trend towards state contraction, retrenchment, and restructuring. Yet, as Raewyn Connell signalled earlier in this volume, while neoliberalism is a global phenomenon, it is always socially heterogeneous. Thus, history, political economy, and cultural circumstances influence the way neoliberal reforms are achieved and their impact on the provision of state welfare in each particular country. This leads to what Leibfried and Obinger (2001) have termed "a global pattern of divergent convergence."

Given the variability in the neoliberal project, Connell's challenge to "understand neoliberalism and trace its consequences" can be met by expanding our analytical lens to include a wider range of social issues as they are articulated in different geographic and sociopolitical settings. Exploring both the commonalities and specificities of diverse realities contributes to a more sophisticated understanding of the significance of neoliberalism in shaping our world today.

This chapter embarks on such a journey. Taking a rather unusual case study – Portugal – I focus on one of the least visible and most neglected groups in society – mothers with disabilities – to illustrate how law and policy inspired by neoliberal principles set in motion processes that create, perpetuate, and in some cases even aggravate social and economic disparities. These processes have much in common with those observed in other contexts, as we have seen, for example, in Thomas's discussion of racialization in the Canadian labour market and Bezanson's study of neoliberal impacts on gender and childcare in Canada.

In this chapter, I draw on in-depth interviews with twenty-one mothers with disabilities living in the metropolitan region of the state capital, Lisbon, to explore disabled women's experiences of motherhood in Portugal as they are shaped by current law, policy, and practices. The study highlights the tensions, contradictions, and paradoxes in values and assumptions regarding disability and citizenship that presently underlie Portuguese society. To situate the discussion, I offer a brief historical account of social policy development in Portugal and then consider how neoliberal reforms in this country have been translated in the domain of disability policy. This analysis shows that, due to the late emergence and development of the Portuguese welfare state, the most critical consequences of neoliberalism there have been *to contain* and *reorient*, rather than dismantle as in other places, a system that is still in need of considerable expansion. In the final part of the chapter, I examine the way notions of disability and dependence are being construed (but also resisted) in the specific context of the Portuguese neoliberal state. To pursue this investigation I focus on three domains: access to disability-related benefits and supports; the introduction of welfare-to-work programs; and the development of rights-based legislation. The analysis reveals the paradoxes of the neoliberal state and its complicity with socioeconomic and political processes that produce the ongoing marginalization of women who are mothering with disabilities.

Recent data show that women with disabilities in Portugal, when compared to non-disabled women and to men with disabilities, tend to present the lowest levels of education and the lowest probability of entering the workforce (Sousa et al. 2007). Disabled women are therefore more likely than any other group to live on welfare and experience poverty and social isolation. Many disabled mothers, however, resist the forces that are shaping their lives. Their personal stories of struggle and strain, as they navigate disabling structures, institutions, and practices to realize their human rights, are powerful political statements. By forging new social relations and identities in the process, these women are also fundamentally disrupting and troubling the primacy of the neoliberal order.

NEOLIBERALISM AND THE PORTUGUESE WELFARE STATE: FROM LEAN AND MEAN ... TO LEANER AND MEANER

To understand how neoliberalism has shaped disability governance in Portugal, we need first to trace the unique circumstances that surrounded the emergence and development of the welfare state in this country. The expansion of the Portuguese welfare state occurred at a much later time than in other industrialized nations: it only took off in the final quarter of the twentieth century, after the 1974 democratic revolution that removed the authoritarian right-wing government that had ruled the country for more than forty years (Adão e Silva 2002). From 1933 to 1974 Portugal lived under a dictatorship of fascist inspiration. One important consequence of this political regime was to delay the modernization of Portuguese society, while reinforcing the role and influence of the Catholic church and the family (in its heterosexual, extended, and patriarchal format) in the provision of welfare. State welfare, by contrast, was rudimentary: large sectors of the population were not covered by existing schemes, important gaps in programs persisted (for instance, there was no protection for the unemployed), and benefits were in general very low (Sousa Santos et al. 1998; Leiria 2000; Veiga et al. 2004).

Right after the revolution, particularly in the period between 1974 and the early 1980s, important changes were introduced in Portugal's social security system, enabling the gradual enlargement of the social risks covered and the increase in the number of beneficiaries. This process of expansion and modernization, however, took place in a context which was already marked by economic recession and the global rise of neoliberalism – forces which dramatically hampered the full maturation of the Portuguese welfare state. Right from the start, Portugal's welfare system was placed under significant financial pressure (Rodrigues 2000). An aging population (Leiria 2000; Marques 1997) and low rates of economic growth in the country (Leiria 2000) have been said to explain the financial crisis that has affected the system almost from the outset. The crisis, however, became more visible from the 1990s onward, when the welfare state came under increasing pressure to act as buffer against the impacts of economic restructuring and global competition – notably through the provision of supports for vocational training measures and early retirement, unemployment schemes and active employment policies (Marques 1997).

In sum, the Portuguese welfare state – an indisputable gain of the democracy installed in the mid-1970s – was still in its infancy and offering only modest (if in most cases universal) programs and benefits when the neoliberal wave hit the nation a decade later. In this sense, the most critical consequence of neoliberalism on the Portuguese welfare state was not so much to dismantle as to contain and reorient a welfare state that was at the time still in need of significant development and expansion.

It was, in fact, an incipient welfare state that came to confront the challenges of neoliberal restructuring. In the early 1990s, with the nation plunged in an economic crisis and under the fiscal pressure exerted by the European Union in the context of the process of monetary and economic integration, restrictions on access to benefits started being adopted as a strategy to control public deficit. Initially, these included the extension of the age of retirement for women, as well as changes in the computing formulas of old age and invalidity pensions that were disadvantageous for workers. In 1995 family allowances lost their universality and became a means-tested benefit.

The "welfare crisis" discourse continued to grow throughout the nineties, prompting a larger reform of the social security system in the year 2000 that was clearly inspired by neoliberal ideals. While this reform only lasted for two years, it opened the way to the privatization of social security in Portugal, a trend that was intensified by the subsequent reforms of 2002 and 2007. For instance, while the right of all citizens to social security and the "primacy of public responsibility" in the provision of welfare were reaffirmed, a new set of principles for welfare policies was gradually put forward. From then on, *complementarity*,[2] defined as "the articulation of different forms of social protection, public, cooperative and social" (Segurança Social 2001), and above all *social subsidiarity*, that is, "recognition of the role that people and families play in providing welfare" (Segurança Social 2005), became guiding notions of the national welfare system. Again, these policy changes strikingly parallel those adopted in other countries, notably Canada, and have served to increase the transfer of care responsibilities to individuals and families (see for instance Bezanson and Luxton in this volume). In line with the neoliberal ideology as well, a new emphasis on "active, preventive and personalized" measures as a means to "eliminate the factors causing marginalization and social exclusion and promote human dignity" was introduced (Lei de Bases da Segurança Social, Law 4/2007 of 16 January 2007).

These successive reforms were explicitly aimed at containing public social spending, despite the fact that meagre benefits and low levels of expenditure are a structural feature of the Portuguese welfare state, traditionally placing the country below the European average (see Table 1). Given the country's unstable financial situation and the tough economic requirements imposed by the current neoliberal policies of the EU, the fragile architecture of the Portuguese welfare state is likely to remain under threat. This is the context in which disability policies have emerged.

RESTRUCTURING DISABILITY POLICY

Unsurprisingly, disability policy in Portugal also has a short history. Prior to the 1974 revolution, public initiatives in this area were sporadic and of limited scope. Few organizations provided services for population with disabilities and their role was limited by the lack of public and private supports. Disability, generally viewed as a "personal tragedy," was individualized and enclosed, relegated to the private sphere of the home as a problem that individuals and families had to deal with on their own.

The end of the colonial war in 1974[3] and the return of many disabled veterans raised the visibility of the disability issue in the public eye. The new constitution, approved in 1976, included a clause about the rights and duties of people with disabilities. For the first time in Portugal, the fundamental law of the nation asserted the state's responsibility to develop "a policy of prevention, treatment, rehabilitation and integration of the handicapped." Nevertheless, developments in disability policy were not among the first priorities in the postrevolution expansion of the Portuguese welfare state (Capucha et al. 2004). Furthermore, the few legislative and programatic initiatives undertaken in this period failed to take a holistic view of the various needs and interests of disabled people. Instead, from the beginning the emphasis was on vocational training, employment, and education.

It was only in 1989 that a general framework for disability policy was adopted through a major piece of legislation, the Prevention, Rehabilitation and Integration of People with Disabilities Act (Act

Table 1
Total Social Protection Expenditure, EU and Portugal

	1996	1998	2000	2002	2004p
As a % of GDP					
EU25	:	:	26,9	27,1	27,3p
EU15	28,4	27,5	27,2	27,4	27,7p
PT	20,4	21,2	21,7	23,7	24,7p
In million EURO					
PT	18 727	22 140	26 574	32 043	35 544p

P: provisional data.
Source: EUROSTAT, European Social Statistics, Social Protection – Expenditure and Receipts (1995–2003 and 1997–2005).

no. 9/89 of 2 May 1989). The law, however, still embedded in the individualistic medical approach, continued to frame disability as personal deficit and general invalidity. Thus, for instance, while the state took on the responsibility of guaranteeing the implementation of disability policy, "in close collaboration with families and non-governmental organizations," disabled people themselves were not identified as important partners in policy development. Rehabilitation was depicted as a "global process" involving interventions in a variety of domains, but the measures proposed were often paradoxical. For example, the law adopted the principle of *equality of opportunity,* requiring "the elimination of all forms of discrimination based on disability"; yet it still supported the provision of special and segregated educational services for children with disabilities.

These paradoxes signal the failure of the act to break with the traditional approach to disability. Informed by an "individual pathology" model (Rioux and Valentine 2006) that aimed at repairing individual dysfunctions so that the disabled could adjust to "a normal life," the act showed very little appreciation of the ways in which society disables some individuals and prevents them from fully participating in social, economic, and cultural life. In short, while the new legislation provided a framework for policies that were already in place, it offered few innovations and had little impact in shaping a new approach to disability.

In 1986 Portugal joined the European Economic Community (as it was then called) and started receiving monies from the European Social Fund directed at supporting initiatives to promote "equality of opportunities in vocational training and employment." The availability of European funds, which reached the country through various programs and initiatives, stimulated national investments; but in line with the hegemonic neoliberal rules of the EU, these too were mainly directed at vocational training and employment programs (Capucha et al. 2004). Consequently, while the number of entities (mostly private not-for-profit organizations) providing vocational training services and the number of beneficiaries of these programs significantly increased, needs related to many other dimensions of disabled people's lives (such as supports to promote independent living) remained largely neglected. Furthermore, due in part to the requirements of the funding structure on which they relied, most of the vocational training programs provided during this period targeted only disabled people. Furthermore, the programs provided training for menial jobs in the service sector, such as house cleaning, garden maintenance, or basic sewing. Since jobs in these areas were scarce, the economic prospects of trainees were minimal; where jobs could be found, they offered little financial reward (ibid.). Thus, while vocational training services for disabled people expanded during this period, the pattern of segregation and marginalization on the basis of disability persisted.

During the last two decades of the twentieth century, disability issues acquired a global dimension particularly as a result of the United Nations Decade of Disabled Persons (1983–92) and the publication of the Standard Rules for the Equalization of Opportunities for People with Disabilities (United Nations 1993). Throughout this time, too, the disability movement gained increasing influence in its push to define disability as an issue of rights. In Portugal, the impact of these initiatives and the dynamics of European integration stimulated the implementation of a number of important policy proposals. New legislation achieved, for instance, the inclusion of children with disabilities in ordinary schools (Act no. 319/91 of 23 August 1991) and the removal of architectural barriers in public buildings and spaces to promote "the enjoyment of full citizenship for people with reduced mobility" (Accessibility to Public Buildings, Collective Facilities and Public Spaces Act, Act no. 123/97 of 22 May 1997).

At the European level, the Treaty of Amsterdam, signed in 1997, opened up new possibilities for a more active role for the European Union in the disability policy arena. The treaty included a new article outlawing discrimination on several grounds including disability. It also included a new chapter on employment establishing the so-called European Employment Strategy and created a new mechanism – the Open Method of Coordination – for policy design and coordination at the European level. National governments were encouraged to develop employment guidelines and National Action Plans (NAPS), which are systematically monitored among member states. National Action Plans have to include measures to improve the vocational training and employment of people with disabilities. A similar mechanism was introduced in 2000 for social policies. National Action Plans to Fight Social Exclusion and Poverty presented by the member states define national priorities and coordinate actions for social intervention at the national level; again, they have to include references to measures aimed at reducing the social disadvantages experienced by people with disabilities.

These developments in disability policy suggested a new orientation towards a rights-based approach. In Portugal a new legal and policy framework was gradually put in place. The main elements of this framework included the Employment Quota System for the Public Sector, installed in 2001 (Act no. 29/2001 of 3 February 2001), and the updating of the fundamental law on disability in 2004 (Act no. 38/2004), proposing "the development of a comprehensive, integrated and transversal disability policy, which promoted equality of opportunities and a society for all." The new act redefined the concept of disability by focusing on limitations to activity and participation resulting from the interaction of individual and environmental factors. Citizenship, non-discrimination, autonomy, and participation became the principles upon which disability policy was to evolve. Further, the act guaranteed the *right* of people with disabilities to employment and vocational training, education and culture, social security, health, housing, sports, and leisure time. Disabled people were *encouraged* to participate in the decision-making process for policies that affected their lives. In the same year, the European Employment Equality Directive prohibiting discrimination in employment and occupation on several grounds including disability (CEU 2000) was transposed to national legislation through the enactment of the new Labour Act (Act no. 35/2004 of 29 July 2004). Finally, in 2006 a new law prohibiting discrimination on the basis of disability was approved (Act no. 46/2006 of 28 August). The law covered a wide range of rights, "economic, social, cultural and others." Together with the new Disability Act this legislation became the fundamental juridical tool for shaping future policy development aimed at improving the situation of people with disabilities in Portugal.

As this brief overview suggests, the EU guidelines and directives of the early twenty-first century played an important role in stimulating the development of laws and policies that addressed disability issues in Portugal. But the EU strategy was increasingly dominated by neoliberal ideas, which tended to subordinate social policy to the imperatives of economic and fiscal sustainability. The impact of the neoliberal agenda on disability policy and law in Portugal thus implied a reorientation of policy goals to favour employment as the main vehicle for social integration. More importantly, this reorientation took place in a context where budget control and cost containment became the primordial concerns of successive governments, discouraging a more holistic approach to disabled people's needs. Such a framework was unlikely to effect a positive change in the life situation of disabled people in general and disabled mothers in particular.

Worldwide evidence indicates that the neoliberal turn has indeed wrought significant transformations in disability-related policy, to the detriment of disabled citizens (Chouinard and Crooks 2005; Parker and Cass 2005; Roulstone 2000; Russell 2002). The impacts of neoliberalism go beyond the design of state laws and policies. They penetrate subjectivities. Neoliberalism has set in motion a new "social ethos," as Connell put it in this volume, that encourages individuals, including disabled people, to develop the qualities of the "active" and "enterprising" citizen. Thus, the solution for disabled people is increasingly conceived as a matter of *individual,* not *social,* change (Galvin 2006; Russell 2002). Programs aimed at improving *individual employability* are chosen over initiatives that fight structural barriers and work to achieve full citizenship for all people with disabilities regardless of their status in the labour market. The new political discourse emphasizing universal rights and inclusion is nevertheless informed by an individualistic conception of disability as a distinct biologic condition, not a relation between embodiment and the social and physical environment (Titchkosky 2003). Such a perspective creates a contradiction in that it presumes that the disadvantages associated with disability can in most cases be overcome, if only the individual with impairments tries "hard enough." Absent from this view is a consideration of the varying

kinds and degrees of needs of the disabled population, or the ac-
knowledgment that oppressive and restrictive environments, including those generated through law and policy, are contributing to
their ongoing marginalization.

In what follows, I examine how notions of disability and dependence, particularly as they affect mothers with disabilities, are construed (but also resisted) in the specific context of the Portuguese
neoliberal state.

Access to Disability-Related Benefits and Supports

As everywhere, welfare reform in Portugal has been closely tied to
cost-containment efforts. Due to the particular dynamics that
marked the late emergence and development of the Portuguese welfare state, however, cutbacks in Portugal have not been as severe
as in other places (see for instance Drake 2000, and Grover and
Piggott 2005 on the situation in Britain; Chouinard and Crooks
2005 for Canada; and Parker and Cass 2005 for Australia). This is
largely because Portuguese levels of social expenditure have historically been low. Benefits and supports, including those related to disability, have nevertheless been under growing pressure in the first
decade of the 2000s.

One critical factor in the shaping of EU policy was the 1997 Stability and Growth Pact binding the EU member states, Portugal
among them, that had adopted the single currency. Infused with neoliberal ideals, the pact established strict economic criteria that imposed severe constraints on national budgets. A key principle of the
Pact was the rule that all Member States keep their budgets close to
balance. In a downturn, national deficits were generally not to exceed three percent of the GDP, otherwise corrective measures or
even fines could be imposed. The Portuguese economy was in recession through 2005 and presented an annual deficit in 2006 of
4.6 percent (Banco de Portugal 2007). Social security expenditures
were identified as one of the main contributors to the national deficit; hence greater "budgetary discipline" was recommended in this
area (Comissão para a Análise da Situação Orçamental 2005).

Since people with disabilities are particularly exposed to poverty
in Portuguese society (see for instance Conselho de Ministros
2003), measures aimed at restraining public expenditure in the area
of social protection are likely to have a negative impact on them.

That such measures are being suggested further demonstrates that despite the new strategies for social inclusion that emerged in the last decade, economic rather than social goals dominate the political agenda at the EU and national levels (Carvalho da Silva 2000). This has serious consequences for Portugal, where, as we have seen, the welfare state developed later and less generously. Significant policy development and public investment were still needed to ensure that all citizens, including those with disabilities, enjoyed an adequate standard of living.

One way in which the neoliberal Portuguese state sought to decrease pressure on social programs was by imposing stricter eligibility criteria and introducing more complicated mechanisms of access. In 2008 the provision of disability pensions, adaptive equipment, and attendant care allowances offset the costs of being disabled only in a modest way. As in other neoliberal states, however, accessing those supports was a complex process that brought a significant degree of regulation into people's lives (Jones and Marks 1999). In order to qualify for entitlements, people had first to prove that they were disabled. This meant going through a battery of medical examinations and complex, intrusive, and time-consuming administrative procedures. Moreover, medical examinations and administrative procedures were repeated on a regular basis to renew welfare benefits, even when the impairment condition was known to be stable. Such processes reflect the prevalence of medical interpretations of disability and convey a lack of respect for the dignity of the person, as many of the women I spoke with could attest. Manuela,[4] for instance, recounted this experience:

> Some time ago I requested a new wheelchair … I went directly to the IEFP[5] … But the bureaucracy is such, and the amount of paper work they request despite knowing that it's hard for us to move around in the city is something … tremendous! I was shocked! I handed in everything, but the places I had to go to, the money I had to spend – I often had to take a taxi to go somewhere and get yet another document – it's a shame! … And this leads me to conclude [that the whole process] is made to make people give up! … That's how I see all these barriers, all the difficulties they place to give us a wheelchair … when they know we depend on it completely!

Manuela was a single mother of three who worked full time outside the house. Having lost both of her legs in a train accident fifteen

years previously, a wheelchair was essential to her ability to go about
in life, to get to work, and to care for her daughters: in other words,
the device was necessary for her to achieve the "independence" and
"autonomy" Portugal's neoliberal state has been so invested in promoting. Yet, rather than finding aids like this readily available,
Manuela encountered only obstacles and difficulties. The hardships in
accessing disability-related supports were so significant that many
people, though not Manuela, eventually give up and are forced to accept "dependency" on family and charities to survive. Manuela's story
thus reveals one of the inherent paradoxes of neoliberalism: the emphasis on independence is not coupled with the provision of adequate
supports that would enable a larger number of citizens, notably those
with disabilities, to live fulfilling lives. The result is an approach which
blames the victims for not achieving what actually the system in place,
pervaded with injustice and inequality, prevents them from realizing.

Disabled women who choose to become mothers have been particularly penalized and face multiple disadvantages. Policy domains of
greater relevance for the woman who is mothering with a disability
have received little attention in the Portuguese neoliberal state. Supports that would help her fulfil her care roles are non-existent or
insufficient: there is a lack of basic supports such as accessible
transportation and inadequate childcare arrangements. Above all, income rates make it hard to meet basic needs such as accessing secure
housing and buying healthy food for her and her children (Masuda
1998). This is without mentioning the physical inaccessibility of many
medical facilities and equipments, and health providers' insufficient
training regarding disability, as many women in this study reported.
One of them, Marta, recounted her experience during pregnancy,
labour and delivery in these terms:

> I had the luck to always have my husband with me. If I didn't it
> would have been impossible. To climb to the examination tables
> to do the exams, the ultrasounds, it would have been impossible,
> there's no accessibility! He had to take me in his arms, it was very
> complicated... Both times I gave birth I spent two days in the hos-
> pital. [My OB] sent me home as soon as possible – she knew I'd be
> better there. The hospital had no accessibility. I practically couldn't
> leave the bed or take a shower – essential things like that!

Besides making their lives ever more complex, the lack of supports in these areas sent disabled women a powerful message – they

were not expected to live sexual and reproductive lives. These pervasive assumptions situated disabled women in a passive dependent situation in which they were regarded as childlike, asexual beings, without desire or the ability to mother. The neoliberal state was complicit with, and reinforced, this view. In neoliberal societies, it is the "independent" subject who represents the political subject or citizen (Kittay et al. 2005). To the extent that they are represented as unable to fulfil traditional adult and female social roles, many women with disabilities have been denied citizenship, not in a formal sense but, as Richard Devlin and Dianne Pothier (2006) described it, in a substantive way: their specific needs are ignored in the design of social and economic environments. They are assigned a subordinated position, a "de-citizen" status (Devlin and Pothier 2006:2). This is visible even at the policy level, as Sónia's account poignantly shows:

> I've tried to apply for disability allowance, because I'm entitled to it. I went there twice and they don't want to give it to me ... They say I've got good arms for working. And they said that if I'm really disabled I don't have the right to have a partner or a daughter! ... That's what they told me. I find this sad, really sad! I showed them my papers proving my degree of incapacity. I have 84 percent incapacity. That's almost 100 percent. They had the guts to ask my partner if I had 100 percent incapacity, if he'd still be with me!

In order to be able to claim supports from the state, Sónia would have to renounce her roles as a loving partner and a mother. She would have to give up the life she has built to fit with the dominant image of disabled women as dependent, incapable and unlovable. Only then would she really "prove" she deserved the supports she was claiming.

Neoliberal reform of welfare and disability support programs are often said to aim at improving *choice*, *autonomy* and *responsibility* for benefit claimants. Sónia made "choices" but the price she paid for them was unfairly high –living below poverty level, sharing an apartment with twelve other members of her partner's family on the second floor of a building with no elevator, depending on her partner to carry her up and down the stairs every single day. For many persons with disability like Sónia, the expression of personal autonomy remains as Wareing and Newell (2002) put it, "the choice between no choice," that is the choice that one makes when one is not having really a choice (p.428). Indeed for those with disabilities, particularly if they are women, fewer resources, greater professional and state authority, and prevailing disablism in a society dominated by neoliberal principles and norms, has increasingly construed "choice" in a very limited and oppressive way.

Welfare to Work Programs

A second critical shift in disability policy with profound consequences for the daily lives of disabled people and disabled mothers has been the renewed emphasis on employment as an important outcome and the path for social integration (Burton and Kagan 2006). As already discussed in this chapter, Portuguese disability schemes, under the influence of EU initiatives and funding mechanisms, have tended to emphasize employment over other dimensions of people's lives.

There are two important things to say about this trend. First, it seems relevant to ask the critical question who benefits from this kind of policy orientation? Then, it is necessary to understand how policies that equate employment with social inclusion shape social identities and construct disability and dependence, particularly for disabled women and mothers.

While on the surface the economic integration of disabled people has been promoted on rights grounds, in fact their participation in a regular working environment is an asset for the European Union (Hantrais 2000) and the Portuguese state. Confronted with high rates of unemployment that threaten social cohesion, diminish competitiveness in the global economy and place an added burden on social protection systems, the EU and its member states have focused attention on active labour-market measures deemed to have a positive impact on beneficiaries, but mostly on the economy at large. This kind of policy, however, disregards the fact that jobs may be lacking, or that there will always be people who could not work even if jobs were available for all (Galvin 2006). Equally overlooked is the changing nature of employment relations (notably the increase of part-time and short-term contracts) as well as the intensification of labour processes, which are fuelling the economic exclusion of growing numbers of workers, many of them with impairments (Wilton 2006). This shouldn't perhaps come as a surprise. As Grover and Piggott (2006) in the UK have argued, and Thomas also discusses in this volume, neoliberal policy changes serve the needs of capital, not those of disadvantaged groups such as disabled people. Through compulsory workfare-type policies even *non-employed* disabled people are now being "reattached" to the labour market and reconstructed as an important part of the "reserve army," thus helping to place downward pressure on overall wage levels. As evident in other areas too, the shift to neoliberalism has not meant the wholesale deregulation of the economy but its reregulation in ways that better support the interests of capital. For too many disabled people, however, this shift has only produced growing marginalization, dependence, and impoverishment.

People with disabilities in Portugal are thus less likely to participate in the labour force than their non disabled peers. A recent study (Sousa et al. 2007) showed that the unemployment rate among disabled people (aged eighteen to sixty-five) is more than twice the rate found in the general population, while their rate of employment is just below half. The same study further indicated that distribution along the occupational structure is uneven for people with disabilities, with larger concentration in blue-collar and unqualified occupations, particularly for women. This reflects the lower levels of education attained by many people with disabilities compared to those of the non-disabled population, and it has been the direct outcome of vocational training programs, which have prioritized traditional and low-qualified areas of activity for disabled people (Capucha et al. 2004). It is also related to the long standing prejudicial attitudes of employers, whose cultural perceptions of disability have been deeply entrenched in the individualistic, medical model (Martins 2007). In short, the few persons with disabilities (mostly male) who entered the labour market have remained in the lowest ranks of the occupational ladder. Thus, despite the fact that they "benefited" from programmes specifically designed to increase their *employability*, these workers can hardly be viewed as the group most advantaged by this kind of policies.

This brings me to my second point. Approaches that equate employment with inclusion define, as a focus for change, the disabled individual, and not the larger social and economic context (Roulstone 2000). It has been assumed that economically inactive disabled people were not in paid employment because they do not have the skills for, and attitudes to, paid employment that make them attractive to employers. Therefore, new schemes for persons

with disability have offered training packages aimed at improving
the individual's motivation to return to work, including training in
confidence building and personal skills. No consideration has been
given to local labour market conditions or, as Parker and Cass note
(2005 under "Moving Towards a Post-Welfare State") to "the promotion of disability-friendly work practices such as job redesign,
flexible hours, workplace modification, adaptive technologies and
accessible transportation." Yet these are of utmost importance to
deliver substantive equality, and not just *equality of opportunities*
for disabled people. Such a holistic perspective would be particularly relevant for those with disabilities who are parenting and have
to juggle family and work responsibilities. Bárbara's story illustrates
this well. Bárbara had rheumatoid arthritis, a condition that affected her mobility and can cause severe physical and mental distress. She held a university degree and worked full time for a large
company. To prevent the risk of a second spontaneous abortion
when she got pregnant Bárbara had to take a sick leave for the
whole period of her pregnancy. When her daughter was born,
Bárbara stayed home with her on maternity leave for five months,
as typical working mothers in Portugal do. After this period she returned to work, but two months later her symptoms worsened.
Bárbara was again forced to go home on a sick leave – "One of
these days they are going to fire me," she told me in our interview.
And she continued:

> 'Cause people ... they are always very nice, very nice but ... they
> don't really understand! Maybe I had to use a cane, I had to look
> awful so that they could realize what this is. I have this condition
> for ten years now ... Many people can't understand what a dis-
> ease like this is until they see the person deformed, or in a wheel-
> chair, I don't know ... [they only understand when they see the
> person] no longer able to move around, very sick, looking awful,
> unable to live a normal life, unable to get married or live with
> someone else, unable to have children or go on vacation. If you
> have a normal life, or if you try to look normal, people don't be-
> lieve you. And I feel discriminated by many people, even those
> who are close to me and know the condition I have.

The dilemma facing Bárbara, and so many others, is that they want
to be able to participate as others do in the social and economic

spheres of life, but to take part in neoliberal society and its market, they are expected to adhere to certain standards of performance. Such standards are usually defined with the male, able-bodied, "independent" citizen in mind. They are therefore incompatible with Bárbara's (and others') personal characteristics and lives, and the reality of their distinct needs. If Bárbara had been "deformed," "in a wheelchair," or looking "awful," then perhaps people would have recognized her in need of special treatment. But then also, Bárbara's "special" needs would have provided the grounds on which to promote and justify her exclusion and marginalization.

The paradox is that individuals like Bárbara should and *could* participate if only their needs and conditions were properly acknowledged and accommodated. Neoliberal welfare reform, said to aim at facilitating the restoration of passive, dependent individuals who are "at risk of long term unemployment" to their roles as "active citizens," has actually preserved the very conditions that have disabled so many people with impairments in the first place (Galvin 2006). In such a context, mothers with disabilities may be faced with particular difficulties, as Fernanda, one of the women interviewed, noted: "[Finding a job] is always hard – it's hard being a disabled person, it's hard being a woman, and it's hard being of a certain age. All three factors together ... form a big snowball that's sometimes complicated."

In a society where work has been increasingly utilized as a fundamental organizing concept in drawing the division between the included and the marginalized, the productive and the "burdensome," women with disabilities who have chosen to mother are apt to be considered "double trouble."

Development of Rights-Based Legislation

While the neoliberal emphasis on training and employment schemes has contributed to making the lives of disabled women and mothers ever more difficult, the passage of disability rights legislation may suggest a significant advance on the road to their full citizenship. Since the turn of the century, following an international trend in disability law, Portugal has issued anti-discrimination protections for their citizens with disabilities. In 2007 the Portuguese government also signed the Convention on the Rights of People with Disabilities recently adopted by the United Nations. When examined more closely however, such frameworks fall short of what they seemed to promise in the paper.

Parker and Cass (2005), reiterating Rose Galvin, note that when disability activists and governments use the language of rights they seldom attach to such discourse identical meaning and conse- quences. For disability activists, claiming rights is demanding social justice and radical social transformation; in other words, disability rights, although firmly based on the recognition of the equal worth and dignity of individual human beings, only gain expression as *col- lective* rights involving all spheres of life – civil, cultural, economic, political, and social. But neoliberal governments have appropriated and reformulated these concepts into "an individualized, contrac- tual approach to disability law and its administration" (Parker and Cass 2005). This narrow conception of rights sits well with the neo- liberal worldview that prioritizes freedom for individuals and mar- kets. Thus, while activists insist on structural and systemic change within social institutions, workplaces, and communities, the neolib- eral state "infers that access and participation can be achieved through individual behavioural change" (Parker and Cass 2005). The sense in which the language of rights gets deployed under neo- liberalism reflects the liberal concept of citizenship and rights in which equality is defined as sameness (Young 1998). This under- standing, feminists have long claimed, operates to exclude all those who do not conform to the norms of the "good," active, and "inde- pendent" citizen. Contrary to what is often stated, those norms are not neutral; instead, they reproduce the interests and values of dom- inant groups and therefore only serve to perpetuate their privilege. Anti-discrimination laws, if they only offer equal treatment and fail to address power inequalities and structural barriers that affect dis- abled people as a group in contemporary capitalist societies – and particularly the impact of competition, profit maximization and ef- ficiency – in practice will not deliver substantive equality for dis- abled people (Russell 2002). Substantive equality does not mean uniformity of treatment; instead, it demands that difference is "rec- ognized, given meaning and valued" (Rioux and Riddle, forthcom- ing). Perhaps more than any other group in society, disabled people remind us that to promote equality, different measures need to be put in place.

The rise of neoliberal ideas in Portugal, as elsewhere, has thus created new contradictions and tensions. While citizenship and rights have become recurrent topics in official documents, the neo-liberal approach to disability has undermined the citizenship of disabled people, particularly disabled women and mothers, in a number of ways. First, it has emphasized individualistic and biomedical conceptions of disability, rather than recognizing that social and legal constructions result in disadvantage for some. Further, neoliberal values of personal responsibility, freedom, and "choice" obscure the structural barriers that have shaped disabled people's lives. As well, implicit in these conceptions has been an assumption of what counts as "autonomy" and "inclusion" for disabled people. Increasingly these notions have come to be narrowly defined in terms of access to the competitive market. "Choices" in other arenas of life, for instance relative to sexuality, reproduction, and mothering, are regarded as irrelevant and made invisible and hence have not been adequately supported or provided for in existing rights-based law and policy, as the story of Claudia, another participant in this study, clearly shows.

Claudia acquired her disability in consequence of a stroke that occurred two weeks after the birth of her second child. The brain injury she suffered caused her to lose the ability to produce and comprehend language but left intact her cognitive abilities. During her long hospital stay her children were kept in the charge of their paternal grandparents, with whom they remained at the time of our interview, despite the fact that Claudia had significantly recovered since the accident. Abandoned by the father of her child soon after, then involved in an abusive relationship for a while, Claudia eventually gained access to social housing. However, the bachelor apartment she was assigned, and which she shared with her partner, had no room for her children. Being removed from her two sons, whom she visited regularly on weekends, caused a great deal of pain and suffering to Claudia. For three years, she had been attending vocational training and was completing an internship in a company, where she hoped to be hired as a cleaner. She was proud of her job, but her greatest ambition in life was to move to an apartment where her children could live with her. Had Claudia not been a disabled woman, her needs and responsibilities as mother would have most likely been taken into account in any housing solution arranged by social services and would have been accepted by her family. But since Claudia was a disabled mother, her disability identity took over any other personal feature or role, and she was denied the basic right of living with her own children. Ironically, for all the efforts that social services and the extended family seemed willing to go to in order to help her regain her place in society, the lack of respect for her dignity, personal choices, and rights, both as a woman and a mother, that was systematically demonstrated in the arrangements provided was remarkable.

It is interesting to note that the Portuguese disability anti-discrimination law, said to cover "all economic, social, cultural and other rights," dedicates a substantial number of paragraphs to outline employment- and work-related discriminatory practices, which come in addition to those already defined in the Labour Code of the state. No clause, however, exists in the same law to protect mothers with disabilities like Claudia from discriminatory practices that allow them to be separated from their children, or force others like Manuela and Celmira to spend long hours away from home and loose important moments of their children's lives because the accessible public transport they need in order to travel to and from work has irregular and limited schedules. This systematic neglect of women's concerns and needs is reinforced by neoliberal goals of fiscal restraint, which impose the underfunding of disability related programs and benefits, including those aimed at promoting full citizenship (Rioux and Valentine 2006). In short, despite a discursive commitment to equality and rights, the neoliberal turn in Portugal has provided a context in which experiences of oppression and exclusion for many persons with disabilities, particularly mothers, have only intensified.

CONCLUSION

As I hope to have demonstrated above, patterns of disability discrimination and inequality (which to some extent were always present) have intensified in Portuguese law, policy, and practices of the early twenty-first century. Insufficient resources, great professional and state authority, and prevailing disablism in a society dominated by neoliberal principles and norms have reinforced relations of oppression and dominance, constructing disability and dependence in the everyday lives of many women with impairments, while undermining their citizenship.

A substantive approach to citizenship for women with disabilities would instead require *redistribution* of resources, social *recognition*, *representation* of women with disabilities' voices and concerns in political spaces (Fraser 2005a; Fraser 2005b), and the *reconfiguration* of social and physical environments in ways that better reflect their characteristics and needs and thus enable access, participation, and genuine inclusiveness.[6] This implies an approach that reconciles the goal of equality *with* the *reasonable accommodation* of disabled mother's diversity, notably through adaptations in work environments, transport systems, educational establishments, health care facilities, and other public or private services. A framework of justice combining *redistribution, recognition, representation,* and *reasonable accommodation* may in fact work best to address not just disability-related but *all* current struggles against injustice, whether these involve gender, race, or other forms of social inequality. A recent example was provided in the conclusions of the Bouchard-Taylor Commission (2008).[7] Convened in Quebec to debate the issue of "reasonable accommodation" over the inclusion of religious minorities, the commission's final report highlighted needs for "accommodation" in the context of broader economic, social, and cultural disadvantages experienced by members of racialized minorities in the Province of Quebec and thus advanced recommendations that addressed the complexities of these intersecting forms of injustice.

Hegemonic neoliberal tendencies, however, have seemed unlikely to deliver such a holistic approach. In Portugal, for instance, under conditions of profit-driven economic rationality, global competitiveness, and welfare restructuring, "equal opportunity" seems at best what a narrowly defined rights-based approach to disability has been able to offer. This has been clearly insufficient, as it has only served to perpetuate the privilege of those already privileged: predominantly able-bodied men, whose norms and standards dominate, and to which all other groups have to be compared and measured (Young 1998). Such processes operate to marginalize disabled women, because they fundamentally ignore the specificities of their lives and needs. Historically, women with disabilities have been regarded as unfit sexual partners and mothers. They are either presumed to be asexual beings or conversely feared for their "uncontrolled sexuality." The reproductive abilities of disabled women have always been tightly policed, notably through institutionalization, forced sterilization, and social control (Kallianes and Rubenfeld 1997). For a number of disabled women therefore, the choice of childbearing is an important political act that defies the social oppression they have been subjected to (Morris 1995).

In the early twenty-first century, a disabled woman in Portugal who engaged in mothering, however, risked being further disadvantaged. Her choice was not supported and her needs went largely unacknowledged. Because the role of a mother has not been one that society or the state expect (or approve) from a woman with disability, she is punished for her "bad" choice. Yet as Foucault taught us, where there is power there is resistance. So these women have resisted. Their lives are accounts of struggle and strain which in every day defy the stereotypes of vulnerability and dependence usually associated with disability and female gender. Fernanda, a woman with a physical disability and a mother of three, summarized it all well when she said:

> I don't allow being pushed aside by others. When I go somewhere, anywhere, whether for working or anything else, I make myself visible. – "I'm here, don't you see me? I'm here!" I make … I make people notice me, with or without the disability, I make them seeing I'm there! And when people start saying "Oh I'm so sorry for you," I show them there's nothing to be sorry about! I have a disability that's true, but I'm not to be pitied. I can do everything other people do! Of course it takes more effort – for example my daughter she can do the dishes in ten minutes and maybe I take longer, but I can do it, and I can do it well! … I think that we, people with disabilities, what we want is just to participate in the community at all levels, just that … it's mostly that.

Resisting oppression means for Fernanda and others, claiming the equal worth and dignity of their lives and contributions, and an equal status as citizens. Mothering is often the site where such forms of resistance take shape, as Manuela narrated: "I raised questions, I asked around, and I let people know that it was not because I have a disability that I should be treated differently. I always emphasized that! Having access to the places where I have to go … to fulfill my responsibilities as a mother, as a parent, that's what I want. Other than that, I don't feel different, I don't want to be treated differently, and I don't allow that to happen!"

What Manuela demanded (though scarcely obtained) was the right to have her needs accommodated, not a demeaning treatment based on any patronizing notion that she could not fulfill her roles as competently as others. Neoliberal ways of governing disabled mothers' lives, however, have rendered them invisible and powerlessness. Many like Manuela resisted, but others perhaps have succumbed. If instead disabled women were all supported in their "efforts to care and be cared for" (Kittay et al. 2005, 467) they could, like the rest of us, enjoy "flourishing lives" in ways that would rather nourish their capacity for loving and caring, and preserve their human dignity.

NOTES

1 I want to thank the women who participated in this study for generously sharing their stories with me. I am particularly grateful to the editors, Susan Braedley and Meg Luxton, for providing me the opportunity, inspiration and supporting advice to write this piece. A final thank you goes to the two anonymous reviewers for their helpful comments to previous versions of this chapter.

2 This and subsequent pieces of legislation cited throughout the chapter were translated from Portuguese by the author.

3 Between 1961 and 1974 Portugal sustained armed conflicts with guerrilla groups who were fighting for the political independence of former colonies of Angola, Mozambique, and Guiné-Bissau. Bringing an end to the colonial war was amongst the motives that precipitated the 1974 revolution.

4 To protect participants' confidentiality, all names used throughout this paper are pseudonyms. Interviews were conducted in Portuguese by the author who was also responsible for the translation into English of the excerpts presented here.

5 IEFP stands for Instituto do Emprego e Formação Profissional (*National Institute for Vocational Training and Employment*) an agency responsible for promoting and supporting employment policies in Portugal.

6 Here I am elaborating upon Nancy Fraser's framework of "democratic justice". In recent publications (see for example *Mapping the feminist imagination: From redistribution to recognition to representation* (2005, Constellations, 12(3)295–307) and *Reframing justice in a globalizing world* (2005, New Left Review, 36: 69–88)), Fraser theorizes a model of justice incorporating the economic, cultural, and political dimensions, and accordingly suggests that struggles for justice in our globalizing era revolve around the politics of *redistribution, recognition* and *representation*. I argue that this framework is helpful but insufficient to theorize struggles for justice when disability is factored in, since "parity of participation" for people with disabilities requires yet a fourth dimension: a politics of *reasonable accommodation, accessibility and universal design* in order to create disability-friendly social and physical environments.

7 I am indebted to Susan Braedley for pointing me to this example.

"Accidental" Health Care

Masculinity and Neoliberalism at Work

SUSAN BRAEDLEY

INTRODUCTION

Since the advent of neoliberal governance in Canada, Canadian health care has been dramatically redistributed. Subject to continual public debate, public scrutiny, and policy change, neoliberal governance has reconstituted not only who provides health care but the form that this care takes (Armstrong and Armstrong 2002).

In this chapter, I describe the "accidental" assignment of some health care provision to publicly provided professional fire services, in order to delineate the redistribution of health care to a public service that is not usually considered, or funded as, a health care service. Further, this assignment has shaken the hyper-masculine core of fire services and firefighting culture. I trace the path of this accidental assignment and its gendered implications to demonstrate not only how neoliberal governance is dismantling and reconstituting health care but how it is shaking gendered divisions of labour in ways that reveal its own gendered character.

While some health care policy outcomes have been the planned result of policy objectives, others appear to be the unintended or unconsidered consequences of policy plans. The increasing involvement of fire services in health care seems to be the unintended consequence of a number of policy directions. One such direction has been the reorganization of health care services at hospitals and elsewhere to focus on acute care needs,[1] and the simultaneous withdrawal from all kinds of chronic care provision. As a result, some people with chronic illnesses are receiving more of their health care through episodic, rather than continuous, care modalities, not only at walk-in clinics and emergency departments but through 9-1-1. Another neoliberal policy direction has been to push a broad range of people into the labour market. In order to achieve this goal, public income support schemes and buffers such as social assistance, unemployment insurances, public housing, and disability pensions have been cut or restricted in scope, or are no longer adjusted for inflation. Unsurprisingly, those who use episodic health care are more likely to be people who have chronic illnesses or are poor, elderly, disabled, without adequate housing, or living in circumstances that make day-to-day living precarious. They are people without adequate income to buy services and without the resources to look after themselves. It seems likely that changes to income support are implicated in sending more of these people to episodic health care services.

A third neoliberal policy direction has been to streamline public services using for-profit business logic in order to render them more efficient and productive. This has meant that services, including fire services, have been encouraged to "cut the fat" and maximize productivity. Fire services have also been pushed to expand their scope of practice. All three of these policy directions, therefore, are implicated in the fire services' increased role as emergency health care providers.

The basis for this analysis is a research project in which I investigated changes to the work at two fire services in Ontario, Canada. Toronto Fire Services is the largest fire service in Canada, employing over three thousand staff. Mnjikaning Fire Rescue Service, located in the First Nations community of Rama, Ontario, has a total non-unionized staff of thirty-seven people. Through background research, individual and small group interviews, and work observation,[2] I have explored the circumstances that have shaped the dramatic increase in emergency "medical" responses provided by fire services, and how firefighters and fire services are dealing with this change.

This discussion proceeds in four sections. Drawing on data from my research, the first section describes the context of fire service involvement in health care by delineating the ways in which the organization of fire services has challenged, and is challenged by, neoliberal policy logic. The second section looks at the doubly accidental character of firefighters' involvement in emergency health care. Here, questions about what constitutes an emergency and what constitutes health care come into sharp focus. The third section explores the ways in which this policy "accident" reveals the deeply gendered consequences of neoliberal governance, dimensions that penetrate not only decisions about who provides service and what services are provided but gendered divisions of labour, and gendered subjectivities. The final section reflects on how this case study contributes to understandings of the gendered nature of neoliberal governance, and its influence on social arrangements.

Firefighters' increasing role in health care has developed during a period in which neoliberalism has been the dominant social and political influence. Neoliberalism has been described as a political ideology that privileges economic concerns and assigns primacy to markets and market logics, such as those of efficiency and competition (Brodie 2007). According to neoliberals, the restructuring of public services is an unavoidable, even inevitable, requirement for maximizing efficiency, enabling "choice," and meeting the stringent demands of global competitiveness through reductions in state spending and regulation (Bakker 1997). The family is hailed and elevated as the responsible agent for social welfare, and public services are reshaped by the "New Public Management" into pseudo-businesses (Barrows and Macdonald 2000). Fire services, as a "core business" of municipalities, have been dramatically affected.

Like other municipal services, fire services experienced the Canadian municipal budget squeeze that resulted from the economic turmoil of the late 1970s and 1980s. This turmoil precipitated federal and provincial government downloading of services and responsibilities to municipalities, markets, communities, households, and families. These moves precipitated associated neoliberal restructuring at every level of governance. A decrease in the occurrence of fires, particularly since 1980, had left many Canadian fire services with a trained, ready, but relatively inactive labour force (Baird 1986). Yet fire services have proved to be a difficult target for cost reductions and reorganization, for three reasons. First, the firefighting labour process does not produce a quantifiable measure of service per unit but rather is designed to produce an intangible quality of readiness

sufficient to respond to accident and disaster, and to prevent loss of
life and loss of property value. This makes firefighting a poor target
for typical neoliberal cost reduction strategies such as reducing the labour force or using on-call labour. Second, insurers insist upon the
availability of fire services as a precondition for medium- to large-
scale property insurance coverage. The history of Mnjikaning Fire
Rescue Service is a case in point. This small professional force replaced an existing volunteer department due to fire protection needs
associated with the construction and establishment of a large casino
and hotel complex on this First Nations Reserve.[3] Indeed, historically, insurers have been strong advocates for publicly provided fire
services in order to protect capital interests (Baird 1986).

Third, while the number of fires is decreasing, the severity and
complexity of those that do occur is increasing, and quick response
remains the most significant factor in saving life and property.
These factors militate against the implementation of other typical
neoliberal strategies – borrowed from the private sector – such as
increasing response times, using on-call labour, or outsourcing.

In spite of the fire services' awkward fit with neoliberal policy orientations, some reorganization of emergency services did occur. The
development of coordinated tiered emergency response systems in the
late 1970s and early 1980s, known as 9-1-1 systems in Canada, came
at an ideal moment for fire services and firefighter unions in that it
provided a justification for the preservation of services, jobs, and
wages in a period of public service reductions. This tiered response
placed firefighters first on the scene in most emergency situations,
due to their availability and their hallmark fast response times. Emergency medical care has become fire services' largest service category,
generated by the introduction of 9-1-1 emergency response. Although
some fire services have historically provided ambulance and paramedic support and most have played a part in providing emergency
first aid at accident and disaster sites, the introduction of 9-1-1 emergency response systems shifted medical care provision to fire services
in unprecedented ways.

In the City of Toronto in 2006, fifty-two percent of firefighter
responses were deemed to be for "medical" reasons, and there
were almost nine thousand more medical emergency responses
than in 2004, an increase of fourteen percent over two years
(Toronto Fire Service 2006). In Rama, more than eighty percent of
calls in 2006 were for medical responses. These statistics are typical

of fire services throughout North America with similar mandates within a tiered emergency response system (Smeby Jr. 2005). Within this "medical" category is a host of emergency and non-emergency health care situations to which firefighters respond. A "medical" call is usually precipitated by a report of shortness of breath, chest pain, fainting, seizure, a shooting, car accident, or suspected death. Firefighters also respond to calls from long-term care homes and seniors' residences, based upon pre-established protocols. As well, they respond to a range of less easily categorized calls for help.

In my research observations, a routine day of firefighting work included training, equipment checks, cleaning, responding to false alarms, traffic accidents, and medical calls, doing physical workouts, and filling a quantity of downtime with sleeping, cooking, eating, grooming, watching TV, playing games, or engaging in other "leisure" activities. These circumstances, when perceived from the perspective of a neoliberal logic of efficiency, situate firefighters as an available municipal labour force whose paid time could easily be used for other purposes, with appropriate preparation and training. Since the 1980s, fire service mandates have expanded to include not only medical emergencies but hazardous materials disposal, heavy urban search and rescue, water/ice rescue, and many other emergency situation responses, including those associated with terrorist attacks. In Cleveland, Ohio, during the summer of 2007, "idle" firefighters were sent out to cut the grass on municipal lawns in order to maximize productivity, travelling to their work sites by fire truck and keeping firefighting gear with them in case of an emergency call.[4] The neoliberals' objective to promote ideal conditions for business means that they must support the preservation of public fire services. However, their concerns for efficiency make fire services' labour process susceptible to intensification. Fire service emergency health care work has developed within this tension.

DOUBLY ACCIDENTAL: EMERGENCY HEALTH CARE

The accidental aspects of health care provision by fire services are not evident in available statistics from the Office of the Ontario Fire Marshall or elsewhere but come to light only when the specifics of firefighters' emergency medical calls are explored.[5] At the time of this writing, I had collected details on more than sixty emergency medical calls, as well as opinions and impressions from firefighters, union officials, and administrators. This data suggests that health care provision by fire services has a doubly "accidental" character.

First, it appears to be an accidental or unanticipated outcome of policy directions that have reduced social services. In Ontario, the 1990s brought neoliberal policies that stripped away many services geared to prevent or treat chronic illnesses, provide income support or housing, or provide twenty-four-hour care. Further, public health care changed to focus on acute-care needs, often at the expense of ongoing care programs. One firefighter, who has worked at many halls in two fire services, made the following observations.

> Just about everywhere you go you get – it's an odd mixture of – it's just the people that kind of slipped through the cracks. Like they don't have – they've got health problems – often there's some form of psychological or emotional problem. They don't have a big support net and you know they just can't cope. And a lot of that picked up a bit a few years back when they started, kind of, phasing down a lot of programs, like disability or mental health and you know mainstreaming people back out into the public. And yeah, there was marked increase, like almost the day that policy went into effect. And there's just a whole bunch of people that have been institutionalized for a large portion of their life and they just cannot cope and now suddenly it's like, "okay you're free." (Chuckles.) "I don't want to be free." They don't know how to cope. And they're just at a loss. Some other people because they're not coping sometimes they call because they realize, "you know what I'm just scared. This isn't good. Like I don't have anybody coming by to tell me to take my meds." They don't have – you can see they're just not coping … You know they don't know any other way to act other than [to dial] 9-1-1 and they know that whenever they've called that in the past, they get people. And we'll come and they, you know, take them into the hospital and get all their meds sorted out. And you know, basically get them back into a – some sort of a decent shape and then they'll come back out again. And they'll kind of hold together for a couple of weeks and then there'll be another couple of weeks where they start to taper off and get more erratic on their meds and then they'll end up calling again. And they're – yeah pretty much every station you go to has their ones like that. (266i)

This firefighter associated the increase in medical calls for care
with the deinstitutionalization of people with mental illnesses and
those with developmental delays that culminated in dramatic
changes in Ontario in the mid-1990s, but that had been developing
throughout the previous decades (Dear and Wolch 1987). This
change was brought about through a combination of neoliberal
economic policies that stressed the need to curb social spending and
activism on behalf of patients who were "warehoused" in the institutional system. It has resulted in inadequate and overburdened systems of community care. It is likely that other changes in healthcare
and social services are implicated in the increased demand for emergency care. In the mid-1990s changes to social welfare reduced levels of benefit and eligibility (Mosher 2000). Hospital discharge
policies that send patients home "quicker and sicker" and the real-
location of resources from hospital care to inadequate and poorly
conceived community-based care are two of a host of health care
system changes that have taken place throughout the period of neoliberal reform, commencing in the early 1980s (Armstrong et al.
1997; Armstrong et al. 2000; Armstrong and Armstrong 2002).
Firefighters describe themselves as backfilling a public services system riddled with holes.

> I think what has happened is that other public services have their
> niche and the nature of their work is more defined now perhaps,
> and I think in some ways the fire service picks up the slack for
> other services. I mean, we don't do policing but we see every day
> people that the police deal with and we have to have maybe a bet-
> ter rapport with them than police do. I mean if they need help then
> we have to help them and we don't care if they're before the courts
> and because of the ambulance and hospital situation where one's
> always trying to put the work on the other, then a large percentage
> of the time, we're first response on medical calls. (155i)

This firefighter links increased firefighter emergency health care
and the narrowing of public service mandates, as well as issues such
as increasing wait times in hospital emergency departments and the
requirement that paramedics stay with their patients until a physi-
cian takes over. When paramedics are tied up at hospital emergency
departments, it is firefighters who end up spending more time
with people who call for help in the meantime. When people cannot

access other services and their lives hit a crisis point, they call emergency services. Leaner health care and other public service systems appear to be involved in transferring care to firefighters. When care is constrained or eliminated in hospitals, doctors' offices, and other community settings, care needs shift and change but they do not disappear, despite neoliberal policy efforts to promote individual responsibility for health as well as for economic and social welfare.[6]

This discussion has set out the ways in which firefighters' health care provision has been significantly shaped by neoliberal policy and logics, although not as an intentional policy direction. Firefighter involvement in health care has evolved as an accidental implication of neoliberal moves that have hollowed out health care and social services, reduced staffing in many care facilities, and put pressure on fire services to justify their budgets in ways that "activate" a labour force whose product is the intangible quality of "readiness." While my research was not designed to establish clear causal links between these changes and the rapidly developing demand for emergency care, documented increases in demand for 9-1-1 emergency response services in Toronto and Rama, as well as elsewhere (Cochrane Times Oct 12,2006; International Association of Firefighters AFL-CIO 2001; Toronto 2005; Toronto Fire Service 2006), have taken place within the context of significantly reduced health care and social services sectors. Neoliberal social policy, designed to get the state out of some kinds of health care provision and reallocate it to markets, households, and communities, seems to have accidentally allocated some of this work to municipal fire services.

The second "accidental" aspect of care provision by the fire services is the way in which an emergency response transforms peoples' chronic-care conditions into a series of emergencies or accidents. People who have no other resources to deal with their chronic health conditions can and do receive help through the 9-1-1 emergency response system. Yet fire services address these needs within their relatively limited scope of practice. An excerpt from an interview describes some typical emergency medical calls:

If alcohol is a factor, we'll go in and we got a lot of talkers. Like I can go in. We had someone who needed a psych evaluation but I could go in and I listen ... So we go in, and say, What's going on? Talk to me, what's going on? I hear you're giving everyone a hard time. And he says blah, blah and I say I can hear you on that, so

... they tried about ten times to get this guy to go ... to get evaluated at the hospital and they were going through hell day and night with this guy 'cause he couldn't get settled ... He went to get the help that he needed ... Sometimes we get people to calm down but then there are other times, you think you are just getting called to routine medical and you're walking through the door and the door slams on you and you see something funny and you go, holy crap ... get me backup. So sometimes you are not getting all the information you need. But some people – we have a lot of diabetics and people can get quite aggressive and mean, with alcohol and with other things going on, so you need to be aware of that. (245i)

Fire services emergency response was not designed to provide this kind of health care. Rather, it is organized to provide brief crisis intervention for medical needs that cannot easily be anticipated. The rapid onset of heart attack, stroke, or seizure, the immediate crisis of a car accident, and the sudden strike of a shooting or stabbing all qualify as circumstances in which people are rendered instantly dependent on others to meet their immediate needs and to sustain life. Firefighters are trained to respond to the initial and most immediate aspects of medical need generated by these situations. They find themselves responding, however, to many situations, such as the one described above, in which people's ongoing and complex health care needs remain unmet by more appropriate services. Next, consider this situation, recounted by another firefighter:

We had a guy, got gangrene. He was a street guy, he didn't want to get help, and ah, ah ... it was really ugly. He was sitting on the steps of the bank and he was getting in the way of the customers so the bank called. So when we got there, I guess we got there first. And he just was telling us to fuck off, he didn't want any help. He had big dirty long hair and a big dirty long beard and obviously hadn't had a bath in months and he stank and he was very angry that we were intruding on his life, and the ambulance guys got there and he didn't want any help and the cops showed up, and it was like there was seven, no, eight, eight people there, trying to take care of this guy, and he's fighting us the whole way. And finally, the ambulance guy is realizing that he doesn't want any help so he says, well, you are going to have to sign something for us to say you didn't ... you declined help. And the guy said fuck you and finally this guy said, If you can get up and walk away, we'll let you go, but if you can't walk away, we'll take you to the hospital in the stretcher or in the back of the cop car. So the guy tried to walk away and he couldn't. So we [the firefighters] picked him up and put him on the stretcher and the ambulance started to check him up, because he wasn't answering any questions or ... And the paramedic got down by his feet and he sniffed and he said, "oh-oh" and he took the guys shoes off and he peeled off the guy's sock and this guy's foot was, uh, it was disgusting. It was totally gangrenous. And, ah, so there's a guy living on the street with gangrene, and he ended up losing his foot. And ah, he's refusing our help, despite his gangrene. I can't imagine how painful that was. And ah, it was disgusting ... So he got towed to the hospital and we went back to the hall and the guys were, like, uh, do you know how much fucking money it is going to cost the system to deal with that freaking guy and you're pissed off at him because he's a burden to society, you know. And that was the reaction of all three crew members other than myself and I think there is a lot ... I mean how lost a soul must you be to refuse help when you've got gangrene? (1931)

In this case, health care was provided by the three emergency services that responded. The man was in need of medical attention, public services became involved; but what needs did the services meet? What was the primary concern of the services that intervened? Was it to meet this man's needs, address public concerns, or meet the bank employees' concern that he be removed? Did he get the care he needed? The firefighter who told me the story indicated that the man's foot was amputated after this incident. When I inquired further, I was told that the man was back living in neighbourhood shelters and on the street. In the absence of appropriate, accessible, and continuous health services, social services, and housing, it is difficult to see how his needs might have been addressed other than through emergency response.

Here is yet another situation, taken from my field notes and interviews. "Maisie"[7] is a woman in her late seventies, well known to every shift at this particular hall. She calls 9-1-1 regularly due to shortness of breath brought on by chain-smoking. Sometimes they respond to her three or four times in the same night. She is thought to be alcoholic by the firefighters, as she is often intoxicated and alcohol is always in evidence in her apartment. She has a small filthy apartment up a dark stairwell lined with garbage. I was told she sometimes has a man staying with her, sometimes not. When the voice on the fire hall loudspeaker announces her address, the firefighters all yell MAIS -EEE, and off we go.

The firefighter with the first-aid bag is first to talk. Maisie looks relieved to see them, knows the crew by sight, if not by name. The firefighter tells her things will be fine. He asks her how she is, listens carefully to her breathing. Asks what she's been up to today. Teases her, asking what man "took her breath away" while he takes a pulse. The other firefighter puts the oxygen mask on her face. She helps. He tells her she looks great. The paramedics arrive. They perform their checks and want to take her to hospital. She refuses, motions to sign their paper. Her colour improves. The captain empties an ashtray and puts some dishes in the sink. Another continues to chat to her about her general well-being and the weather. Everyone leaves.

One of the firefighters had this to say: "Some people would say she's a nuisance, but she needs help and she needs to be checked on and there is no one else. So we do it. We are the service that HAS to go when we're called. That's what we do. For everyone. That's why we are a real public service" (236g).

This firefighter recognized that the fire service is responding in the absence of other services and further, that the emergency response system must by definition respond to everyone who calls, regardless of their situation. He characterizes this universal response as the hallmark of a "real" public service.

Another firefighter had a different perspective:

The station takes care of her. We've had to go take care of her three and four times a night. It was just terrible. The paramedics would say the same thing, they know. They'd hear the address and go "here we go." You'd say, oh Maisie. And you'd lose your compassion, you'd lose like okay, what is it now. Its unfortunate but its just … And all she wants is the ventalin … I think she's lonely, you know … It's not just the expense for the [community] and for taxpayers, you're taking trucks. Now someone is really having a heart attack, and someone is trying to respond and having to come a distance. So I don't think that is really in their thought. I don't think they look at that. I think all the regulars in this area are drug and alcohol related. They get drinking and falling down and ... It's not the same as a person who has a real medical problem. No. (236g)

This firefighter's distinction between a "real medical problem" and Maisie's situation might be restated as the contrast between an emergency situation – the fast onset of a short-term need for emergency medical care – and incidents typical of long-term chronic conditions such as alcohol and drug dependencies, emphysema, mental illness, and poverty. This example also illustrates the kind of health care that firefighters provide. Firefighters routinely went into Maisie's home and tended to her immediate need for company, reassurance, and breathing support. Their labour provided them with incomplete but significant knowledge about the condition of her body and about her home, habits, health, and problems. Her needs were not fully understood or met by the firefighters, but they, with paramedics, provided her with the care they had available when and where she requested it. They were frustrated and concerned for her and they did what they must, and what was in their power, to make her life more livable. It is also one more instance of the transformation of a long-term chronic health care need into a series of "accidents" or pseudo-emergencies.

As these quite typical situations make clear, firefighters appear to be responding disproportionately to people who are poor, disabled, mentally ill, or elderly, and those with chronic health care conditions. Neither of the fire services in this study collect or maintain detailed information on their patients or on their interventions that could definitively confirm this impression.[8] However, it is one that was shared by many of the firefighters who participated in my research. Participants also confirmed that the situations mentioned here are typical of the workloads for firefighters in stations across the City of Toronto and Rama. Local socioeconomic conditions appear to have an impact on the number of calls received by the fire hall in any given neighbourhood but have less impact on the kinds of calls received.

Firefighters are able to provide a certain kind of health care, but doing so contains an obvious challenge. The twenty-four-hour tiered response system provides support that maintains people in the community, given the teeter-totter of health care and social service provision. The appropriateness or effectiveness of that support is another matter. Health care provision of this kind has the effect of transforming long-term chronic health conditions into a series of scantily recorded isolated "accidents" in the records of public safety services, which in turn has the effect of hiding the gaps and insufficiencies in the health care system through the deployment of a service not fully integrated with or considered to be part of the health care system.

It is important to point out that this analysis does not situate these needs for emergency medical response as uniformly inevitable. Many of these needs could be prevented through better health care and social policies. The historical success of fire prevention points to these possibilities: fire incidence took a steep decline when comprehensive fire prevention policies went into place. Fire services don't fight nearly as many fires these days. If similar energies could be mobilized to prevent even some of the chronic human health care needs met by emergency medical response, success seems assured. I like to imagine the outcome of such prevention efforts: our emergency room nurses working out, doing training exercises, playing ping-pong or watching TV, like firefighters at a fire hall, ready and waiting for a call to attend to a patient.

THE MASCULINITY OF NEOLIBERALISM: INVISIBLE HEALTH CARE?

It is not insignificant that neoliberal health care governance has unintentionally shaped the conditions in which men, employed in a masculinized public service, have been drawn increasingly into health care provision. In the neoliberal view, it is appropriate for the state to be involved in public safety, law and order, and security concerns (see Côté-Boucher in this volume), domains that historically include fire services since they are an "essential service" and central pillar of public safety. The increased emphasis on public safety, law and order, and security, emerging since the advent of neoliberal regimes, has been explained as necessary to city gentrification processes associated with capitalist accumulation (Smith 1996) and has assisted in disciplining the working class to wage labour (Gordon 2005); it was also exacerbated by the events of September 11, 2001. Whatever the rationale, there is no question that these arenas, deemed legitimate state activity under neoliberal doctrine, are strongly associated with masculinity.[9]

Further, neoliberal governance has a tendency to conceive the state as inappropriately involved in the areas of health and social welfare (see the chapters by Bezanson and Pinto in this volume).

Traditionally services in these areas have been provided by women in occupations such as nursing, social work, childcare, and personal care,[10] and they tend to operate with feminized norms. Thus, neoliberal policy direction reveals a gendered quality in sanctioning state provision of masculinized services while relegating feminized services to other sectors, even if they are directed or managed by the state.

The case of firefighter involvement in health care provision contains a fascinating contradiction. Here, a masculinized service traditionally oriented to the provision of public safety has become increasingly involved in the more feminized domain of health care, albeit in a limited way.[11] As I described earlier in this chapter, the hollowing out of many of state's feminized service sectors has left service gaps that remain unfilled, despite neoliberal strategies of enticement and coercion to foist responsibility for care onto individuals and families (see Bezanson and Luxton, both in this volume). These gaps are pulling the services that remain strong – masculinized public security services – in their direction.[12] Fire services have also been pushed to take on more work by neoliberal policies of productivity and efficiency.

Fire services and their workers face a multidimensional dilemma. In order to maintain their status within neoliberal regimes, fire services must retain their profile as highly effective *public safety* services. This identification also preserves the robust masculinity that is woven through firefighters' occupational culture, a gender position that appears particularly compatible with neoliberal orientations. On the other hand, firefighters are responding to more and more emergency health care calls, and they must be adequately trained and prepared. Yet the type of work involved undermines both fire service status as a purely public safety service and its conjoined hyper-masculine ethos. Apart from emergency health care, recent expansions in fire services' scope of practice, such as Hazardous Waste Disposal and Urban Search and Rescue, fit neatly into the categories of public safety and security: in other words, they are all evocative of a protective masculine presence.[13] When emergency health care work "rescues" people from immediately life-threatening circumstances, it can be perceived as protective and masculine public safety work. But when it comes to dealing with the day-to-day crises experienced by people with inadequately treated chronic illnesses and conditions – diabetes, alcohol and drug addictions, mental health problems, disabilities, poverty, and social isolation – notions of public safety break down. The work is more feminized and much less acceptable to firefighters.

The conflicts between increasing health care provision, the occupational culture of firefighting, and firefighters' understanding of themselves as masculine beings jump out of the interview transcripts and field notes. Gordon, Benner, and Noddings have argued that, "because of their socialization ... men have very specific, gender-related caregiving problems. Because of gender ideology, traditional stereotypes, and the formal identification of men only with public life and economic activity, their caring practices are overlooked and understudied. These activities suffer a legitimization crisis and are constantly said to contradict current definitions of power and status"(Gordon et al. 1996, ix).

My research on masculinized occupational health care provision sheds some light on these "gender-related caregiving problems" that have contributed to the relative invisibility of firefighters' emergency health care provision. Indeed, many of the firefighters I interviewed were surprised and disappointed that the primary focus of this study was their provision of emergency medical care. Even those who entered firefighting within the last decade indicated that they had not anticipated doing so much of this kind of work. *Fighting fires* is still the main focus for most firefighters. Of the thirty-seven firefighters I interviewed, all but four expressed sentiments ranging from discomfort to outright rejection of their work in health care provision while completely accepting their expanded roles in hazardous material disposal, urban search and rescue, water/ice rescue, and emergency preparedness.

"The things they're asking us to do are really so far outside the realm of what we anticipated it was going to be, that you almost feel like I'm losing some of what I was really meant to be ... You know? If all I do is run medical calls for the rest of my life, I'm still a fireman. And that's what I do. Fight fires" (58i).

To an outsider this attitude seems all in the name, "firefighter." Yet for some firefighters at least, health care provision is the one addition to a panoply of expanded services that constitutes a loss of "who I was really meant to be." The majority of my respondents told me that they came to this employment to be "fire*men*." Somehow health care provision is construed as a challenge to that self-understanding, in a way that other new duties are not. The rejection of identification with health care provision combined with a reassertion of masculinity came through over and over in the interviews, including interviews with a number of women firefighters. As one woman firefighter put it, "Don't think we're prissy because we do medicals. You have to be tough to do this job" (158i).

At Mnjikaning Fire and Rescue Service, firefighters continued to identify fighting fires as their prime function, even though some of the workers had never fought an actual structural fire. Willingness to take physical risks is constitutive of many masculinities, according to a number of accounts (Kimmel 1990; Burstyn 1999). My research participants' identification with the activity of firefighting and other rescue work that involves physical danger is evidence of its importance to the production and maintenance of an honourable masculinity. Even those who became firefighters during the time that emergency medical care provision had become dominant on the job were quick to describe firefighting as their occupational raison d'etre and the most enjoyable aspect of the job: "Going to a fire. That's the greatest thing for us. To do what we're trained to do and it worked. You're just happy because you get to do what you're trained to do" (46i).

This strong overall identification with firefighting together with a common and related ambivalence towards, if not a rejection of, emergency health care provision was evident not only at the subjective level of individual firefighters but also within firefighter culture and fire services organization and regulation. The masculine identification with public safety work within fire services is being eroded; but, in 2008, it was also being protected through strategies and practices at every level that render emergency health care provision nearly invisible. These strategies permit firefighters, fire services, and their regulators to maintain their masculine heroic public safety image, while also performing the day-to-day health care interventions described earlier in this chapter. Further, this unvalued work in health care provision is in some ways facilitated by the "brotherhood" culture of firefighting, which offers workers an occupational context of caring relations that underpins and supports firefighters' often risky and difficult work with the public.

The invisibility of firefighters' emergency health care provision is produced through both the structure and culture of firefighting. Structurally, the invisibility of what firefighters actually do in emergency health care has been maintained and extended by a general failure within the broader organization of fire services to collect and collate detailed information about who firefighters serve and what they actually do on emergency medical calls. In June 2008, despite the predominance of emergency medical calls in firefighting, the Ontario Fire Marshall still did not require the collection of specific data on emergency health care, beyond the recording of call types from a standardized list.[14] Neither the Toronto Fire Service nor Mnjikaning Fire Rescue Service maintained statistics on the details of emergency medical calls or whom they serve. This was in striking contrast to the detailed information maintained on fire responses. This pervasive denial of any identification with the dominant service category of contemporary fire services and the continual affirmation of the identification with firefighting itself was evident not only in interviews but in the physical spaces and documents of both fire services under study, Office of the Fire Marshall reports, and in most union information.[15] The invisibility extended further. For example, Toronto Fire Service annual reports for 2002–07 are decorated with photographs of firefighting and feature reports on "significant" incidents, yet they are entirely silent on issues related to medical calls other than mention of the SARS outbreak in 2003.

These silences exist in a context where firefighters were involved in more and more emergency health care work. Medical training is now a significant component of firefighter training.[16] Respondents also indicated that they have acquired interpersonal skills, such as expressing empathy, calming volatile people, and de-escalating situations, by watching other firefighters and making mistakes. Firefighters, as an occupational group, were learning to provide this care. Significantly, the general public has accepted them as providers of health care, even though in many situations men are not trusted to provide care (Fine 2007). Firefighters may be accepted by the public in this role due to their occupations' status as most trusted (Leger-Marketing 2005). But their work in emergency health care has yet to be structurally woven into the reporting, statistical data, recognition programs, and formal training of fire services.

Firefighting culture also works to discursively hide firefighters' work in emergency medical care. But, paradoxically, it also supports and facilitates it. Both aspects are related to the close knit and supportive occupational culture or "brotherhood" of firefighters. This "brotherhood" has been well documented (Scott and Myers 2005; Yarnal, Dowler, and Hutchinson 2004; Chetkovich 1997; Lasky 2006). These accounts, whether sociological, psychological, historical, or based in fire engineering, and whether about volunteer, professional, urban, or rural fire services, are strikingly similar. Firefighting has a robust and seemingly ubiquitous dominant culture nurtured in the social relations of the fire hall and facilitated by the distinctive position of firefighters as workers who are willing to risk death to assist faceless others. This culture is not only well known to firefighters: it is disseminated through everything from children's picture books and cartoons to movies and the news. While "brotherhood" is a term maintained through union activity in other workplaces, the brotherhood of firefighters, while certainly entwined with union activity, should not be reduced to it. It predates and transcends the solidarity of unionization to take in non-unionized and volunteer firefighters as well as firefighters in management positions. This culture seems pervasive and was actively maintained within fire hall life in every fire hall that I visited.

That a familial metaphor, "brotherhood," is so generally applied by firefighters to their relations with each other seems particularly appropriate. First, fire halls are intimate domestic spaces, much like a home. Second, firefighters have downtime on the job, when they are not preparing for or responding to emergencies. During these "slow" times at the fire hall, they pursue many activities that are usually associated with home life. Third, senior workers are responsible for initiating and training probationary firefighters to get along at the fire hall as well as deal with the realities of emergency response. The more experienced workers nurture, protect, and mentor new workers, who are known by diminutives such as "probies" or "pups." All of these factors are implicated in the continual production of a close communal masculine culture amongst an overwhelmingly male labour force.

At the two fire services I studied firefighters were assigned to work together in permanent "crews" of four to six. Crews work on permanent servicewide "shifts," so the group of co-workers at a fire hall and across fire halls on any shift remained fairly static, with occasional disruptions due to promotions, transfers, leaves, illness, and retirement. In Ontario, provincial regulations require either twenty-four-hour shifts for firefighters, as in Toronto, or rotating shifts of ten-hour days and fourteen-hour nights, as in Rama. These staffing arrangements suit firefighting and other emergency work, according to the people I interviewed, because they allow workers to get to know one another, learn to trust each other, work well together, and understand each others' reactions when under pressure. Workers acquired intimate knowledge of each other's bodies, habits, tastes, and foibles. One captain commented that it was only in a job like firefighting that everyone knew what a co-worker's hair did if she didn't use a blow dryer to style it (236g). Many workers told me who snored or talked in their sleep. They knew each other's food preferences: at one fire hall I saw separate plates being prepared for those who didn't care for onions or salad dressing.

The notion of "brotherhood" is also appropriate given the homogeneity of firefighters. This labour force is overwhelmingly dominated by white men in most communities across Canada and the United States (Bossarte and Larner 2004; Chetkovich 1997). Many firefighters come to the field through long-standing connections with family and friends. Although it is no longer the case, for many years it was official policy in Toronto to hire firefighters' male family members and friends. In Rama, most of the current firefighters have family connections to the job. In the eleven Toronto fire halls I had visited at the time of writing, I met more than ninety firefighters, of whom two were white women, five were men from visible minorities, and one, also a man, was professedly gay. In Rama, there were two women firefighters. Most of the senior officers on the Mnjikaning force were white, due to a reported lack of experienced aboriginal firefighters, and they brought the dominant culture of firefighting into their work environment where it has been adopted in varying degrees by the predominantly aboriginal firefighters there.

The intimacy of the fire hall and the production of masculinity are interwoven with the crisis-laden and life-threatening nature of firefighting. Responding to emergencies requires workers to perform under duress. Firefighters use the relations within the fire hall to "engage in the emotions work necessary to deal with the multiple stresses of being public workers who routinely face private issues such as death and suffering" (Yarnal, Dowler, and Hutchinson 2004). Firefighters routinely debrief and support one another emotionally in ways that both provide care and maintain the hyper-masculine culture, while at the same time erasing their unease about the health care component of their job. The following example from my field notes will suffice to provide some insight into these intertwined relations.

On one occasion I watched two firefighters gently transfer a very ill and very disabled young man from his bed in an extended care facility to an ambulance gurney. Every move brought a cry of pain from the patient. One firefighter, Ray, maintained eye contact with the patient, verbally preparing, reassuring, and praising him, while both firefighters moved in skilful concert. A third firefighter, Will, held high an IV bag attached to the patient and moved with the others carefully, while the paramedics looked on.

When we returned to the truck, I complimented Ray on his caring manner. He quickly responded with sarcasm, "That's my problem. I feel too much." Then he said, more loudly, addressing the other firefighters, "If I ever get like that, I couldn't live in a place like that. I think if I knew I had to live like that, I'd just get me a big block of some crack cocaine and a couple of beautiful women, and after I'd had a real good time, I'd get someone to take me up in a plane and I'd push out over the house of someone I had it in for, and splatter all over the place." The other firefighters immediately entered the conversation, with lively and vivid discussion of how they would end their lives if they were confined to a wheelchair and had no alternative but to live in as depressing a surrounding as the facility we had just left. Women as objects, drugs, alcohol, and life-defying stunts figured largely in these tales.

Ray empathetically engaged with the patient in ways that helped him to ease suffering, ensure safety, and retain his patients' self-respect. Ray's distress as a result of this "emotion work"(Hochschild 1979) emerged within the context of the normative hyper-masculinity of firefighting. His fellow firefighters reassured Ray by sharing in his feelings and his mode of self-expression. They cared for him in a way that maintained their individual and collective subjectivities as risk-taking heterosexual masculine beings; in fact, as prototypical firefighters. This peer support also effectively erased Ray's health care provision through a conversation that turned the focus away from his work and toward recuperating a thoroughly hetero-masculine position. Firefighter culture and the masculinity it produces seem to "survive" health care work through such erasures.

A further example of these erasures and how they contribute to the invisibility of firefighters' emergency health care provision can be seen in the design of the Toronto firefighter badge. On one fire hall visit, I noticed that the shield of the Toronto Fire Services, printed on the firefighters' T-shirts, had a fire ladder on one side and a medical caduceus on the other. On the firefighter badges, however, I noted that the caduceus had been replaced by a hydrant. When I asked about it, I was told, "That's ... um, you know ... politically incorrect ... kind of a little ... well, it just takes a little bit back ... you know, everyone of us who came on this job came to be firefighters. We had to accept the fact the majority of our job is going to be medical based. I know why we do that and that's fine. Right? But still, we're first and foremost firefighters" (58i). My understanding is that the badge was designed by Toronto firefighters themselves.

Although the close culture of brotherhood helps to disguise and erase firefighters' health care work, it also supports it through tight supportive fraternal relations that are difficult to overstate. Whether in travelling to attend firefighter funerals, memorializing firefighters who died in the course of duty, providing important supports to those who have been injured on the job, offering emotional support, teaching a new skill, or socializing, firefighter solidarity extends well beyond the workplace. These activities of "brotherhood," which are continually enacted in the lives of firefighters, offer workers a particular form of socialization in caring and support to deal with at least some of the trauma and risk associated with their work. It is a caring relation grounded in homogeneity, an implicit expectation of reciprocation, and a sense of shared fate as men "who run into burning buildings when everyone else is running out" (89i). Firefighting culture is cultivated in the intimate life of the fire hall, and in the sense of affiliation to an honourable international brotherhood, not only producing gender but producing caring relations between and among firefighters. Although these bonds have historically supported these men who confront life-threatening circumstances in the course of their work, my research suggests that these relations may also serve as a resource for health care provision to the community, as well as producing and maintaining masculinity through ambivalence and rejection of this same work.

This tight culture has been under pressure to change, however, not only through increased involvements in health care provision but by employment equity initiatives. The diversification of the fire service labour force has been a major pressure on fire services. In Toronto, City Council and advocacy groups have applied pressure, and the fire service initiated innovative recruiting strategies to attract a more diverse group of recruits. In Rama, the pressure has been different. After forming as a professional service in 1997, the department initially hired some white senior officers because of a perceived shortage of experienced aboriginal senior officers; otherwise, hiring has been closed to non-aboriginal people, and it is now limited to aboriginal people who are band members from Mnjikaning First Nation. In order to facilitate recruitment and retention, Mnjikaning Fire Service developed its own unique training program that takes into account recruits' backgrounds.

Employment equity moves in both Toronto and Rama have aimed at addressing peoples' claims to the right to work in their own community services. Yet when asked directly, none of my respondents suggested that the cultural brotherhood of firefighting needed to shift substantially in order to include and retain non-white or non-male workers. In Toronto, anecdotal reports indicated that women and non-white firefighters tended to choose employment outside of the fire hall, for example in fire prevention, human resources, training, or mechanical divisions. The general white masculinity of firefighters that was woven into most aspects of fire hall life and fire services organization, even in the First Nations fire service at Rama, did not perceive itself as gendered or racialized. Instead, in Toronto, fire services administrators, union representatives, and senior staff expressed confusion and frustration about why women and non-whites fail to apply and fail to stay on the job. In Rama, senior officers emphasized the need to induct into the firefighting culture young aboriginal firefighters who had not been exposed to firefighting through their family backgrounds or communities. While recognizing that aboriginal culture was distinctive, in Rama as in Toronto there was an expectation that workers from all backgrounds would and could adapt to firefighting culture in their occupational lives.

In Rama, the close social relations of reserve life offer another basis for caring for each other and for the community that challenges the "brotherhood" of firefighting. For some of the aboriginal workers, firefighting culture seems to be an unnecessary alternative to the close affiliations within their First Nations community. Some of the officers and firefighters – among them those who hold the keys to promotion in this non-unionized department – said that their new firefighting force needs to assume the highest standards of firefighting expertise and community service, which, in their opinions, are tied to the traditional culture of firefighting life. The officers and those who report to them, however, are aware that the cultural norms of this First Nations community sometimes conflict with the norms of traditional firefighting culture: "Some of us, well, we don't want to be promoted. That would mean we'd have our buddies reporting to us. And

I don't want to have to bust my friend's asses. I mean when they call in sick when I know they're gone hunting. We gotta go home and have our friends, you know? That comes before any job" (218i).

For this respondent solidarity with co-workers as friends took precedence over opportunities to compete and advance on the job. Indeed, firefighting for these workers was perceived as a "job" rather than as a way of life and a way of being. In this case, entering the higher ranks of the fire service meant leaving the ranks of aboriginal workers and joining the primarily white officers. Although developing a cadre of aboriginal officers is an overt organizational goal, there is some sense among firefighters that to advance is also to "whiten." Community attachments offered an alternative to the firefighter brotherhood as a basis for caring to the community, albeit one with its own problems:

> It's kind of neat here. Well there's a couple of things. There's a guy here on this shift, he's a really good guy ... And he knows everybody. And you get a call, and he, you know "Myra (or whatever your name is) you know, oh how you doing? Tim is everything okay?" And they'll talk back and forth and he'll be a real calming factor for the person. [He'll] calm them down. And that's a really good thing. I think it's a helpful thing. Now for him, I don't know how stressful that is for him, seeing his friends or family like that. (196i)

At the call just described, involvement in a close community allowed firefighters to provide an effective response, even though the emotional costs to the firefighters were not well understood. Taken together, these examples show that the white masculine firefighter culture is being challenged in this First Nations community.

The case of firefighters' health care provision demonstrates some of the "gender-related caregiving problems" faced by men as they have surfaced in Canadian health care provision. Here, a masculine occupation has become a workforce of reluctant health care providers who continually erase any identification with health care provision in order to protect their collective masculinity. Further, their socialization to caring has been at least partially located in their homogeneous "brotherhood" – the very relation of gender production that requires that any occupational association with health care provision be erased. The complexities of these relations do not seem to point to any obvious resolution or crisis but rather point out the complexities of social change.

THE MASCULINITY OF NEOLIBERALISM: TENSIONS IN CARE

This discussion has set out a series of accidents, opacities, erasures, and unrecognitions. I began by describing an allocation of health care that operates outside of the health care system and the purview of health care data collection; while it maintains people it fails to provide the support they need to thrive. This whole situation is shored up by the neoliberal deployment of economic models that do not recognize value in certain labour processes. In this case, firefighters' labour that produces a readiness to respond, as well as most non-technical emergency medical work, has gone unrecognized.

Dominant firefighting culture is complicit in this unrecognition, generally finding health care provision inconsistent with its masculine project. It operates to erase and disguise health care work, while at the same time producing a brotherhood of care, which, I have suggested, serves as a relational basis for firefighters' health care provision to the public. This culture is being destabilized, however, by the affirmative action and anti-oppression projects within the fire services, as well as by their involvement in health care provision.

Redistribution of care from provincial formalized health care and social services to municipal public safety services, and from qualified feminized workers in health and social services to differently qualified masculinized workers in public safety occupations, has been accompanied, in this case, by a transformation of the form that health care has taken. Moves to acute care throughout the health system shape a kind of care that is more consistent with the logic of the masculinized domains of public safety. This care, based upon the logic of rescue, is more episodic, impersonal, and technical than the continuous relational care that is the hallmark of good feminized care, as portrayed in the standards set for nursing or social work (Tanner et al. 1996). Yet even this relation is unstable, as masculinized workers encounter the need for a more relational type of care and find themselves responding to it, albeit without the skills or time necessary to do it well.

This tension within health care provision is due to an incomprehension about care relations at the level of policy; an incomprehension that may be a defining feature of neoliberalism, tied deeply to the history of masculine domination in liberal governance. Neoliberalism recoups many of the characteristics of the laissez-faire liberalism of the late eighteenth and early nineteenth centuries in order to address the perceived excesses of the social liberalism that has dominated welfare state developments of the twentieth century. In Canada, it has worked toward a societal configuration in which care, whether for children, or people who are ill, frail, elderly, or disabled, is more exclusively the concern of private households, families, and individuals, while the state withdraws from care provision. This withdrawal has shifted the focus of publicly provided health care to acute care and eroded many other forms of social support that have buffered people from extreme need. These changes are some of the factors involved in the "unparalleled inequalities in income wealth and life chances" (Brodie 2007,93) fuelled by the neoliberal project.

That people do not just emerge into the labour force fully created and ready to work evaded liberalism. The work of social reproduction that women have performed has gone unrecognized in the liberal tradition, as one hallmark of its masculinist orientation (Brown 1995). But as this case shows, neoliberal policy makers are aware that such work is necessary but are determined that it is not the role of the state to provide or support it. Rather, it is the duty of the state to withdraw from care. But while neoliberal governance has removed and reconfigured services, it has failed to remove the expectations of, and pressures from, the Canadian public that the state *will* provide, particularly in the realm of health care. The logic of neoliberal policy is that some series of magic adjustments to policy change will occur, which, while painful in the transition, will produce social good in the form of economic prosperity. The state has yet to catch up with its populace, at least in Canada, where despite decades of neoliberal policy there remains a strong public expectation that the state will be involved in providing quality health care.

In the early twenty-first century, the dynamic of masculine domination interwoven with neoliberal logic seems profoundly contemporary in that its tensions parallel the societal relation between dominant masculinities and women's calls for men's involvement in care more generally. The state and its agents have dealt with the pressure to provide care with arguments that it is too costly, that they are too busy elsewhere, that it is someone else's job, that people should look after themselves, or that people don't really need care at all. When they find themselves having to be involved despite their best efforts, ongoing care needs are dealt with as short-term emergencies and the masculinized people involved are perceived not as publicly funded health care providers but as hyper-masculine protectors of public safety; as "firemen." This mis-recognition is supported by a policy logic that mis-recognizes needs and expectations for care, and the social relations that constitute it.

NOTES

1 I am indebted to Dr Pat Armstrong for pointing out this connection between the reorientation to acute care in hospitals and emergency health care responses to chronic care needs. I deeply appreciate the generosity of Pat, Meg Luxton, Leah F. Vosko, Karine Côté-Boucher and Tom Johnstone, who all provided feedback on the arguments and early drafts of this chapter.

2 I am very grateful to the firefighters who agreed to participate in this research, and to the Toronto Fire Service, Mnjikanging Fire and Rescue Service and the Toronto Association of Professional Fire Fighters, who facilitated this research. At the time of writing, I had conducted thirty-seven interviews and put in forty-seven hours of work observation at twelve fire halls. All data from Mnjikaning Fire Rescue Service is from interviews. Interviews have been assigned a number, followed by the letter I to indicate an individual interview or g to denote a group interview.

3 In fact, the Ontario Lottery and Gaming Corporation, a provincial body, pays seventy-five percent of the Rama Fire Rescue Services' annual budget. This unusual funding arrangement was reached due to the casino and hotel insurance requirements for a full-time professional fire department.

4 See iafflocal502.com/modules/news/article.php?storyid=45

5 Fire services data collection from emergency medical calls is minimal and does not describe most interventions or give any detailed information about the patient. In my view, these factors are implicated in the invisibility of firefighters' health care work, a topic discussed in the last section.

6 Neoliberal policy logic, discourse, and interventions urge people to take responsibility for their own care, well-being, and decision-making. These important aspects of neoliberal governance have been extensively researched. See (P.Armstrong et al. 2000) and Luxton, this volume. The failure of this policy orientation is certainly a component of the dynamic described in this case study. The important point for the purposes of this chapter, however, is that profound health care needs remain unmet – particularly those of working-class men and women.

7 All names in interviews and field notes have been changed to preserve anonymity.

8 The Toronto Fire Service has a plan to begin to collect data on interventions.

9 This argument may appear to essentialize gender forms. That is not my intention but rather follows in the footsteps of authors such as Wendy Brown, Judith Stiem, Iris Young, and others who have traced the masculine dominance inherent in modes of state power. See W.Brown 1995; Stiehm 1982; Young 2003.

10 Although the health care and social services labour force consists primarily
of women, it has been directed primarily by men, who serve as physicians
and administrators.

11 The case of paramedic services is also involved in this shift but is beyond
the scope of this research. See (J.Ross 2000; Bledsoe 2007)

12 *Crisis Call* is a stunning documentary film on police involvement with
those who are mentally ill, another striking example of the "pull" on public safety services shaped by health care and social services gaps (Sky 2003)

13 For more on protective masculinity and neoliberalism, see (P.Glasbeek
2006; Hubbard 2004)

14 See (Ontario Fire Marshall 2007) http://www.ofm.gov.on.ca/english/
Publications/sir/default.asp

15 An exception to this portrayal is found in International Association of Fire
Fighters 2001, their submission to the Romanow Commission on the Future
of Health Care in Canada. This document advocated the use of fire services
in responding to critical medical emergencies, stating that firefighters "are
health care workers who play a critically-important role in Canada's health
care system, especially in the vital area of pre-hospital care"(2).

16 There appears to be no formal training to teach skills to deal with the interpersonal aspects of medical care provision. Training is purely in technical procedures.

8

Doing Neoliberalism

Perverse Individualism in Personal Life

MEG LUXTON

Neoliberalism, the reassertion of free market capitalism that was developed in the late 1970s, represented a direct challenge to feminist, labour, and left-wing demands for greater social responsibility for care (Luxton 1997).[1] Committed to promoting the unfettered investment of capital and to a growing reliance on markets and private profit making, neoliberalism emphasizes the reduction of the role of the state in providing services and protections for the population as a whole, while strengthening its activities in support of business interests and private profit making (Gill and Bakker 2003). It implements privatization wherever possible by offloading services that were formerly provided by the state to private enterprise. Central to this initiative are the claims that individuals and their families should take more responsibility for their own care, that government provision of services is inefficient and costly, that reliance on state services weakens individual initiative and undermines family and community ties, and that caregiving is best arranged through voluntary familial and community networks (Cohen 1997; Luxton 2001; Luxton and Corman 2005).

In countries such as Canada with established welfare states, the success of neoliberalism rests on widespread acceptance that individuals and their households must absorb more of the work necessary to ensure the livelihoods and well-being of their members. As various levels of government have implemented specific neoliberal policies, people have typically had fewer supports and resources available to them, making personal caregiving more difficult and fraught. However, opposition to neoliberalism's agenda for caregiving has been fragmented and largely ineffectual. In a context where oppositional movements such as feminism, labour, and the left are weak, efforts to mobilize support for greater social investments in caregiving face complex challenges.

In this paper, I draw on interviews conducted in the Greater Toronto Area in Ontario, Canada, to show some of the dynamics that enable neoliberalism's care agenda. The study was designed to probe the dynamics involved when, in the context of changing job markets and government cutbacks to social services, people do rely, informally, on families, friends, neighbours, or others in their communities. Many of the people I interviewed accepted basic neoliberal assertions that individuals are primarily or even solely responsible for interpersonal and family care. That claim was closely tied to beliefs about individual identity, choice, and responsibility. I argue that neoliberal assertions are successful in part because they resonate with widespread and deeply held convictions. At the same time, as neoliberal ideology becomes hegemonic, it becomes difficult for many people to envision alternatives. Many of the people I interviewed were dissatisfied with their life circumstances but unable to imagine how to change things. Their sense of resignation and passivity strengthened neoliberal politics. However, I suggest that at the same time, they also expressed contradictory beliefs that recognized a degree of collective responsibility and challenged the defeatist implications inherent in neoliberal policies and practices to do with care. This recognition potentially offers a political basis for opposition to neoliberalism and support for an alternative vision of caregiving.

NEOLIBERALISM AND THE POLITICS OF CARE

Advocates of neoliberalism are fundamentally opposed to state provision of care, arguing instead that care is a personal responsibility and its services should be provided either voluntarily by family and friends or by the market where for-profit services may be purchased. Neoliberalism claims that changing international realities put roughly the same demands on all governments (Brodie 1996, 4). Representing the interests of the business or corporate sector, it calls on governments to adopt as priorities: the creation of free markets and the pursuit of free trade policies (such as the North American Free Trade Agreement, or NAFTA) to maximize exports and enable market forces to restructure national economies as parts of transnational or regional trading blocs;

the reduction of government regulation of the economy to free business from "oppressive" government controls, especially by weakening labour market regulation (such as repealing anti-scab legislation or eliminating pay and employment equity policies); reducing taxes on corporations; reducing government spending on social programs; and privatizing public services (Brodie 1996, 16). One of the main assumptions motivating this agenda is that "private choice is better than public regulation as a mechanism for allocating resources and ordering social affairs" (Phillipps 2002, 1).

Part of what fuelled the emergence of neoliberalism, and especially its most conservative wing, the new right, was the revitalization of existing, and the emergence of new, activist, equality, and liberation movements in the 1960s and 1970s.[2] These movements organized collectively to challenge the inequalities and discriminations faced by members of socially recognized groups: labour, women, aboriginal peoples, visible minorities, immigrants, people with disabilities, people with low incomes, lesbian, gay, bisexual, and later, transsexual and transgendered peoples. Activists from these movements demanded improved working and living conditions for working and poor people. They also revealed how existing welfare policies and practices sustained and reproduced prevailing assumptions about class, gender, race, disability, and sexuality, actively reproducing the subordinate and marginalized status of these and a range of other social constituencies. Some of the more radical activists put forward an analysis and critique of prevailing family ideologies and practices, reiterating a long-standing claim that nuclear family forms are profoundly antisocial and calling for social policies and practices that would eliminate the privileging of such family forms (Barrett and McIntosh 1982; Luxton 1997, 2001). They argued strongly for collective responsibility for individuals and caregiving, advocating, for example, for policies such as extended maternity and parental leaves, free universal childcare, affordable housing, an expansion of health care provisions such as dental care and home care, and a range of other benefits. These services and benefits, they insisted, should be available to everyone and should be paid for out of general revenues by increasing taxation of corporations, the wealthy, and superprofits.

What neoliberalism and especially the new right attacked was not just the existing welfare state and social security net already in place, but what they might have become in response to the expansionist and transformative demands of socialists and equality-seeking groups.

Central to that counterattack was an effort to reassert the centrality of a sexual division of labour, nuclear family forms, private responsibility for individual well-being (Connell 1998), and a racialized division of labour that anchors racism (see Thomas, this volume).

The neoliberal attack has had significant success. As Marjorie Cohen has argued, it has orchestrated a shift from a period in which "the deep contradictions in capitalism were modified by a system of social welfare based on the assumption that the well-being of the economy depended on the well-being of the people in it" to a situation in which "social and economic well-being for people is subordinate to the well-being of the corporate sector" (1997, 5). Governments changed from a redistributive state model to one that more openly justifies and reinforces market outcomes by rewarding those who place the least demand on public social programs and cajoling everyone else to follow their example.[3] This involved a strong move away from collective responsibility to individual initiative with a concomitant acceptance of greater insecurity for increasing numbers of people and growing inequality among people.

These changes in economic and social policy have both required and produced a change in the dominant assumptions about social life. As David Harvey noted in *A Brief History of Neoliberalism*: "For any way of thought to become dominant, a conceptual apparatus has to be advanced that appeals to our intuitions and instincts, to our values and desires, as well as to the possibilities inherent in the social world we inhabit. If successful, this conceptual apparatus becomes so embedded in common sense as to be taken for granted and not open to question" (2005, 5).

To support neoliberalism's claim that individuals and their families should take more responsibility for their own care, its advocates argue that government provision of services is inefficient and costly, that reliance on state services weakens individual initiative and undermines family and community ties, and that caregiving is best arranged through voluntary familial and community networks. In most welfare state economies family caregiving, and particularly women's unpaid labour, has been a crucial but unrecognized part of welfare provision. State policies both have assumed that families have always been the main provider of welfare and have also produced the conditions that require family members to work out their own solutions to the problems of combining paid employment and unpaid domestic labour. Typically women have had the primary responsibility for implementing those solutions (Luxton and Corman 2001). The women's and labour movements have challenged such arrangements, calling for state support for women's economic independence (for example through equal work and pay legislation, and the provision of childcare services and maternity and parental leaves). They have also called for public recognition and valuing of the activities such as love, caregiving, mutual aid and duty that are so central to unpaid work in the home (Armstrong and Armstrong 1994; Maroney and Luxton 1997).

However, the success of neoliberalism rests on widespread acceptance that households must absorb more of the work necessary to ensure their subsistence and the livelihoods of their members. In neoliberal discourse, support for privatization carries a double meaning, implying both the private sector of the economy and the private realm of the family. A whole range of developments have reduced or eliminated government services, enforcing "self-reliance," that is, compelling people to rely on earnings, on support from friends, family and voluntary organizations, and on privatized services, or to do without. This perspective was articulated quite explicitly in Ontario by the Conservative Harris government when, in 1995, as part of their efforts to create a climate of public opinion supportive of their neoliberal program, they urged people in Ontario to rely less on government services and more on families, friends, neighbours and their communities (Luxton 2001).

THE STUDY

The study discussed here investigated what happens when people who had no other options had to rely on informal caregiving provided by families, friends, neighbours, and others in their communities. Between January 1999 and January 2002, I interviewed a total of one hundred and thirty seven people in the Greater Toronto Area (GTA) and did follow-up interviews with sixty-four of them at least six months after the first interview (see the appendix for details). The people were selected because they had been directly affected by neoliberalism, by both economic restructuring and government downsizing and restrictions on programs, and because they were responding to the resulting situation by relying on voluntary family and community assistance. The medical emergency substudy included thirty-one people who had each suffered an unexpected medical emergency as a result of which they spent at least two weeks at home unable to care for themselves and without much formal support. It also included forty-two people who looked after them. The co-habiting sub-study included sixty-four people in twenty-five households who had formed new households of adult children and parents because at least one member could no longer sustain an independent household.

Each of the patients in the medical emergency substudy had only limited access to formal care provided by health or social services. They mobilized care, and their caregivers provided care, in a context in which most of them thought there were few alternatives. Most of the patients were convinced that cutbacks to health care forced them to rely on their own personal ties to provide the care they needed. Most of their care providers likewise assumed that if they failed to provide the care they were offering, no one else would step in.

In the cohabiting substudy, parents and children were living together because at least one of them was unable to maintain an independent household for financial reasons. In each case, the financially strapped person said that, if family cohabiting had not been an option, they would be in dire straits, facing the possibility of living on the street or seeking welfare services. Their financial difficulties were caused by layoffs (11); the end of a marriage and the resulting loss of the spouse's income (9); the loss of resources following a divorce settlement (5); the long-term impact of low-income jobs (4); job loss due to illness (2); or some combination of these circumstances.

By relying on and providing informal care arrangements, instead of having access to state services such as home care or income supports, these people were practising what neoliberalism demands of its adherents. However, their conformity to neoliberalism's ideals was strengthened by their implicit affirmation of neoliberalism. By accepting it, they validated its claims and entrenched its hegemony and so normalized their own life circumstances and undermined any efforts to protest against such circumstances as unacceptable or warranting changes. In doing so, they lent legitimacy to neoliberalism's inevitable production of greater social inequality and hardship for the majority.

THE CONTEXT OF THEIR LIVES

Throughout the 1980s and 1990s, as secure well-paid employment became more scarce and various government income and social supports were reduced and access was increasingly restricted, making a living became more difficult for many people in Canada generally, and in Ontario specifically (Bezanson 2006). In the late 1990s, according to the United Nations statistics on poverty in industrialized nations, 11.7 percent of people living in Canada had incomes below fifty percent of the national median income (Townsen 2000, 14).[4] The number of people with low incomes increased after the early 1980s and the degree of poverty experienced by those living on low incomes deepened.[5] The National Council of Welfare in its 1999 *Poverty Profile* reported that the number of individuals and families living at less than half the low-income cut-off level had also grown. By the late 1990s income inequality had grown as the income differences between the wealthiest and poorest groups in Canada increased dramatically (Yalnizyan 1998; Toronto *Globe and Mail*, 16 March 2001, A3). This class inequality was also deeply racialized, as systemic discrimination against aboriginals, immigrants, people whose first language was not English, and people of colour intensified (see Thomas, this volume; Galabuzi 2006). Likewise, discrimination against people with disabilities increased. The growing inequality was profoundly gendered as women were discriminated against in the paid labour force, where they still typically earned less than men (Drolet 1999) and their responsibility for providing unpaid family-based caregiving kept many out of the paid labour force for significant periods of time (Armstrong and Armstrong 1994). Women were more likely to be poor than men, in part because of their major responsibility for caregiving (Statistics Canada 2000, 137, 205, 259). As a result, women more than men relied on social services and were disproportionately affected by government cuts (Day and Brodsky 1998).

Increases in the number of people living on low incomes were obviously related to changes in the kinds of jobs available and rates of pay, hours, and benefits. Restructuring in manufacturing and government downsizing significantly reduced the number of full-year, full-time unionized jobs that paid a living wage with benefits. Legislative changes reduced health and safety protections, permitted extended hours of work, and eroded employment and workplace protections to the advantage of employers. More and more new jobs were part time, paying low wages and offering few or no benefits. These labour market changes affected men, especially young men who in previous generations would have been able to get industrial and manufacturing employment, undermining their ability to support families. They also significantly reduced the number of "good jobs" available to women, especially in the public sector (Luxton and Reiter 1997, 213). Those labour market changes were reinforced by government policies that backed away from employment and pay equity measures, allowing the historic discriminations in access to jobs and gender differences in pay rates to continue (Drolet 1999, 32).[6] Through the 1990s the growth of low-paid temporary jobs created a female-dominated contingent workforce of people who rarely earn a living wage (Vosko 2000). Inevitably, the social groups that were already oppressed were hit hardest by such contractions: people earning low incomes, members of First Nations, people of colour, immigrants, people with disabilities (Thomas, this volume; Wallis and Kwok 2008).

Changing government policies, especially cuts to unemployment/ employment insurance, social services, and welfare, had a disproportionately negative impact on women. The federal government's 1990 cap on the Canada Assistance Plan (CAP), which cut federal support to Ontario, Alberta, and British Columbia, followed by its 1996 decision to eliminate CAP and replace it with the Canada Health and Social Transfer (CHST), pushed provinces and territories to cut welfare funding. Simultaneously, many provincial and territorial governments were already making eligibility for welfare more stringent and subjecting its recipients to demeaning scrutiny and control. Concurrently, changes to the federal (un)employment insurance benefits in 1997 meant that proportionately fewer women than men were eligible. To some extent this was because more women had part-time jobs where it was harder to get enough qualifying hours, and because it became more difficult to qualify after time out of the labour force (Toronto *Globe and Mail*, 23 March 2000, A1, A6). Throughout the 1980s and 1990s the percentage of women living in poverty steadily increased. In 1980 1.8 million women had low incomes; by 2000 about 2.2 million adult women had low incomes. Almost nineteen percent of adult women were poor. When women have low incomes, their children live in poverty too. About twenty percent of low-income women were mothers raising children on their own; another fifty-one percent were coparents in low-income families (Townsen 2000, 12). The National Council of Welfare estimated that the total welfare income for a single parent with one child ranged from a low of fifty percent of the low-income cut-off level in Alberta to a high of sixty-nine percent in Newfoundland. For couples with two children, welfare incomes averaged around fifty to fifty-five percent of the low-income cut-off level (National Council of Welfare 1999).

In 1995 Ontario's newly elected Conservative government led by Mike Harris implemented a dramatic restructuring of provincial government operations, based on massive cuts to taxes and social services (Bezanson 2006). One of their explicit goals was to reduce the number of people eligible for state support, so one of their first acts was to cut welfare benefits by 21.6 percent for all recipients except the aged and people with disabilities, a decrease that hit single parents particularly hard (*Toronto Star*, 28 September 1995, A14). Later, Harris cut a nutritional supplement for pregnant women with low incomes because, he claimed, they would only spend the money on beer (Toronto Star 16 April 1998, A2). The increasing poverty rates and levels offer one measure of the impact of neoliberalism on people living in Canada in general and people living in Ontario in particular.

What is less well documented and, to date, less widely discussed is the impact of the changing economic and political order on the ways in which people understood individual and family responsibility for caregiving. Precisely because personal life is private and individualized, what happens to individuals, or in individual family households, or among personal friends, neighbours, and co-workers is often difficult to assess. Even more occluded from public scrutiny is the way neoliberal assumptions have become normal, to the point where most people assume there are no alternatives. Certainly, all of the one hundred and thirty-seven people interviewed for this study talked about the negative ways in which economic restructuring and government cuts to social services had affected their lives and reduced their well-being. A few of them identified neoliberalism as the problem, explicitly denouncing it and arguing for alternatives; the majority did not. However, most (although not all) of the people I interviewed maintained that most of their life circumstances were both inevitable and an outcome of the choices they had made.

ACCEPTING NEOLIBERALISM

Two things from the interviews were striking. First, most people were convinced that no real alternative help was available from social or health care services (even when such help was available) because such services, which they believed had once existed, apparently did so no

longer "because of the cuts." Second, many expressed a resigned
sense of the inevitability of their situation, despite their conviction
that things had been different in an earlier period. Few had any
sense that more services might be available if they sought them
out; fewer had any sense of outrage at the limited availability of
services. Fewer still had any sense that they could ask, or fight, for
more. Over and over, people described difficult or painful circumstances, then shrugged and said some version of "But what can you
do? That's just the way things are." While most of them recognized
some of the social forces shaping their practices, they typically asserted that such forces – described variously as luck, god's will, or just
the way things are – were external to them and inevitable. Few people expressed any sense that they could affect the context in which
they made their choices. A former industrial worker said: "Well,
what can you do, eh? The company made lay offs and I was one of
them – nothing I could do about it."

At the same time, and apparently without recognizing the contradiction, most of them tended to accept a degree of personal responsibility, even when they assumed that the forces shaping their lives were
beyond their control. The same worker continued: "Of course, I
chose to work there, didn't I? I guess if I'd made other choices I
wouldn't be unemployed today, would I?"

Repeatedly people explained that because they had made the
choices that had culminated in their current situation, it was their private problem, not a social issue. It was something to be coped with,
not something to mobilize against politically. I argue that this is an
example of a perverse form of individualism – an obstinate and persistent belief that blames the victim by privatizing social problems. It
is a belief that is central to neoliberalism as neoliberalism simultaneously depends on widespread acceptance of this worldview for its
success and imposes this worldview on those subject to its workings.

What was also striking when people talked about their choices
was their strong sense of individual responsibility for decision making. A woman in her fifties talked in ways that show how deeply
such notions of individual responsibility permeate people's understandings of their lives. She had left high school after grade ten and
moved away from home because her father was sexually abusing
her. Although she lived on the streets for four years, she managed to
get a series of low-paying jobs, save money, and, at the age of nineteen, get a clerical job that she held for thirty-six years. Despite a

stellar work record she never earned very much. When the company closed, terminating her employment, she had few savings. She could have described herself as a self-made woman who had overcome unacceptable treatment by her parents (who never spoke to her again after she left home although she tried to keep in touch with them), had worked hard and done well until the layoff. She could have protested that managers were given hefty severance packages while employees received only employment insurance. She could have argued that the company should bear some responsibility or that government has responsibilities for people who are unable to make a living income. Instead she blamed herself for her situation: "So at fifty-five, I have no income. No one wants to hire women my age and I am desperate. Now I realize I should have done things differently, got more education. I could have gone back to school I guess, although there never seemed to be time for that. I could have saved more, found a cheaper place to live and put the money in the bank. Looking back, I just see how I made so many mistakes that got me here."

Like many of the other people I interviewed, this woman expressed a core ideological position of neoliberalism, that individuals are responsible for themselves and that the choices they make determine the outcome of their lives. The people who articulated this position seemed to assume that their situation was in effect the sum of the choices they had made over the years and that the problems and difficulties they faced were a result of poor choices. They expressed very little appreciation of the ways in which circumstances that were largely out of their control had shaped their lives. They seemed to have no sense that they could intervene to change those circumstances.

In a similar way, most of the individuals who had succeeded financially, professionally, or in other ways attributed their success to their own efforts and reaffirmed the belief that those who failed to do well had only themselves to blame. A successful businessman said: "Well, I did well, but it was because I worked hard, kept my eye on the goal, and didn't get distracted by other things. Anyone can succeed if they do that. I have no use for the whiners and complainers who want government handouts because life treated them unfairly."

Even a woman who, as a trade union organizer for many years, had witnessed the power of employers over workers and who presented herself as a socialist, had inculcated elements of neoliberalism in her analysis:

When I was younger and active in the women's liberation movement of the 1970s, I thought the problem was the capitalist system. You know, bosses have power. Workers have to work or
starve so have to do what bosses tell them unless they organize
together. Well, I'm a union organizer. I still know that workers
standing together have strength where workers on their own have
none. But now I think, you know, that people sort of make
choices. Like if they don't want to be part of a union, stand up
for themselves, then they have made a choice to have crappy
working conditions. And anyway, now I know that the way the
economy works, there's not much we can do about the jobs that
are available.

While the change in her political analysis over the years could be attributed to a variety of causes, it illustrates the ways in which neoliberal perspectives are entrenched and shows how readily they can
immobilize potential opposition.

THE POWER OF CHOICE

Woven throughout the interviews was the idea of choice. Anthro-
pologist Marilyn Strathern (1992) has shown how ideas about
choice are related to concepts of individuality in western European
and North American thought. In that tradition, an individual is
seen to be defined by their innate capacity to make free choices and
choices are deemed to be expressions of individuality. This understanding has permeated people's subjectivity so that a sense of individuality is constituted through the capacity to make choices and
the choices made.

   The ideas about choice and individuality expressed in the interviews confirmed Strathern's analysis. The belief in individual choice
was widespread. For most, it involved a sense that there is an autonomous self capable of, and responsible for, deciding how to act
on the basis of personal beliefs and predilections. Most assumed
that their decisions were also statements about themselves. When
they were pleased with a decision and its outcome, they could take
satisfaction from their sense of accomplishment and confirm their
identity as a good person contributing something valuable to their
social relationships: "I made a decision and I wasn't sure at all if it
was okay. But as I saw him get happier, and knew that I was making

him feel better and getting back on his feet, then I felt good about myself. I could see I had made a difference, by what I did."

Reverberating through the interviews, however, was a sense of confusion about how to make decisions, what criteria might inform their choices, and how their decision making might reflect on them as individuals. A nurse who contrasted the experience of caring for her brother with her experiences on the job said: "At work what's at stake is my skill at my job, what kind of a nurse am I. But when I'm here looking after my brother, it's very different. It's our whole relationship, it's like what's at stake is who I am. Everything I do, or don't do, for him, is like a statement about this is the kind of person I am."

The deeply held belief in the importance of choice permeated all aspects of caregiving negotiations. Although many described agonizing over certain decisions, most claimed that having made particular choices, they had to accept the consequences even when things did not unfold as they had expected them to. Many said that their choices reflected their essential self: "I just had to let him move in. What other choice could I make, given who I am? I don't think it's a good choice for me, but I couldn't do anything else, not and be true to myself."

The idea of individual responsibility for choice combined with a sense that choices reflect identity imposes a considerable burden. A mother of young children contrasted her parenting responsibilities, about which she assumed she had no choice, with her care for her mother, where her responsibilities were less clear. The clarity of the former required less choice and so was less confusing: "With my kids, there's no choice. I am their mother. I take care of them. I don't even have to think about it. But with my mother, every little thing is a choice. Will I do this? Will I do that? Do I want to help her this way? If I say no, what does that mean about who I am? It's endless and it's all up to me and I have to think about every little thing."

One of the most insidious features of neoliberalism is its denial of social structure, and of the ways in which individuals, as members of communities and societies, are both formed by and subject to the prevailing values and practices. Margaret Thatcher, at the height of her power as a champion of neoliberalism, stated: "There is no such thing as society. There is only the economy and families" (Thatcher 1987). This claim remains central to neoliberalism, and the more people believe it, the harder it is for them to recognize the impact of "society" on individuals and the choices they make.

However, while many of the people I interviewed expressed a strong sense of identity as unique individuals, they also acknowledged a sense of identity as part of a social group whose members share characteristics and explained their choices with reference to the group. Some, like the woman who said that as a mother "there's no choice," insisted that they had to act as they did, and most attributed their lack of choice to the social responsibilities they had accepted and the system of morality by which they lived their lives.

Their discussions revealed confusing tensions between the two aspects of identity. If individuals can make free choices about how to act, how are they to understand the social pressures they experience? If they recognize themselves as subject to social pressures, how are they to understand themselves as individuals? As one person said: "Like, I know it's all up to me to decide what I want to do in my life, but I know there's all this stuff – like my mother keeps telling me what she thinks, and her friends, they are always on me about what's right. The priest, he has a whole thing about how I should live, and then I see my friends. Like, who am I? And then, how do I figure out what's right for me?"

Most described an uneasy relationship between both identities. One man's hesitant comment was typical: "Well, it's kind of, like, you know, it's up to me, eh. It's my choice, what I do. But I know I have values that are, well, they're not my parents' values. I'm a different generation, but when I make decisions, I have to think about where my values come from because they're not just out of my head. They come from the world I live in."

Many people echoed this man's confusion as they tried to reconcile a sense of themselves as independent individuals making choices with the recognition both that they are affected by the world they live in and that they have a sense of accountability to it. Their confusion was compounded by a distinct lack of analysis about how their own individuality or identity was shaped by that world. I suggest this results in another aspect of perverse individualism, a belief that attributes social values and morality to individual consciousness. After describing in detail how looking after an ailing neighbour had created serious difficulties for him, including lost pay and a major fight with his girlfriend, a man tried to explain why he continued to care for the neighbour: "Well, like I know it's just crazy and I should stop. I am seriously screwing up my life. But that's just who I am. It's the way I'm made and I can't change me. Maybe if I were smarter, or more together, I would figure out a way to do it better. But I also just think, like, that's what people should do, eh? Help each other. It's just how I am, no matter what the world says. I guess you just got to be who you are, regardless."

While conflating social values with individual consciousness obscures the ways in which people are part of their society, most of the people who did so also articulated a sense of a shared morality. Recognizing that something is "right" and what people "should" do implies a sense of accountability to a larger system. The same man went on to say: "I just know it is the right thing to do."

CHANGING SOCIAL OBLIGATIONS

Ideas about individual responsibility and choices are further complicated by one of the key features of contemporary social life: most interpersonal relationships, including kin, are increasingly diverse and largely voluntary. Only nuclear family relationships are subject to state regulation and to a strong degree of social agreement about mutual obligations. Parents are obligated to provide for their underage children and risk losing custody and access if they are deemed to have failed to do so. Spouses are legally required to pool and share key resources such as the matrimonial home or pensions but are free to terminate their relationship if they wish. Under certain circumstances, parents can make financial demands of adult children. And, as the interviews showed, there are deeply held assumptions about caregiving obligations and responsibilities among nuclear family members that are reinforced by the prevailing familial ideology of contemporary society. But even nuclear family relationships are increasingly diverse and relatively easy to terminate. Such ideas reverberated through the interviews when people talked about themselves in relation to their families. A sixty-three-year-old woman living with her daughter said:

It's much harder for young women today. My grandmother and mother, they knew what to do. My mother didn't like what was expected of women, where women just looked after the home and the family and did what the men said. She complained endlessly, but she knew what to do. Women just had to look after anyone in the family who needed it, no matter what. Things are different for me and even more for my daughter. We face choices

my mother never had about what to do. I don't think men can tell
women what to do any more and I don't even think women know
what looking after their families really means any more.

Beyond the nuclear family, interpersonal obligations are relatively
optional. The more people believed that they could choose whether
or not to take responsibility for their kin, the stronger their sense of
the possibility of individual choice. A woman, who had just told
me, with considerable bitterness, that neither of her siblings took
any responsibility for their aging and ill mother, went on to say: "I
guess I could choose that too, and not look after her. But I would
feel so guilty because, really, I think I should look after my mother. I
think it would be so much easier if I just knew I had to do it. Now
every time it seems too hard, I think why am I doing this? It's my
fault my life is so impossible. And then I realize that if I just was
more organized and dealt with things better, I would be okay, so
then I get mad at myself."

This critique echoes both the multiple discourses of capitalist time
management and neoliberal rationality arguments that efficiency produces greater productivity. Neither recognizes that the circumstances
this woman finds herself in, which are not of her choosing, might
make demands on her that she is unable to meet satisfactorily, no
matter how well organized or competent she might be.

Another feature of contemporary social life is that there is considerable diversity in the practices that are socially recognized as acceptable.
Established conventions are deeply embedded and constantly reinforced. While they may be constraining, they do provide the security of
knowing what is expected. Trying to do things outside those conventions requires innovation and often incurs questioning or criticism. The
breakdown of convention produces greater social uncertainty. For example, people who came of age in the 1930s knew that having babies
outside of marriage was completely unacceptable. The mothers were
often ostracized, the children were legally illegitimate and the fathers
were often under considerable pressure to marry. Those coming of age
in the early 2000s may still be subject to similar pressures from families
or religious communities, but the legal penalties no longer exist and
there is little general social stigma. Many women have and raise children without ever marrying. As a result, individuals are forced to make
decisions about which social practices they associate themselves with
and about how to act in myriad situations. As one woman said: "My

girlfriends and ·me, we talk about that all the time. Like we can't decided what's right for us so we are always having to think – what to do
now? Sometimes I just wish I didn't have to think so much, that I
would just know what to do and do it, or even not do it and feel bad.
But I always have to, you know, what should I do, how do I feel. It
makes me crazy. Then I feel bad that I can't cope!"

Even the most socially isolated and the most fiercely independent
made their personal choices in a larger social context that shaped
their decision making. However, the power of beliefs in individual
identity and personal responsibility made it difficult for many people to recognize the impact of social forces on the way they lived
their lives. "Ultimately it's all up to me, what I choose to do. Of
course I know I have to think about what will people think. And I
know what my church says is right and I try to live by that. But it's
finally up to me. It makes me feel lonely you know, all alone deciding what to do."

Most not only accepted the idea that they were individually responsible for either finding their own care or providing care for others,
they also tended to attribute the success or failure of that caregiving to
their own actions and to the specific relationship between care provider and care receiver. By holding themselves accountable and deny-
ing the social context, they were "doing neoliberalism" – enacting the
practices advocated by neoliberalism and normalizing them, confirming neoliberalism's hegemony.

CONCLUSIONS

I suggest that this lack of vision, combined with a lack of appropriate
social support, contributes to a climate of resignation and sometimes
despair that shapes peoples' caregiving practices and their response to
changing business and government policies. This lack of vision left
many of the people in this study with a sense that there was little they
could do to improve their circumstances – that their only options were
to accept the inevitable and make the best of it – a perspective which
left them vulnerable to neoliberal cutbacks and downloading. At the
same time, they all had quite clear ideas about the kinds of care they
wanted to offer others and many of them were providing care, often at
considerable personal expense. In this sense, they offer credence to neoliberal assertions that people should (and by implication, can) rely on
voluntary familial and community networks.

The strength of neoliberal politics lies in its articulation and production of a commonsense hegemonic ideology based on the fundamental liberal concept of self-actualizing individuals whose relative successes in the competitive labour and consumer markets depends on the rational choices they make and their own skilled and diligent work (Lloyd 1984). The widespread acceptance of personal responsibility lends credibility to neoliberal demands. At the same time, the experiences of living under a neoliberal regime encourage people to narrow their vision of what is possible and to accept responsibility for their own circumstances. This perverse individualism easily immobilizes people, making it hard for them to envision alternatives and rendering them politically inactive. Their sense of individual agency is reduced to a notion of choice, the concept of collective political action seems increasingly unimaginable, and they are inclined to assume that their circumstances are a result of poor choices they have made, rather than that the choices available were problematic or wrong. The net effect is to obscure or even deny the class, gender and racialized relations that are fundamental to contemporary society. The extent to which people accept personal responsibility both reveals the depth to which neoliberal ideologies have penetrated personal life and shows the centrality of such ideologies for the success of neoliberalism.

However, despite their sense of individual responsibility for their own lives, the people in this study also took for granted an important commitment to the well-being of others. They valued their caregiving and described their socially responsible contributions with pride. They expressed a strong sensibility about themselves as moral actors, as people embedded in, and shaped by, social values they share with others and to which they are accountable. That sense of a shared morality, which they took into account when deciding how to act, included a strong sense of their responsibility to care for others and a vision of a world in which people provide care for each other. Their comments show that they were trying to implement their values in the way they lived their lives. That sense of being part of a system of social values and of obligations to others offers a potential antidote to the neoliberal vision of a fully marketized society of competing individuals. The challenge for those opposed to neoliberalism is to develop a conceptual apparatus that taps into those values in order to offer a different common sense that invites people to question neoliberalism.

APPENDIX A: THE TAKE CARE STUDY

Interviews conducted in Toronto, Ontario January 1999 – January 2002

1. The Medical Emergency:

31 individuals (18 years of age or older)

who had experienced an unexpected medical emergency as a result of which they required short term help (such as getting around the house, shopping, cooking, errands, medical treatment)

> Total: 31 interviews: 18 women, 13 men
> Follow-up: 13 interviews: 12 women, 1 man

42 care givers (for 29 of the individuals who needed care)

> 1 care giver for 20 individuals (19 women, 1 man)
> 2 care givers for 5 individuals (8 women, 2 men)
> 3 care givers for 4 individuals (10 women, 2 men)
> Total: 42 interviews: 37 women, 5 men
> Follow-up: 29 interviews: 26 women, 3 men

Medical Emergency Total: 73 people (55 women, 18 men)
      Follow-up Total: 42 people (38 women, 4 men)

2. The Intergenerational Households Study: Adult Children and Parents Cohabiting (after at least two years living separately)

28 adult children, 27 parents, 7 children's spouses, 2 parent's siblings = 64 individuals

25 households (H)(where the child was 18 years of age or older):
> 17 households: one adult child and one parent
> (H 1–9: 9 households: a male child and a female parent)
> (H 10: 1 household: a female child and a male parent)
> (H 11 – 17: 7 households: a female child and a female parent)
> Total: 34 interviews: 24 women, 10 men
> Follow-up: 16 interviews: 13 women, 3 men
> 5 households: one adult child, one partner of adult child and one parent:

(H 18–20: 3 male children, their 3 female partners,
3 female parents)
(H 21: a female child, a male partner, a female parent)

(H 22: a female child, a male partner, a male parent)
Total: 15 interviews: 9 women, 6 men
Follow-up: 4 interviews: 3 women, 1 man

2 households: 2 children, a spouse of one and two parents
(H 23: a male child, a female child and male spouse,
a female and male parent)
(H 24: 2 female children, a female spouse, a female and
male parent)
Total: 10 interviews: 6 women, 4 men
Follow-up: 2 interviews: 1 woman, 1 man

1 household: 2 adult children, one parent, 2 siblings of parent
(H25: a male child, a female child, a female parent,
1 female sibling of parent, 1 male sibling of parent)
Total: 5 interviews: 3 women, 2 men
Intergenerational Households Total: 64 people (42 woman,
22 men)
Follow-up: 22 people (17 women, 5 men)

TOTAL INTERVIEWS: 137 people (97 women, 40 men)
Total follow-up interviews: 64 people: (55 women, 9 men)

Ethnicity/Country of Origin:

Canadian	37
American	17
Caribbean	17
British or Irish	12
Eastern European	10
Southern European	10
Vietnamese	9
East African	9
Chinese	7
First Nations	5
West African	2
Philippines	2

NOTES

1 Jim Petersen read the original draft of this paper. His comments led me to re-write it. Then Susan Braedley and Jane Springer patiently read and reread further drafts. Their intellectual challenges and personal support prove once again the importance of friends and community and I thank them.

2 Such movements were also linked to international solidarity movements that supported anti-colonial and national liberation movements, as well as defending socialist regimes and opposing international corporate and military power.

3 This description of neoliberal state orientation derives from Lisa Phillipps's important paper on tax law and social reproduction in which she documents the ways in which tax laws regulate social reproduction showing how the changes in the 1990s imposed more of "the costs of social reproduction on women, undermining women's economic security, autonomy and equality" (2002, 1).

4 This is compared to five to seven percent in European countries and 19.1 percent in the United States.

5 Statistics Canada identifies people as low income if they need to spend more than fifty-five percent of their before-tax income on food, shelter, and clothing. Actual figures are calculated each year and vary by the number of people in a family, and by the number of people living in a region. This approach has been used for more than thirty years in Canada (National Council of Welfare 1997).

6 For example, in 1989 the arbitration board determined that female public sector workers in Newfoundland were owed $80 million in back pay because their wages had been discriminatory. The province appealed. In 2004 the Supreme Court of Canada upheld the arbitration but also found the province justified in withholding the payment because it was in such dire financial straits (National Union of Public and General Employees http://www.nupge.ca/news_2005/n07deo5a.htm).

9

Neoliberalism in Action
Canadian Perspectives

PAT ARMSTRONG

According to economist and Nobel laureate Joseph Stiglitz, a professor at Columbia University who has worked with the World Bank: "Neo-liberal market fundamentalism was always a political doctrine serving certain interests. It was never supported by an economic theory. Nor, it should now be clear, is it supported by historical experience. Learning this lesson may be the silver lining in the cloud now hanging over the global economy" (2008, A17). It is because we need to learn this lesson, and learn it, as Connell reminded us in chapter two of this volume, within the specific context of the social forces operating within each country, that the articles in this book are so important. Clearly inequality in general, and inequality linked to racialization, gender, ability, and class in particular, did not originate with the neoliberal hegemony of the last thirty years or so. What Connell and the other contributors have addressed, however, are the ways in which current neoliberal practices differ from those of earlier welfare states, the consequences for both equity and resistance, and various alternatives to this far-too-pervasive understanding of, and approach to, the world.

In this conclusion I bring together the multiple aspects of neoliberalism set out in these chapters, using forms of privatization as a frame and linking them to previous feminist discussions of private and public. The purpose is to provide another lens through which to learn the lessons drawn by the contributors. I shall then raise a few theoretical and empirical questions stimulated by the book in order to suggest some additional ways forward to Stiglitz's silver lining.

SHIFTING BOUNDARIES: PUBLIC AND PRIVATE

Underpinning discussions of neoliberalism are particular notions about public and private, collective and individual. Even before neoliberalism became the fashion and before talk of privatization emerged, feminists were exploring the meaning of the terms. They sought to understand how different constructions of public and private in ideology and in practices shaped women's lives and the lives of women in various social, physical and economic locations differently. The understanding of what constitutes private and public has developed over time, through intellectual debate and empirical investigation. It has been reconstructed at the same time as the public and private are themselves being reconstructed under neoliberalism, as this book makes clear. Sorting through the meaning of public and private helps provide a frame for understanding what is different about neoliberalism and the consequences of those differences for inequality. In the 1960s and 1970s, feminists talked about public and private mainly as a single divide, with women relegated primarily to the private sphere of the household. As Canadian feminists explored how a public/private divide influences women's relations, they refined their conceptual tools in ways that emphasized differences among women and the complexity of, as well as the contradictions in, divisions between private and public. It has become increasingly obvious that private and public connote several things (Armstrong and Armstrong 2005). First, there is a distinction between households (which may be called private) and the spaces outside them (which may be called public), especially the formal economy but also what is often called the third or voluntary sector. Second, there is the distinction between public and private sectors within the formal economy, government-funded and -controlled operations being separate from the private ones. And within the private sector of the formal economy, there are for-profit and not-for-profit concerns. Finally, there is the distinction between private or individual rights and responsibilities and collective or shared ones.

From the 1970s onward, feminists in Canada began demonstrating how the development of capitalism encouraged the separation of public and private into what appear to be quite different spheres, each with a different underlying logic, a different construction of time, and different social relations. At the same time they showed the interpenetration between households and formal economies, communities and markets (Armstrong and Armstrong 1978; Fox 1980; Hamilton 1978; Luxton 1980; Morton 1972; Seccombe 1974). The path to the separation of public and private has been uneven and incomplete, variable from region to region, class to class, and between people of different genders and races. The whole is shaped by capitalism in numerous and often contradictory ways, as well as by resistance. Canadian feminists have documented the general tendency toward separation of private and public in the twentieth century and analyzed its implications with regard to struggle and inequality.

This theoretical and empirical work touched in part on the lives of a majority of women. During the postwar period in Canada, the various distinctions between private and public became clearer, although there were some contradictory trends. Most women were not in the labour force and most did domestic work in their homes. Within what was lumped together as the public sphere, distinctions among state organizations, private, for-profit, and not-for-profit concerns also became clearer. The search for profit remained dominant throughout society but a somewhat different logic applied to the public and private spheres, as well as to the public and private sectors. Though they perpetuated many forms of inequality (Ursel 1992), the distinctions made by the welfare state between private and public sectors and the different spheres within them had some positive effects. In its role as legislator, regulator, funder, employer and service provider, the state helped to promote the idea of shared rights and responsibilities, as Bezanson explained in relation to childcare (see chapter five). Major aspects of education, infrastructure, social services, and health care were provided with state funding and by public or non-profit agencies in the formal economy, and their delivery was based on an assumption of service rather than of profit (Armstrong 1997). They were not commodified, that is, they were not being exchanged on the market. Especially within the state sector in the Canadian formal economy, women had some success in drawing the distinctions between public and private in ways that brought them more recognition, pay, security, and control. Overall, income inequality declined under what Luxton called the redistributive state (see chapter eight), and some racialized groups made gains through human rights claims, labour standards legislation, and new immigration policies. Collective rights were recognized, to some extent.

The emergence of neoliberalism has brought an increased blurring of the distinctions between the different kinds of private and public as well as within them. Some of the distinctions have been reinforced, however, thanks to the increased privatization that has resulted from neoliberal reforms. At the same time, as Thomas pointed out in chapter four, employment for women in general, and for particular categories of women such as those from racialized groups, has become more precarious. Indeed, life has become more precarious for growing numbers of people, even as the precautionary principle is applied in the name of national security, and services are redrawn or withdrawn in the name of choice (see the chapters by Côté-Boucher, Braedley, and Luxton in this volume). We can see these trends and contradictions more clearly by looking at various forms of privatization (Armstrong et al. 1997; Armstrong et al. 2002).

SORTING THE FORMS OF PRIVATIZATION

Privatization of Responsibility

The privatization of responsibility, which has been addressed throughout this volume, is often sold as individual choice or individual rights. Private responsibility emphasizes individual rights to the exclusion of collective rights. The nanny state will no longer provide. Gone is the notion of collectively pooling risks. It is difficult to imagine Prime Minister Stephen Harper saying, as Leonard Marsh did in his 1943 *Report on Social Security for Canada*, that "it is impossible to establish a wage that will allow every worker and his family to meet the heavy disabilities of serious illness, prolonged unemployment, accident and premature death. These are budget shattering contingencies that strike most unevenly" (Marsh 1975, 10). Rather, individuals or their families are expected to take responsibility for themselves and earn enough through the market to provide for their own needs. This form of privatization provides a rationalization for inequality through the assumption that we get what we deserve as a result of our efforts. It is an ideology, as Connell put it, that "implicitly justifies the social inequality that allows proper rewards for 'winning.'" It unites a wide range of neoliberal approaches, from what Bezanson called the libertarian-leaning neoliberal Theo-Cons of Stephen Harper (see chapter five) to the third way of many premiers.

Indeed, central to the neoliberal ideology of the third way is "equality of opportunity rather than equality of outcome or status," which is based, as Pinto explained in chapter six, on the notion of tying rights to responsibilities and of individuals gaining human capital so they can enter the labour market and take responsibility for their own support. It leaves out people with disabilities and ignores structural and other constraints that create inequalities.

Luxton described the "move away from collective responsibility to individual initiative" that comes with the increase in private responsibility for care; firefighters have become caregivers, as Braedley showed, now that the closing of institutions, shorter patient stays, and limited homecare have forced many more people to assume responsibility for their own health. Similarly, individuals are called on to take responsibility for their location within the market; for their jobs, their benefits and their income. Thomas shows how labour protections for the most vulnerable workers have been reduced, leaving individuals with no choice but to consent to their excess hours of paid work. Even the way border management conveys "a sense of status to concerned individuals," as Côté-Boucher put it, can be understood as a means of shifting responsibility for security to individuals.

In Canada and elsewhere, the move to privatization is framed as a reduction in state involvement. It is important to note, however, that this ideological shift is accompanied by a real shift in responsibility. As Luxton pointed out, the state now plays a critical and direct role in "compelling people to rely on earnings, support from friends and family and voluntary organizations and privatized services." The hundred-dollar allowance for childcare, Bezanson argued, reinforces women's responsibility for care without offering collective means for providing that care. The Conservative government in Ontario introduced new legislation that did not simply remove the rules, according to Thomas: it improved employers' rights. And of course, as Côté-Boucher showed, the precautionary principle applied to border crossings allows all kinds of state intervention in private life, just as the deinstitutionalization of people with disabilities, taking Pinto's example, requires more state surveillance for the purposes of determining eligibility for meagre benefits. Indeed, we have heard Prime Minister Stephen Harper on the virtues of "banning child pornography, raising the age of sexual consent, providing choice in education and strengthening the key institution of marriage" (Bezanson, chapter five). The state is moving back into the bedrooms of the nation, the same bedrooms former Prime Minister Pierre Trudeau was intent on leaving. Such interventions not only contradict the claim of less state involvement but they are internally contradictory as well in that they reflect state intervention in the very private lives of people who are in theory to be allowed choice, responsibility, and rights. It is done in the name of protecting society. The result too often is a blurring of the lines between public and private, less individual control, greater precariousness, and greater inequality.

Nor should we assume that some of the recent investments of the federal government reverse this shift toward individual responsibility. The emphasis on supporting training through employment insurance, rather than by extending the right to benefits and upholding the centrality of legitimate support through legislation, reflects a continuing stress on individual failure. Similarly, calculating the need for public housing on the basis of the few groups that are defined as vulnerable perpetuates the notion that only a few unfortunates are at risk and ignores the dramatic changes in the economy that have made economic security precarious for everyone.

Privatization of Work

The privatization of responsibility is closely tied to the privatization of work, which results in more work being done without pay, both outside and inside the formal economy, through a process known in political economy as decommodification. Bezanson's chapter on childcare sheds light on the process of ensuring that care work is done in the home, primarily by women provided with barely enough money to pay for diapers. We also saw how health-care services are in some ways being decommodified, as the tasks involved are largely shifted from women who are paid to provide care to those without pay and often without formal training (Luxton, chapter eight; Grant et al. 2004). Increased reliance on unpaid work is evident at the gas pump as we fill our own tanks, in banks as we input our own data on the instant cash machine, in airline travel as we check ourselves in. It is evident as well among paid workers. In her study of social services (2004), Baines documents how workers in the private and public sectors of the formal economy are increasingly expected to put in unpaid overtime. This is the case especially for women who provide care. As

Thomas pointed out, government legislation now allows overtime work without overtime rates and that the more vulnerable the worker, the likelier this is to be the case.

There are contradictions. The most obvious is that, while the transfer of work is described as a choice, it is those who are not in a position to exercise choice, particularly those from equity-seeking groups, who are most compelled to do the unpaid labour – for example, women without significant economic resources who have to provide unpaid care (Guberman 2004). Those interviewed for Luxton's study saw no real alternative to providing unpaid care and had become "resigned to the inevitability of their situation," even accepting the work as their responsibility. Côté-Boucher's piece on surveillance suggests that some people feel privileged to do the work of surveilling themselves.

Yet as Connell pointed out, there has never been widespread public support for the cutbacks in public services. The National Forum on Health (1997,19), a group appointed by the prime minister in 1997 to look at the future of health care, found that women rejected the idea of being "conscripted" into unpaid caregiving. Pinto described mothers with disabilities agitating against neoliberal strategies aimed at shifting the work of care. From a different perspective, Braedley's firefighters could also be seen as resisting unpaid labour. Research indicating the negative consequences for employers of women's unpaid caregiving offers another example of how neoliberal strategies to privatize work can undermine the efforts to make everyone reliant on selling their ability to work for a wage; that is, on working for pay at the mercy of the employer (Lilly et al. 2007).

Thus, to reiterate, the lines between paid public labour and unpaid private work are blurring. While there are some contradictory developments and signs of resistance to the shift to unpaid work, new public investment that seems to contradict neoliberal approaches is primarily about creating jobs in the private, for-profit sector where many more men than women work for pay. Meanwhile, jobs in the public sector are being reduced and those that remain are subjected to further restraints, leaving more of the work to be done without pay.

Privatization of Public Assets and Institutions

The privatization of public assets and institutions is spurred by pressures from the search for profit. As Pinto noted, this particular form of privatization is directly linked to the crisis in capitalism that became evident with the 1970 oil slump. Profits were falling and corporations were searching for new places to invest. One solution was "the universal commodification of services," especially "the privatization of public assets and institutions" (Connell, chapter two). Some of this involved the outright sale of public assets to the for-profit sector, assets such as airlines and water supplies. More recently, there has been a shift to public/private partnerships through which hospitals, schools, and roads have been created.

The rationale behind public investment and ownership in these areas included the need to provide equitable access to necessary services, often as a matter of collective rights, and the failure of the for-profit sector to offer services at all in many places where a profit could not be made. In northern Canada, for example, before the federal government became involved, people had no electric lights, no water or sewage systems, no highways, and no airline service mainly because of the perceived unprofitability of delivering services to small and widely scattered populations.

Public involvement was also justified in terms of the collective good, an important investment in the future of society as a whole. People who were poor could not afford to feed their children properly, send them to fee-charging high schools so that they could find decent jobs, or get medical care so that they could be healthy workers and citizens. In addition, public institutions offered the most efficient means of providing necessary services. Health care offers one clear example. Having started from a pro-private perspective, the 1964 Hall Royal Commission on Health Services nonetheless found that it was more efficient to create a universal public scheme than to support a fragmented private one with some public support for those deemed worthy and unable to support themselves (see also Taylor 1987). The Romanow Report (Canada 2002) confirmed this finding, concluding that a universal public plan was both more efficient and more equitable, a public good for the future of Canada.

A similar range of arguments has been used to support the move away from public ownership. The most important claim is that the market and for-profit organizations are more efficient and effective than the public sector. Neoliberals pointed to the debt and deficit as indicators of poor management, and to social programs as examples of inappropriate and reckless spending. They pointed as well to what they portrayed as the privileged conditions in public sector employment, the hard-won gains of unions that meant that women in particular but also, to some extent, members of other equity-seeking groups had decent employment (Armstrong and Laxer 2006). Such claims reflect what Connell called "the missionary faith" of the neoliberals rather than any evidence that the for-profit sector is more efficient or effective than the public sector. Research published in the *Canadian Economic Observer* (Mimoto and Cross 1991) showed that the debt crisis in government was primarily the product of tax cuts and interest rates, along with the slowdown in the for-profit sector. Spending on social programs had little to do with it. Nor is there evidence that acceding to worker demands had forced costs up unreasonably. Take the health-care workforce for example. According to the Canadian Institute of Health Information (2005, 43), "census data show that, on average, employment incomes for full-time workers in health occupations rose at about the rate of inflation between 1995 and 2000. That compares to a 6 % after-inflation increase for all earners."

Furthermore, there is little evidence that the for-profit sector is more efficient and effective than the public sector. Again health care provides an excellent example. The fastest-rising costs in Canadian health care derive from areas that are dominated by the for-profit sector, namely, drugs and technologies. Economist Robert Evans (1993) has shown that what kept health-care costs down in Canada as compared to the United States was our public system. As for the public/private arrangement now in effect, research from the United Kingdom (2003) has clearly demonstrated that such partnerships are more, rather than less, expensive than public institutions alone. The Ontario Health Coalition (2004) has provided similar evidence in the case of Canadian hospitals. The contracting out of some services is similarly inefficient in cost terms and has particularly negative consequences for women and others from equity-seeking groups, leading to lower wages, fewer benefits, and less job security (Cohen and Cohen 2004). In short, the neoliberal faith in the efficiency and effectiveness of market and for-profit health-care provision is challenged by the evidence.

The neoliberal claim that corporations and institutions run on neoliberal principles rely on the market rather than government is contradicted by various instances in which the government has provided direct support to corporations. The most obvious example is the way governments throughout the West moved to rescue banks despite the crisis they created with their subprime mortgages. The Canadian government has also provided direct support to Bombardier and to the auto industry. In July 2008 the federal government, having previously given it $22 million, quietly invested a further $25 million in Suncor's ethanol plant (*Toronto Star* 2008, A19) despite considerable public debate about the merits of ethanol and growing concerns that the shift to ethanol production is a significant factor in the creation of global food shortages. Less obvious is the way governments support monopoly control by drug companies over their products, long after the companies have made a handsome return on their research investments.

The privatization of public assets and institutions further blurs the line between the private and public sectors. With public/private partnerships it is hard to know who is in charge or where to lay blame. With the contracting out of services in the public sector, it is hard to tell a public servant from a private one. In the process, many of those previously employed in the public sector have lost their collective and individual rights.

There are some contradictory trends, however. In Manitoba, for example, the government ended its experiment in the contracting out of home-care services to a for-profit firm after it was demonstrated that public care was at least as efficient (Shapiro 1997). Not only did the most vulnerable receive more reliable services through public care but the care workers, many of whom are from racialized groups and most of whom are women, had better jobs compared to those in the private sector.

The January 2009 federal budget allowed for some new public investment. There was little indication, however, that this would mean a significant expansion of the public sector or an end to public/private partnerships. Indeed, most of the money went to the for-profit sector, with government using its investment as leverage in its effort to reduce the wages, benefits, and rights of workers in this sector.

Privatization of Managerial Practices

The privatization of managerial practices is very much related to the shift in assets and institutions to the private sector. It refers to the adoption of for-profit practices within governments and the public sector more generally and the adoption of market strategies by governments carrying out their other functions. Consistent with this form of privatization, states have been contracting out to the for-profit sector elements of the institutions that remain public.

The introduction of competitive bidding for home- and long-term care services in Ontario is one example. Public funds are paid mostly to for-profit providers to offer services, based on a selection process that is intended to replicate the market. Another example is the New Public Management mentioned by Connell. This term refers explicitly to the management practices taken from the for-profit sector and to the idea that governments should shed anything they can hand over to the private sector (Osborne and Gaebler 1993). The government of British Columbia was following this strategy when it cancelled some union agreements in the health sector and contracted work out to the for-profit sector (Cohen and Cohen 2006). Market principles have been extended across the public sector as well as within public sector organizations (Exworthy and Halford 1999). In others words, governments are to act like businesses; the notion that governments operate on the basis of a commitment to public service is removed. A third example comes from labour standards in Ontario, earlier discussed by Thomas, where the market principle of the flexible worker has been written into law.

Like the selling off of public assets on the grounds that for-profit companies are more efficient and effective, the privatization of managerial practice is based more on faith than evidence. It assumes that for-profit practices deliver what they promise and that methods that work in the for-profit sector will work as well in public sectors such as health, education, and air travel. In other words, it has been accepted as doctrine that the free operation of the market ensures that all businesses are efficient and effective, and that market principles can be applied with equal success to car making and baby catching. Yet as Henry Mintzberg, McGill University's famous professor of management studies, wrote thirty years ago in his book *The Structuring of Organizations* (1979), public services are very particular kinds of organizations that require their own forms of management, in part because they put service before profit. More recently, he has railed against the application of private sector practices to public institutions and the assumption that within public organizations one form of management fits all (CBC,1999). The superiority of market principles is based on the notion that organizations and institutions that are run according to those principles have to be good or they close. However, governments regularly shore up private sector firms that fail and we cannot easily allow schools or hospitals to close.

As with other forms of privatization, there are contradictions in the processes themselves and there is resistance. In the wake of health-care cuts, Braedley showed, firefighters in Ontario have actively resisted pressures to take over elements of care work by using various strategies to limit their involvement. Equally important, the very nature of their work has prevented full application of for-profit practices to their jobs. One part of capital (i.e., the insurance companies) is insisting on the need for a fire brigade to prevent insurance claims. For-profit managerial strategies, on the other hand, might dictate elimination of a service that does so little so much of the time: the amalgamation of fire, ambulance, and police services in Ontario was a move in that direction. Thanks to their efficiency, moreover, firefighters have often undertaken care work because they were first on the scene. The need for a skilled firefighting force, however, and the nature of firefighting has prevented a further imposition of market managerial practices.

In another example of resistance, health sector unions in British Columbia together used the Canadian Charter of Rights and Freedoms to challenge the contracting out of their services by the provincial government. On 8 June 2007 the Supreme Court of Canada ruled that sections of Bill 29, the Health and Social Services Delivery Improvement Act (2002), violated the Charter (Health Services and Support Facilities Subsector Bargaining Association 2008). Referring to the Charter's freedom-of-association provision, the court struck down key sections of the act that eliminated many of the bargaining rights of health care workers and paved the way for massive job losses, primarily among women, and especially women from racialized groups. Unfortunately, the court did not uphold the claim that the government action was particularly discriminatory towards women. Nevertheless, the case demonstrates that there are limits to state privatization strategies and that people can indeed resist.

The blurring of private and public is particularly obvious as governments imitate businesses. They come into the private sphere through the application of market principles to government services, as Pinto showed in the case of access to entitlements for mothers with disabilities. The blurring is perhaps less obvious when it comes to the ways that market managerial principles penetrate the home. They enter through the Internet and the Blackberry, with workers expected to be responding at all times of the day and night to their paid workplace demands, taking home their jobs but doing so without additional pay. The demands for flexibility and even sacrifice on the part of workers and families are increasing with the current economic crisis, with people pushed to allow more and more of their paid work to spill over into their private homes.

The Privatization of Costs

It is not only responsibility but also costs that are privatized in neoliberal strategies. Governments are busily offloading all kinds of costs. More roads have tolls and riders pay for a bigger share of what used to be public transit. Parents pay for more and more of their children's public education. The hundred-dollar allowance for childcare masks the shift of care costs involved in the elimination of the childcare agreements (Bezanson, chapter five), while the unpaid care work is not the only consequence of sending people home quicker and sicker (Luxton, chapter eight). All household costs increase when patients are cared for at home, where they must pay for drugs and other necessities that would be covered by public money if they were in the hospital. Private for-profit employers are also shifting costs to their workers. With the more flexible work arrangements Thomas described, workers absorb more of the costs of unemployment and of lost benefits. Fewer are eligible for employment insurance or protected from injury at work, which forces individuals to absorb the expense of being unemployed or injured (Bernstein et al. 2006; Tucker 2006).

The cost shift is justified, as the papers in this volume explain, not only as a means of reducing government expenditures but also as a move toward greater choice. More is available for purchase and purchasing means choice. Indeed, this seems to be the assumption behind the Canadian Supreme Court's conclusion, in *Chaoulli v. Quebec* (2005), that the Quebec government "has prohibited private health insurance that would permit ordinary Quebeckers to access private health care while failing to deliver health care in a reasonable manner, thereby increasing the risk of complications and death. In so doing, it has interfered with the interests protected by s. 7 of the Canadian Charter." Of course, the right to buy is limited by one's economic resources, something the majority of judges ignored in arguing that "ordinary" Quebecers could buy expensive surgery through private means. Thus the notion of cost and rights means that access to goods and services is increasingly related to class, gender, and race.

Although governments have been shifting the costs of social programs onto individuals and families, they have not been significantly reducing overall expenditures. This is in part because expenditures on other things, such as defence (Bezanson, chapter five) and surveillance (Côté-Boucher, chapter three), not to mention the $13 billion spent on policing, courts, and incarceration and the increases implied by proposed new "tough on crime" legislation (Contenta et al. 2008, A1), are growing significantly. Although women and racialized groups have made some inroads into these sectors, the employment that results from government expenditures is more likely to result in jobs for Canadian-born males. At the same time, taxes have been reduced in ways that significantly favour the rich and increase inequality (Osberg 2008). More and more Canadians are left not only with fewer services but also with less money with which to exercise their "choices" in purchasing services.

As governments add fees for services previously offered without them and fail to expand coverage to new necessary services while cutting back on others, the line between what comes from the public or private purse becomes harder to draw. It is also harder for people to see what they get for their taxes. There has been no significant decline in government spending, even by governments claiming to favour smaller government. Rather, there has been a major shift in the way money is collected and spent. It is a shift away from universal or other programs based on the notion of collective rights and a shared obligation to meet certain fundamental needs towards spending on surveillance and enforcement.

In the current economic crisis, we are seeing the federal government take public responsibility for for-profit failure, with little regulation of the profits that result. Meanwhile, individuals and households are expected to absorb much of the costs of job loss.

WHERE THE SORTING LEADS

Looking at neoliberalism through the lens of privatization highlights aspects of change that are otherwise difficult to see, for example, the simultaneous commodification of some services that were previously provided by non-profit and public organizations and the decommodification of others that must now be provided by families and individuals. This commodification/decommodification spreads the burden of work unevenly and restricts access to services in unequal ways while allowing the conditions of employment to deteriorate, especially for women and those from racialized groups.

We can also see how distinctions between different kinds of public and private are being blurred. As noted above, what is public in the sense of shared responsibility and services is not only increasingly narrowly defined but it is also increasingly penetrated by private for-profit business and practices. At the same time, the private sphere of household and community as well as the private non-profit sectors within the formal economy are increasingly being monitored and held accountable to rigid bureaucratic rules of the very sort that neoliberals so vehemently attack when they impinge on the for-profit sector. Personal lives are also being monitored increasingly in the name of security.

The upshot of the blurring is that it has become more difficult to hold governments democratically accountable. The intrusion of business practices into the public sector, the contracting out of services, and government payment for goods and services delivered by for-profit organizations make it harder to see where our public money goes. The difficulty is compounded by the claim that contracts for public services must be kept confidential in order to ensure competitiveness and enforce patents. It is difficult to monitor the development and application of public standards when the standards are often set outside the legislative process, when public inspections are eliminated in favour of self-monitoring by business, and when the contract between employer and employee becomes private. Thanks to what Connell calls "the new ethos of managerialism," accountability is defined in bureaucratic terms and numerical measures become the basis of accountability and choice. Not only what can easily be measured but what it is important to measure is decided by particular interests pretending to value-free assessment that allows public input. Written "objectives" and reports based on these measures replace the messier processes of democracy and debate. This "cult of efficiency," to use Janice Stein's term (2001), is actually self-referential. Like the Romanow Report on the future of Canadian health care (Canada 2002), Stein draws our attention to the need to begin with fundamental human and social values in any system of accountability rather than with numbers and dollar signs.

Thus we can see the increasing extent to which decision making is being privatized. Individuals get to make more decisions based on the ability to purchase, while corporations make decisions behind closed doors on how to spend our public money. In the political doctrine of neoliberalism, the market inevitably becomes the decision maker, directing us all with an invisible hand. As Brendon Martin (1993) so eloquently put it, the metaphor of an invisible hand running the market hides the grubbier ones that are directing it in fact. And it too often hides the ways in which neoliberal governments intervene to make the market work for specific interests.

LEARNING THE LESSONS

These hidden decision-making processes, along with their consequences, contribute to the conviction that there is no alternative, as Luxton observed. Yet thirty years of neoliberalism have revealed many contradictions that, once exposed, help us to understand that "neoliberal market fundamentalism was always a political doctrine serving certain interests" (Stiglitz 2008, A17). Documenting the contradictions within this political doctrine allows us to monitor the neoliberal experiment and develop ways to hold governments accountable. Recognizing it as an ideology without empirical support paves the way for effective organizing to challenge neoliberal doctrines and work collectively towards alternatives. This book has identified many of the contradictions within neoliberalism and leaves us with many more to explore. In closing I shall suggest some additional issues that need to be addressed before we can see Stiglitz's silver lining.

This book points to the centrality of the various private and public spheres in producing inequity. The state has reduced public services, thus offloading more care work onto private households. Not only has this created more work for members of the household (Bezanson, chapter five, Luxton, chapter eight) but it has also increased demand for the surviving public services (Braedley, chapter seven). It also highlights the interconnections between strategies of governance, social relations, and subjectivity. As we have seen, state efforts to privatize care instilled in some people a sense of loss, while the dictum of responsibility instilled a sense of self-blame (Luxton, chapter eight). Similarly, state strategies to foster private enterprise while managing public security instilled a sense of privilege in some people but imposed a sense of exclusion on others (Côté-Boucher, chapter three). As these examples show, the lines between various forms of public and private are simultaneously blurred and reconstructed, leaving us with the challenge of how to create public and private spaces in ways that promote equity.

We are also left with central questions about time and work organization. Neoliberal strategies have transformed how we work, where we work, and how long we work. Increasingly, paid and unpaid work are being intertwined in new ways. Neoliberal thinking also equates paid work with independence and unpaid work with dependency in ways that render dependency shameful (Pinto, chapter six). Neoliberal policy reforms have emphasized a privatized model of labour regulation that has strengthened employer control over working time, which coincides with the intensification of domestic labour as more work is sent home to women especially (Thomas, chapter four). These reforms raise questions about how our time can be distributed and controlled in ways that support not only the right to decide but also our interdependence. They also raise an important question about free wage labour. Central to the analytical notion of free wage labour is the idea that we are free to sell our ability to work for a wage, leaving the employer in charge while we are at our wage work, but that time spent away from paid work is our own. But how are we to interpret this when the line between waged and unwaged work is increasingly blurred?

And how are we to understand the role of religious fundamentalism? It is no coincidence that the rise of neoliberalism has been accompanied by a rise in religious fundamentalism in many parts of the world. As Connell and Bezanson have shown, the two are not inevitably linked but share some fundamental political assumptions. Certainly religion has played a part in justifying the massive expansion of the military-industrial complex and in the denial of rights; enemies, for example, are often identified in terms of religion. We have also seen how religion as "other" is mobilized in border security (Côté-Boucher, chapter three), raising further critical questions about the relationship between neoliberalism and fundamentalist religions.

These issues suggest an additional question. The authors of this book have identified inequalities based on gender, racialization, class, and ability and shown how these inequalities are intensified under neoliberalism. As Pinto stressed, it is important to devise strategies for the achievement of equity that include accommodation and the removal of structural barriers. But we are still left with the challenge of how to develop collective strategies that do not depend on an idea of equity as sameness or as independence.

Finally, the current economic crisis poses the hardest, and perhaps most obvious, question. How can we ensure that this crisis of capitalism is not used to justify the sort of shock therapy identified by Naomi Klein (2007): How can we effectively demand that public money be employed for public good, through democratic processes of governance? How can we ensure that it means the regulation of corporations and their profits rather than of workers and their incomes? How can we ensure that existing inequalities are undermined rather than strengthened?

The neoliberal project, as Connell argued, has run up against a number of limits that can also be sources of resistance and change. "The claims of mutual care and mutual responsibility, and the fundamental requirement of cooperation in human institutions (including, of course, economic production), are perhaps irreducible barriers to the expansion of competitive individualism. The land is the land, and not just a factor of production and source of profit." But as Connell also reminds us, "a collective practice is always required to turn this possibility into reality" (this volume, 36).

References

CHAPTER ONE

Albo, G. (2008). "Neoliberalism and Canada's Ruling Class." MRzine Retrieved 12 March 2009 from http://www.monthlyreview.org/mrzine/albo070407.html DOI: http://mrzine.monthlyreview.org/

Arat-Kroc, S. 2006. "Whose Social Reproduction? Transnational Motherhood and Challenges to Feminist Political Economy." In *Social Reproduction: Feminist Political Economy Challenges Neo-liberalism*, edited by K. Bezanson and M. Luxton, 75–92. Montreal and Kingston: McGill-Queen's University Press.

Aronowitz, S. 2003. *How Class Works: Power and Social Movement*. New Haven: Yale University Press.

Asia-Pacific Economic Co-operation (APEC). 2008. "Lima APEC Leaders' Statement on the Global Economy." Retrieved 12 March 2009 from http://www.apec.org/etc/medialib/apec_media_library/downloads/news_uploads/2008/aelm/aelm.Par.0001.File.tmp/08_aelm_StandAloneStmtGlobal Economy. pdf

Baker, M. 2006. *Restructuring Family Policies: Convergences and Divergences*. Toronto: University of Toronto Press.

Bakker, I., and S. Gill, eds. 2003. *Power, Production and Social Reproduction*. New York: Palgrave MacMillan.

Bashevkin, S. 1998. *Women on the Defensive Living through Conservative Times*. Toronto: University of Toronto Press.

Brodie, J. 2007. "Reforming Social Justice in Neoliberal Times." *Studies in Social Justice* 1, no.2: 93–107.

Bureau of Labour Statistics. 2009. *The Employment Situation: February 2009*. Washington, DC: United States Department of Labor.

CNBC. 2008. "CNBC Interview Transcript and Video: Warren Buffet Explains his $5B Goldman Investment." Retrieved 12 March 2009 from http://www.cnbc.com/id/26867866

Cohen, M. G. and J. Pulkingham, eds. 2009. *Public Policy for Women The State, Income Security and Labour Market Issues.* Toronto: University of Toronto Press.

Enright, M. 2008. "Misogyny and American Politics." *The Sunday Edition.* CBC Radio, 2 March.

Fanon, F. 1970. *Black Skin, White Mask.* London: Pluto.

Fraser, N. 1997. "After the Family Wage: A Postindustrial Thought Experiment." In N. Fraser. *Justice Interruptus: Critical Reflections on the "Postsocialist" Condition,* 41–66. New York: Routledge.

Gilroy, P. 2000. "Against Race: Imagining Political Culture beyond the Color Line." *Callaloo* 23: 1,147–51.

Glenn, E.N. 1992. "From Servitude to Service Work: Historical Continuities in the Racial Division of Paid Reproductive Labor." *Signs* 18, no. 1: 1–43.

Group of Twenty (G20). 2008. "Declaration: Summit on Financial Markets and the World Economy November 15,2008." Retrieved 12 March 2009 from http://www.g20.org/Documents/g20_summit_declaration.pdf.

Hayek, F.A. 1944. *The Road to Serfdom.* Chicago: University of Chicago Press.

– 1976. Foreword to the American edition. *The Road to Serfdom,* iii-xxi. Chicago: University of Chicago Press.

Honneth, A. 1996. *The Struggle for Recognition: The Moral Grammar of Social Conflicts.* Boston: MIT Press.

International Labour Organization. 2004. "More women are entering the global labour force than ever before, but job equality, poverty reduction remain elusive." Retrieved 13 August 2008 from http://www.ilo.org/global/About_the_ILO/Media_and_public_information/Press_releases/lang--en/WCMS_005243/index.htm.

Kroll, L. 2008. "The World's Billionaires." Retrieved 8 August 2008 from http://www.forbes.com/2008/03/05/richest-people-billionaires-billionaireso8–cx_lk_0305billie_land.html.

Lucas, Linda E. 2007. *Unpacking Globalization Markets, Gender, and Work.* Lanham, MD: Lexington Books.

Luxton, M. 1980. *More than a Labour of Love.* Toronto: Women's Press.

Luxton, M., and J. Corman. 2001. *Getting By in Hard Times: Gendered Labour at Home and on the Job.* Toronto: University of Toronto Press.

McKenna, B. 2008. Millions, Billions, Trillions. Toronto, *Globe and Mail.*

McNally, D. 2005. *Another World is Possible: Globalization and Anti-Capitalism*. Winnipeg: ArbeiterRing Publishers.

McNally, D. 2009. "From Financial Crisis to World Slump: Accumulation, Financialization, and the Global Slowdown." *Historical Materialism* 17, no.2: 35–83.

Mohanty, C.T. 2003. *Feminism without Borders: Decolonizing Theory, Practicing Solidarity*. New Delhi: Zabaan.

Obama, B. 2009. Remarks of President-Elect Barack Obama as Prepared for Delivery American Recovery and Reinvestment Thursday, 8 January 2009. Retrieved 9 March 2009 from http://www.scribd.com/doc/9917224/Obama-Economic-Speech-American-Recovery-and-Reinvestment-January-9–2009

Ong, A. 2007. *Neoliberalism as Exception*. Durham and London: Duke University Press.

Picchio, A. 1992. *Social Reproduction: The Political Economy of the Labour Market*. Cambridge, UK: Cambridge University Press.

Portugal News Online. 2008. Global financial crisis at centre of Portugal-Brazil summit 1/11/08. Retrieved 9 March 2009 from http://www.the-news.net/

Reguly, E. 2008. "How the crisis is taking the 'U' out of the EU." Toronto, *Globe and Mail*, B2.

Robert, A.-C., and J.-C. Servant. 2009. "Africa's imported wealth." *Le Monde Diplomatique*, 16.

Rose, N. 1999. *Powers of Freedom: Reframing Political Thought*. Cambridge, UK: Cambridge University Press.

Rowbotham, S. 1972. *Woman, Resistance and Revolution: A History of Women and Revolution in the Modern World*. London: Allen Lane.

Seccombe, W. 1992. *A Millennium of Family Change: Feudalism to Capitalism in Northwestern Europe*. London: Verso.

– 1993. *Weathering the Storm: Working Class Families from the Industrial Revolution to the Fertility Decline*. London: Verso.

Segal, L. 1999. *Why Feminism? Gender, Psychology, Politics*. Cambridge, MA: Polity Press.

Sen, A. 1993. "Capability and Wellbeing." *The Quality of Life*, edited by M. Nussbaum and A. Sen, 30–52. Oxford: Clarendon Press.

Statistics Canada. 2009. Latest Release from Labour Force Survey, 13 March 2009. Ottawa: Statistics Canada.

United Nations. 1995. "Beijing Declaration and Platform for Action." New York: United Nations Department of Public Information.

Waring, M. 1988. *If Women Counted: A New Feminist Economics*. San Francisco: Harper Row.

Wolf, E. 1982. *Europe and the People without History*. Berkeley: University of California Press.

CHAPTER TWO

Alvarez, José Luis. 1996. "The International Popularization of Entrepreneurial Ideas." In *The Politics of Management Knowledge*, edited by Stewart R. Clegg and Gill Palmer, 80–98. London: Sage.

Amin, Samir. 1997. *Capitalism in the Age of Globalization: The Management of Contemporary Society*. London: Zed Books.

Connell, Raewyn. 2007. *Southern Theory: The Global Dynamics of Knowledge in the Social Sciences*. Cambridge: Polity Press.

Duménil, Gérard, and Dominique Lévy. 2004. *Capital Resurgent: Roots of the Neoliberal Revolution*. Cambridge, MA: Harvard University Press.

Fox, Loren. 2003. *Enron: The Rise and Fall*. Hoboken, NJ: Wiley.

García Canclini, Néstor. 2001. *Consumers and Citizens: Globalization and Multicultural Conflicts*. Minneapolis, University of Minnesota Press.

Hadiz, Vedi R., and Richard Robison. 2003. "Neo-Liberal Reforms and Illiberal Consequences: The Indonesian Paradox." Southeast Asia Research Centre Working Papers No. 52. Hong Kong: City University of Hong Kong.

Harvey, David. 2005. *A Brief History of Neoliberalism*. Oxford: Oxford University Press.

Hewison, Kevin, and Garry Rodan. 2004. "Closing the Circle? Globalization, Conflict and Political Regimes." Southeast Asia Research Centre Working Papers No. 63. Hong Kong: City University of Hong Kong.

Hubbard, Phil. 2004. "Revenge and Injustice in the Neoliberal City: Uncovering the Masculinist Agendas." *Antipode* 36, no. 4: 665–86.

McDonald, David A., and Laila Smith. 2004. "Privatising Cape Town: From *Apartheid* to Neo-Liberalism in the Mother City." *Urban Studies* 41, no. 8: 1,461–84.

Marginson, Simon. 1997. *Markets in Education*. Sydney: Allen and Unwin.

Murray, Georgina. 2006. *Capitalist Networks and Social Power in Australia and New Zealand*. Aldershot: Ashgate.

Naples, Nancy A., and Manisha Desai, eds. 2002. *Women's Activism and Globalization: Linking Local Struggles and Transnational Politics*. New York: Routledge.

Negri, Antonio. 1974. *Crisi dello Stato-piano: comunismo e organizzazione rivoluzionaria*. Milano: Feltrinelli.

Neumann, Franz. 1944. *Behemoth: The Structure and Practice of National Socialism 1933–1944*. 2d ed. New York: Oxford University Press.

Pusey, Michael. 2003. *The Experience of Middle Australia: The Dark Side of Economic Reform*. Cambridge: Cambridge University Press.

Silva, Eduardo. 1996. *The State and Capital in Chile: Business Elites, Technocrats, and Market Economics*. Boulder, CO: Westview Press.

Smart, Barry. 2003. *Economy, Culture and Society: A Sociological Critique of Neo-Liberalism*. Buckingham, UK: Open University Press.

Song, Jesook. 2006. "Family Breakdown and Invisible Homeless Women: Neoliberal Governance during the Asian Debt Crisis in South Korea, 1997–2001." *Positions* 14, no. 1: 37–66.

Stokes, Susan C. 2001. *Mandates and Democracy: Neoliberalism by Surprise in Latin America*. Cambridge: Cambridge University Press.

Vellinga, Menno. 2002. "Globalization and Neoliberalism: Economy and Society in Latin America." *Iberoamericana: Nordic Journal of Latin American and Caribbean Studies* 32, no. 2: 25–43.

CHAPTER THREE

Agamben, G. 2002. "On Security and Terror." *Theory and Event* 5, no. 4.

Alboim, N. and Maytree Foundations. 2009. *Adjusting the Balance: Fixing Canada's Economic Immigration Policies*. Last accessed 7 August 2009: http://www.maytree.com/policy

Amoore, L. 2006. "Biometric Borders: Governing Mobilities in the War on terror". *Political Geography* 25, no. 3: 336–51.

Andreas, P. 2003. "A Tale of Two Borders. The U.S.-Canada and U.S.-Mexico lines after 9/11." In *The Rebordering of North America*, edited by P. Andreas and T.J. Biersteker, 1–23. New York: Routledge.

Aradau, C., and R. Van Munster. 2007. "Governing Terrorism through Risk: Taking Precautions, (Un)knowing the future." *European Journal of International Relations* 13, 1: 89–115.

Arat-Koç, S. 2006. "Whose Social Reproduction? Transnational Motherhood and Challenges to Feminist Political Economy." In *Social Reproduction. Feminist Political Economy Challenges Neo-Liberalism*, edited by K. Bezanson and M. Luxton, 75–92. Montreal and Kingston: McGill-Queen's University Press.

Associated Press. 2008. "Truck Traffic Down at Ambassador Bridge." *Examiner*, 12 January 2009. Last accessed 21 January 2009. http://www.examiner.com/a-1789875~Truck_traffic_down_at_Ambassador_Bridge.html

Association of Professional Executives of the Public Service of Canada. 2006. "NEXUS Highway, a Model of Intergovernmnental Cooperation." Last accessed 13. August 2009. http://www.apex.gc.ca/uploads/awards/ past%20winners/apex%20award_nexus%20highway_final_e-.pdf

Bahdi, R. 2003. "No Exit: Racial Profiling and Canada's War against Terrorism." *Osgoode Hall Law Journal* 41, nos. 2, 3: 293–317.

Baker, T., and J. Simon. 2002. "Embracing Risk." In *Embracing Risk. The Changing Culture of Insurance and Responsibility*, edited by T. Baker and J. Simon, 1–25. Chicago: University of Chicago Press.

Bauder, H. 2006. *Labor Movement : How Migration Regulates Labor Markets*. New York: Oxford University Press.

Bauman, Z. 2006. *Liquid Fear*. Cambridge: Polity Press.

Bell, C. 2006. "Subject to Exception: Security Certificates, National Security and Canada's Role in the 'War On Terror.'" *Canadian Journal of Law and Society* 21, no. 1: 63–83.

Bentham, J. 2008 [1843]. *The Works of Jeremy Bentham. Published under the superintendence of his executor, John Bowring*. Edinburgh. Vol. 1, *The Making of Modern Law*. Gale, 2009.

Braedley, S. 2006. "Someone to Watch over You: Gender, Class, and Social Reproduction." In *Social Reproduction. Feminist Political Economy Challenges Neo-Liberalism*, edited by K. Bezanson and M. Luxton, 215–30.

Brown, W. 2005. "Neoliberalism and the End of Liberal Democracy." In *Edgework: Critical Essays on Knowledge and Politics*, 37–59. Princeton: Princeton University Press.

Browne, S. 2005. "Getting Carded: Border Control and the Politics of Canada's Permanent Resident Card." *Citizenship Studies* 9, no. 4: 423–38.

Butler, J. 2004. *Precarious Life: The Powers of Mourning and Violence*. London, New York: Verso.

Buzan, B., O. Weaver, and J. de Wilde. 1998. *Security: A New Framework of Analysis*. Boulder: Lynne Rienner Publishers.

Canada. 2009a. "Cross Often? Make It Simple." 23 January 2009. Last accessed 13 August 2009. http://www.spp-psp.gc.ca/eic/site/spp-psp.nsf/ eng/00051.html

– 2009b. "Making Smarter, More Secure Borders." 23 January 2009. Last accessed 13 August 2009. http://www.spp-psp.gc.ca/eic/site/spp-psp.nsf/ eng/00056.html

– Auditor General of Canada. 2004. *National Security in Canada -The 2001 Anti-Terrorism Initiative. Report of the Auditor General to the House of Commons*. Last accessed 14 August 2009. http://www. oag-bvg.gc.ca/internet/docs/20040303ce.pdf

- Department of Finance. 2008. "Budget 2008 Responsible Leadership." Last modified 26 February 2008. Last accessed 13 August 2009. http://www.budget.gc.ca/2008/glance-apercu/brief-bref-eng.asp
- Embassy to Washington. 2008. "Notes for an Address by the Honourable Michael Wilson, PC, OC, 14 March 2008." Last accessed 13 August 2009. http://www.canadainternational.gc.ca/washington/offices-bureaux/amb/080314.aspx?lang=eng&highlights_file=&left_menu_en=&left_menu_fr=&mission=
- Foreign Affairs and International Trade. 2001. "The Smart Border Declaration: Building a Smart Border for the 21st Century on the Foundations of a North American Zone Of Confidence." Department of Foreign Affairs and International Trade (Canada). Last accessed 13 August 2009. http://www.dfait-maeci.gc.ca/anti-terrorism/declaration-en.asp
- Office of the Prime Minister. 2006. "The Security and Prosperity Partnership of North America: Next Steps." Last modified 4 July 2006. Last accessed 13 August 2009. http://www.pm.gc.ca/eng/media.asp?id=1084
Canadian Border Services Agency (CBSA). 2009a. "eManifest." Last Modified 23 June 2009. Last accessed 13 August 2009. http://www.cbsa-asfc.gc.ca/prog/manif/menu-eng.html
- 2009b. "Join FAST." Last modified 30 April 2009. Last accessed 14 August 2009. http://www.cbsa-asfc.gc.ca/prog/fast-expres/driv-chauff-eng.html#a1
- 2008a. "FAST Commercial Driver Participant's Guide." Last modified 25 February 2008. Last accessed 14 August 2009. http://www.cbsa-asfc.gc.ca/publications/pub/rc4319-eng.pdf
- 2008b. "NEXUS Reaches the 250,000th Member Mark." 8 December 2008. Last accessed 13 August 2009. http://www.cbsa-asfc.gc.ca/media/release-communique/2008/2008-12-08-eng.html
Canadian Islamic Congress. 2006. "Islamic Congress Condemns Border Treatment of Prominent Imam." Last accessed 14 August 2009. http://www.straightgoods.ca/Election2006/ViewNews.cfm?Ref=63.
Castel, R. 1991. "From Dangerousness to Risk." In *The Foucault Effect: Studies in Governmentality*, edited by G. Burchell, C. Gordon, and P. Miller, 281–98. London: Harvester Wheatsheaf.
Coleman, M. 2005. "US Statecraft and the US-Mexico Border as Security/Economy Nexus." *Political Geography* 24, no. 2: 189–205.
Connell, R.W. 1998. "Masculinities and Globalization." *Men and Masculinities*. 1(1): 3–23
Connell, R.W., and J. Wood. 2005. "Globalization and Business Masculinities." *Men and Masculinities* 7, no. 4: 347–64.

Côté-Boucher, K. 2005. "Governing through Borders. Mobilizing Risk, Anxiety and Biopower in the Canada-United States Smart Border Declaration." Unpublished master's thesis. Toronto, York University.

– 2008. "The Diffuse Border: Intelligence-Sharing, Control and Confinement along Canada's Smart Border." *Surveillance and Society* 5, no. 2: 142–65.

– 2009 (forthcoming). « Interdictions à la mobilité, identités autorisées et échange de renseignements: La frontière intelligente vue du Canada. » In *Mobilité(s) sous surveillance, Perspectives croisées UE-Canada*, edited by A. Scherrer, E.-P. Guittet, and D. Bigo, Montréal: Athéna Éditions.

Council of Canadians. 2008. "Quebec to Become Third Province to Offer Enhanced Driver's Licences." 22 May 2008. Last accessed 14 August July 2009. http://www.canadians.org/integratethis/insecurity/2008/May-27.html

Cowen, D. 2007a. "The Border as 'Seam': Supply Chain Security and the Re-territorialization of The Social." Paper presented at the conference "Securing Citizenship?" Toronto, University of Toronto, 16 November 2007.

– 2007b. "Struggling with 'Security': National Security and Labour in the Port." *Just Labour: A Canadian Journal of Work and Society* 10 (Spring): 30–44.

Crépeau, F., and D. Nakache. 2006. "Controlling Irregular Migration in Canada. Reconciling Security Concerns with Human Rights Protection." *IRPP Choices* 12, no. 1: 1–42.

Deleuze, G. 1989. "Qu'est-ce qu'un dispositif?" In *Michel Foucault philosophe: rencontre internationale, Paris, 9, 10,11 janvier 1988*. Paris: Seuil, 185–95

Deleuze, G., and F. Guattari. 1980. *Mille Plateaux*. Paris: Éditions de Minuit.

Donzelot, J. 1994 [1984]. *L'invention du social. Essai sur le déclin des passions politiques*. Paris: Seuil.

Doty, R.L. 2007. "States of Exception on the Mexico-US Border: Security, 'Decisions,' and Civilian Border Patrols." *International Political Sociology* 1, no. 2: 113–37.

Douglas, M., and A. Wildavsky. 1982. *Risk and Culture. An Essay on the Selection of Technological and Environmental Dangers*. Berkeley: University of California Press.

Engle, K. 2004. "Constructing Good Aliens and Good Citizens: Legitimizing the War on Terror(Ism)." *University of Colorado Law Review* 75: 59–114.

Ericson, R.V., and A. Doyle. 2004. *Uncertain Business. Risk, Insurance, and the Limits of Knowledge*. Toronto: University of Toronto Press.

Ewald. 1986. *L'État providence*. Paris: Grasset.

Ewald, F. 2002. "The Return of Descarte's Malicious Demon: An Outline of a Philosophy of Precaution." In *Embracing Risk. The Changing Culture of Insurance and Responsibility*, edited by T. Baker and J. Simon, 1–25.

Foucault, M. 2004a. *Naissance de la biopolitique. Cours au Collège de France, 1978–1979*. Paris: Seuil/Gallimard.

– 2004b. *Sécurité, Territoire, Population. Cours au Collège de France, 1977–1978*. Paris: Seuil/Gallimard.

Grenier, J.-Y., and A. Orléan. 2007. « Michel Foucault, l'économie politique et le libéralisme. » *Annales HSS* 5: 1,155–82.

Hacking, I. 1990. *The Taming of Chance*. Cambridge: Cambridge University Press.

– 2003. "Risk and Dirt." In *Risk and Morality*, edited by R.V. Ericson and A. Doyle, 22–47. Toronto: University of Toronto Press.

Haggerty, K.D. 2003. "From Risk to Precaution: The Rationalities of Personal Crime Prevention." In *Risk and Morality*, edited by R.V. Ericson and A. Doyle, 193–214.

Hagopian, E.C., ed. 2004 *Civil Rights in Peril: The Targeting of Arabs and Muslims*. Chicago: Haymarket Books/ Pluto Press.

Hobbes, T. 1996 [1651]. *Leviathan*. Cambridge: Cambridge University Press.

Honig, B. 2001. *Democracy and the Foreigner*. Princeton, NJ: Princeton University Press.

Hunt, A. 2003. "Risk and Moralization in Everyday Life." In *Risk and Morality*, edited by R.V. Ericson and A. Doyle, 165–92.

Isin, E. 2004. "The Neurotic Citizen." *Citizenship Studies* 8, no. 3: 217–31.

Jorion, P. 2002. *La gestion des risques après le 11 septembre 2001*. Montreal: HEC.

Larsen, M., and J. Piché. 2007. "Incarcerating the 'inadmissible'; KIHC as an Exceptional Moment in Canadian Federal Imprisonment." May 2007. Last accessed 14 August 2009. http://www.yorku.ca/yciss/whatsnew/documents/WP45–LarsenandPiche.pdf

Lemke, T. 2001. "'The Birth of Bio-Politics': Michel Foucault's Lecture at the Collège de France on Neo-Liberal Governmentality". *Economy and Society* 30, no. 2: 190–207.

Locke, J. 1988 [1690]. *Two Treatises of Government*. Cambridge: Cambridge University Press.

Luxton, M. 2006. Feminist Political Economy in Canada and the Politics of Social Reproduction. In *Social Reproduction. Feminist Political Economy Challenges Neo-Liberalism*, edited by K. Bezanson and M. Luxton, 11–44.

Lyon, D. 2003. *Surveillance after September 11*. Cambridge: Polity Press.

Mackey, E. 1999. Constructing an Endangered Nation. Risk, Race and Rationality in Australia's Native Title Debate. In *Risk and Sociocultural*

Theory, edited by D. Lupton, 108–30. Cambridge: Cambridge University Press.

– 2002. *The House of Difference. Cultural Politics and National Identity in Canada.* Toronto: University of Toronto Press.

Macklin, A. 2005. "Disappearing Refugees: Reflections on the Canada-U.S. Safe Third Country Agreement." *Columbia Human Rights Law Review* 36: 365–426.

McIntire Peters, K. 2008. "Homeland Security Seeks to Bolster Management, Border Security." 4 February 2008. Last accessed 14 August 2009. http://www.govexec.com/story_page.cfm?articleid=39217&ref=rellink

Min, H., and T. Lambert. 2002. "Truck Driver Shortage Revisited." *Transportation Journal* (December). Last accessed 14 August 2009. http://goliath. ecnext.com/coms2/gi_0199–2766031/Truck-driver-shortage-revisited.html

Mitchell, K. 2001. "Transnationalism, Neo-liberalism, and the Rise of the Shadow State". *Economy and Society* 30, no. 2: 165–89.

Mongia, R. 2003. "Race, Nationality, Mobility: A History of the Passport." In *After the Imperial Turn. Thinking with and through the Nation,* edited by A.M. Burton, 196–215. Durham, NC: Duke University Press.

O'Malley, P. 1996. "Risk and Responsibility." In *Foucault and Political Reason: Liberalism, Neo-Liberalism and Rationalities of Government,* edited by A. Barry, T. Osborne, and N. Rose, 189–207. Chicago: University of Chicago Press.

– 2004. *Risk, Uncertainty, and Government.* London: Glasshouse Press.

Ong, A. 1999. *Flexible Citizenship. The Cultural Logics of Transnationality.* Durham: Duke University Press.

– 2004. "Latitudes of citizenship: Membership, Meaning and Multiculturalism." In *People Out of Place,* edited by A. Brysk and G. Shafir, 53–70. New York and London: Routledge.

– 2006. *Neoliberalism as Exception. Mutations in Citizenship and Sovereignty.* Durham and London: Duke University Press.

Parrett, W.G. 2007. *The Sentinel CEO. Perspective on Security, Risk, and Leadership in a Post 9/11 World.* Hoboken, NJ: John Wiley and Sons.

Pellerin, H. 2004. "Une nouvelle économie politique de la frontière." *A Contrario* 2, no. 2: 58–82.

Pratt, A. 2005. *Securing Borders. Detention and Deportation in Canada.* Vancouver: University of British Columbia Press.

Pratt, A., and S. Thompson. 2008. "Chivalry, 'Race' and Discretion at the Canadian border." *British Journal of Criminology* 48: 620–40.

Reifer, T.E. 2004. "Labor, Race and Empire: Transport Workers and Transnational Empires of Trade, Production and Finance." In *Labor versus Empire:*

Race, Gender, Migration, edited by G. Gilbert, R.F. Gonzalez, V. Price, D. Smith, and L. Trinh Vo, 17–36. London and New York: Routledge.

Rygiel, K. 2006. "Protecting and Proving Identity: The Biopolitics of Waging War through Citizenship in the Post-9/11 Era." In *(En)Gendering the War on Terror. War Stories and Camouflaged Politics*, edited by K. Hunt and K. Rygiel, 145–68. Aldershot: Ashgate.

Salter, M.B. 2003. *Rights of Passage: The Passport in International Relations*. Boulder, London: Lynne Rienner.

Salter, M.B., ed. 2008 *Politics at the Airport*. Minneapolis: University of Minnesota Press.

Sharma, N. 2006. *Home Economics. Nationalism and the Making of "Migrant Workers" in Canada*. Toronto: University of Toronto Press.

Simon, J. 2002. "Taking Risks: Extreme Sports and the Embrace of Risk in Advanced Liberal Societies." In *Embracing Risk. The Changing Culture of Insurance and Responsibility*, edited by T. Baker and J. Simon, 177–208.

Sklair, L. 2001. *The Transnational Capitalist Class*. Oxford: Blackwell.

Smith, A. 1979 [1776]. *An Inquiry into the Nature and Causes of the Wealth of Nations*. Oxford: Oxford University Press.

Sparke, M. 2004. "Passports into Credit Cards: On the Borders and Spaces of Neoliberal Citizenship." In *Boundaries and Belonging. States and Societies in the Struggle to Shape Identities and Local Practices*, edited by J.S.Migdal, 251–83. Cambridge: Cambridge University Press,

– 2006. "A Neoliberal Nexus: Economy, Security and the Biopolitics of Citizenship on the Border." *Political Geography* 25: 151–80.

Stalder, F., and D. Lyon. 2003. "Electronic Identity Cards and Social Classification." In *Surveillance as Social Sorting. Privacy, Risk and Digital Discrimination*, edited by D. Lyon, 77–93. London: Routledge.

Stasiulis, D., and D. Ross. 2006. "Security, Flexible Sovereignty, and the Perils of Multiple Citizenship." *Citizenship Studies* 10, no. 3: 329–48.

Stasiulis, D.K., and A.B. Bakan. 2005. *Negotiating Citizenship. Migrant Women in Canada and the Global System*. Toronto: University of Toronto Press.

Taylor, C. 2004. *Modern Social Imaginaries*. Durham: Duke University Press.

Torpey, J. 2000. *The Invention of the Passport: Surveillance, Citizenship and the State*. Cambridge: Cambridge University Press.

United States. The White House. 2001. "At O'Hare, President Says 'Get on Board.'" 27 September 2001. Last accessed 28 May 2008. http://www.whitehouse.gov/news/releases/2001/09/20010927-1.html

van der Ploeg, I. 2006. "Borderline Identities. The Enrollment of Bodies in the Technological Reconstruction of Borders." In *Surveillance and*

Security. Technological Politics and Power in Everyday Life., edited by T. Mohahan, 177–93. London, New York: Routledge.

Vermond, K. "Life in the Fast Lane." Toronto, *Globe and Mail*, 26 September 2007, R10.

Volpp, L. 2002. "The Citizen and the Terrorist." *UCLA Law Review* 49: 1,575–600.

Wright, A. 2007. "Banned from Canada for a Year for War Protest." *Truth Out*, 30 October 2007. Last accessed 14 August 2009. http://www.truthout.org/article/ann-wright-banned-from-canada-a-year-war-protest

CHAPTER FOUR

Acker, Joan. 2006. *Class Questions, Feminist Answers*. Toronto: Rowman and Littlefield.

Adib, Amel, and Yvonne Guerrier. 2003. "The Interlocking of Gender with Nationality, Race, Ethnicity and Class: The Narratives of Women in Hotel Work." *Gender, Work and Organization* 10, no. 4: 413–32.

Arat-Koç, Sedef. 2006. "Whose Social Reproduction? Transnational Motherhood and Challenges to Feminist Political Economy." In *Social Reproduction: Feminist Political Economy Challenges Neo-liberalism*, edited by K. Bezanson and M. Luxton, 75–92. Montreal and Kingston: McGill-Queen's University Press.

Baines, Donna, and Nandita Sharma. 2002. "Migrant Workers as Non-Citizens: The Case against Citizenship as a Social Policy Concept." *Studies in Political Economy* 69: 75–107.

Basok, Tanya. 2002. *Tortillas and Tomatoes: Transmigrant Mexican Harvesters in Canada*. Montreal and Kingston: McGill-Queen's University Press.

Bezanson, Kate, and Meg Luxton. 2006. *Social Reproduction: Feminist Political Economy Challenges Neoliberalism*. Montreal and Kingston: McGill-Queen's University Press.

Block, Fred. 2002. "Rethinking Capitalism". In *Readings in Economic Sociology*, edited by N. Woolsey Biggart, 219–30. Malden, MA: Blackwell.

Bonacich, Edna. 1976. "Advanced Capitalism and Black/white Race Relations in the United States: A Split Labor Market Interpretation." *American Sociological Review* 41, no. 1: 34–51.

Brand, Dionne. 1999. "Black Women and Work: The Impact of Racially Constructed Gender Roles on the Sexual Division of Labour." In *Scratching the Surface: Canadian Anti-Racist Feminist Thought*, edited by E. Dua and A. Robertson, 83–96. Toronto: Women's Press.

Calliste, Agnes. 2000. "Nurses and Porters: Racism, Sexism and Resistance in Segmented Labour Markets." In *Anti-Racist Feminism: Critical Race and Gender Studies*, edited by A. Calliste and G. Sefa Dei, 143–64. Halifax: Fernwood.

Campion-Smith, Bruce. 2009. "Ontario May Delay Minimum Wage Hike." *Toronto Star*, 27 March.

Canadian Labour Congress (CLC). 2009. *The 2009 Federal Budget: Canadian Labour Congress Analysis*. Ottawa: CLC.

Cheung, Leslie. 2005. *Racial Status and Employment Outcomes*. Ottawa: Canadian Labour Congress.

Cranford, Cynthia J., Leah F. Vosko, and Nancy Zukewich. 2003. "Precarious Employment in the Canadian Labour Market: A Statistical Portrait." *Just Labour* 3: 6–22.

Creese, Gillian. 2007. "Racializing Work/Reproducing White Privilege." In *Work in Tumultuous Times: Critical Perspectives*, edited by V. Shalla and W. Clement, 192–226. Montreal and Kingston: McGill-Queen's Press.

de Wolff, Alice. 2000. *Breaking the Myth of Flexible Work: Contingent Work in Toronto*. Toronto: Contingent Workers Project.

Doeringer, Peter B., and Michael J. Piore. 1971. *Internal Labor Markets and Manpower Analysis*, Lexington, MA: Heath.

Edwards, Richard. 1979. *Contested Terrain: The Transformation of the Workplace in the Twentieth Century*. New York: Basic Books.

Employment Standards Work Group (ESWG). 1996. *Bad Boss Stories: Workers Whose Bosses Break the Law*. Toronto: ESWG.

Fudge, Judy. 1991. "Reconceiving Employment Standards Legislation: Labour Law's Little Sister and the Feminization of Labour." *Journal of Law and Social Policy* 7: 73–89.

– 2001. "Flexibility and Feminization: The New Ontario Employment Standards Act." *Journal of Law and Social Policy* 16: 1–22.

Fudge, Judy, and Eric Tucker. 2000. "Pluralism or Fragmentation? The Twentieth-Century Employment Law Regime in Canada." *Labour/Le Travail* 46: 251–306.

Gabriel, Christina. 1999. "Restructuring at the Margins: Women of Colour and the Changing Economy." In *Scratching the Surface: Canadian Anti-Racist Feminist Thought*, edited by E. Dua and A. Robertson, 127–64.

Galabuzi, Grace Edward. 2004. "Racializing the Division of Labour: Neoliberal Restructuring and the Economic Segregation of Canada's Racialized Groups." In *Challenging the Market: The Struggle to Regulate Work and Income*, edited by J. Stanford and L.F. Vosko, 175–204. Montreal and Kingston: McGill-Queen's University Press.

– 2006. *Canada's Economic Apartheid: The Social Exclusion of Racialized Groups in the New Century*. Toronto: Canadian Scholars Press.

Glenn, Evelyn Nakano. 2001. "Gender, Race, and the Organization of Reproductive Labor." In *The Critical Study of Work: Labor, Technology, and Global Production*, edited by R. Baldoz, C. Kroeber, and P. Kraft, 71–82. Philadelphia: Temple University Press.

Hawkesworth, Mary. 2006. *Feminist Inquiry: From Political Conviction to Methodological Innovation*. New Brunswick, NJ: Rutgers University Press.

Harvey, David. 2006. *The Limits to Capital*. London and New York: Verso.

INTERCEDE. 1993. *Meeting the Needs of Vulnerable Workers: Proposals for Improved Employment Legislation and Access to Collective Bargaining for Domestic Workers and Industrial Homeworkers*. Toronto: INTERCEDE.

Jackson, Andrew. 2005. *Work and Labour in Canada: Critical Issues*. Toronto: Canadian Scholars Press.

Jain, H., and S. Muthu. 1996. "Ontario Labour Law Reforms: A Comparative Study of Bill 40 and Bill 7." *Canadian Labour and Employment Law Journal* 4: 311–30.

Jenson, Jane, Rianne Mahon, and Susan D. Phillips. 2003. "No Minor Matter: The Political Economy of Childcare in Canada." In *Changing Canada: Political Economy as Transformation*, edited by W. Clement and L. Vosko, 135–60. Montreal and Kingston: McGill-Queen's University Press.

Jessop, Bob. 1993. "Towards a Schumpeterian Workfare State? Preliminary Remarks on Post-Fordist Political Economy." *Studies in Political Economy* 40: 7–39.

Kinley, John. 1987. *Evolution of Legislated Standards on Hours of Work in Ontario*. A Report Prepared for the Ontario Task Force on Hours of Work and Overtime. Toronto: Ontario Task Force on Hours of Work and Overtime.

Krahn, Harvey, Graham Lowe, and Karen Hughes. 2006. *Work, Industry and Canadian Society*. 5th ed. Toronto: Thomson Nelson.

Macklin, Audrey. 1994. "On the Inside Looking In: Foreign Domestic Workers in Canada." In *Maid in the Market: Women's Paid Domestic Labour*, edited by W. Giles and S. Arat-Koç, 13–39. Halifax: Fernwood.

McKeen, Wendy, and Ann Porter. 2003. "Politics and Transformation: Welfare State Restructuring in Canada." In *Changing Canada: Political Economy as Transformation*, edited by W. Clement and L. Vosko, 109–34. Montreal and Kingston: McGill-Queen's University Press.

Miles, Robert. 1989. *Racism*. London: Routledge.

Mitchell, Elizabeth. 2003. "The Employment Standards Act 2000: Ontario Opts for Efficiency over Rights." *Canadian Labour and Employment Law Journal* 10, no. 2: 269–86.

Monsebraaten, Laurie. 2009. "The Bitter Reality of Employment Insurance." *Toronto Star*, 25 January.

Murji, Karim, and John Solomos. 2005. *Racialization: Studies in Theory and Practice*. Oxford: Oxford University Press.

Murray, Stuart, and Hugh Mackenzie. 2007. *Bringing Minimum Wages above the Poverty Line*. Ottawa: Canadian Centre for Policy Alternatives.

Ng, Roxana, Renita Yuk-Lin Wong, and Angela Choi. 1999. *Homeworking: Home Office or Home Sweatshop?* Toronto: UNITE.

Ontario. 1991. *Employee Wage Protection Program*. Background No. 91–05. Toronto: Ministry of Labour.

– 2001. *Who Is Covered by the ESA*. Toronto: Ministry of Labour.

Progressive Conservative Party of Ontario (PCPO). 1995. *The Common Sense Revolution*. 7th printing. Toronto: PCPO.

Peck, Jamie. 1996. *Work-Place: The Social Regulation of Labor Markets*. New York and London: The Guilford Press.

– 2001. *Workfare States*. New York and London: The Guilford Press.

Polanyi, Karl. 2001. *The Great Transformation: The Political and Economic Origins of Our Time*. 2d ed. Boston: Beacon Press.

Rubery, Jill, and Frank Wilkinson, eds. 1994. *Employer Strategy and the Labour Market*. Oxford: Oxford University Press.

Saunders, Ron. 2003. *Defining Vulnerability in the Labour Market*. Ottawa: Canadian Policy Research Networks.

Satzewich, Vic. 1991. *Racism and the Incorporation of Foreign Labour: Farm Labour Migration to Canada since 1945*. London and New York: Routledge.

Schenk, Chris. 1995. "Fifty Years after PC 1003: The Need for New Directions." In *Labour Gains, Labour Pains: 50 Years After PC 1003*, edited by C. Gonick, P. Phillips, and J. Vorst, 193–214. Halifax: Fernwood.

Sharma, Nandita. 2006. *Home Economics: Nationalism and the Making of "Migrant Workers" in Canada*. Toronto: University of Toronto Press.

Stasiulis, Daiva K., and Abigail B. Bakan. 2005. *Negotiating Citizenship: Migrant Women in Canada and the Global System*. Toronto: University of Toronto Press.

Statistics Canada. 2008. *The Canadian Immigrant Labour Market in 2007*. Ottawa: Statistics Canada.

Sugiman, Pamela. 2001. "Privilege and Oppression: The Configuration of Race, Gender, and Class in Southern Ontario Auto Plants, 1939 to 1949." *Labour/Le Travail* 47: 83–113.

Teelucksingh, Cheryl, and Grace-Edward Galabuzi. 2005. *Working Precariously: The Impact of Race and Immigrants Status on Employment Opportunities and Outcomes in Canada*. Toronto: Canadian Race Relations Foundation.

Thomas, Mark. 2004. "Setting the Minimum: Ontario's Employment Standards in the Postwar Years, 1944–1968", *Labour/Le Travail: Journal of Canadian Labour Studies* 54: 49–82.

– 2007. "Toyotaism Meets the 60 Hour Work Week: Coercion, 'Consent' and the Regulation of Working Time." *Studies in Political Economy* 80: 105–28.

– 2009. *Regulating Flexibility: The Political Economy of Employment Standards*. Montreal and Kingston: McGill-Queen's University Press.

Vosko, Leah F. 2000. *Temporary Work: The Gendered Rise of a Precarious Employment Relationship*. Toronto: University of Toronto Press.

Wilkinson, Frank, ed. 1981. *The Dynamics of Labour Market Segmentation*. London: Academic Press.

Winsa, Patty. 2009. "Poor Neighbourhoods Growing across Toronto." *Toronto Star*, 8 February.

Wood, Ellen. 1998. "Labor, Class, and State in Global Capitalism." In *Rising from the Ashes? Labor in the Age of 'Global' Capitalism*, edited by E. Meiksins Wood, P. Meiksins, and M. Yates, 3–16. New York: Monthly Review Press.

Workers' Action Centre (WAC). 2007. *Working on the Edge*. Toronto: WAC.

Workers' Action Centre, and Parkdale Community Legal Services (WAC and PCLS). 2008. *Response to "A Consultation Paper on Work through Temporary Help Agencies."* Toronto: WAC.

Yanz, Linda, Bob Jeffcott, Deena Ladd, and Joan Atlin. 1999. *Policy Options to Improve Standards for Women Garment Workers in Canada and Internationally*. Ottawa: Status of Women Canada.

Zeitinoglu, Isik Urla, and Jacinta Khasiala Muteshi. 2000. "Gender, Race and Class Dimensions of Nonstandard Work." *Relations Industrielles/Industrial Relations* 55, no. 1: 133–67.

CHAPTER FIVE

Adkin, L., and Y. Abu-Laban. 2008. "The Challenge of Care: Early Childhood Education and Care in Canada and Quebec." *Studies in Political Economy* 81 (Spring 2008): 49–77.

Bakker, I., and S. Gill, eds. 2004. *Power, Production and Social Reproduction: Human In/security in the Global Political Economy*. London: Palgrave Macmillan.

Bashevkin, S. 2002. *Welfare Hot Buttons: Women, Work, and Social Policy Reform*. Toronto: University of Toronto Press.

Bashevkin, S. 2002. *Women's Work Is Never Done: Comparative Studies in Caregiving* New York: Routledge.

Battle, K. 2006. "Modernizing the Welfare State." *Policy Options* (April-May): 47–50.

– 2008. *A Bigger and Better Child Benefit: A $5,000 Canada Child Tax Benefit*. Ottawa: Caledon Institute of Social Policy.

Battle,K., S. Torman, and M. Mendelson. 2009. *The Red Ink Budget*. Ottawa: Caledon Institute of Social Policy.

– 2006. *More Than a Name Change: The Universal Child Care Benefit*. Ottawa: Caledon Institute of Social Policy.

Battle, K., S. Torjman, M. Mendelson, and E. Tamagno. 2007. *Mixed Brew for the 'Coffee Shop' Budget*. Ottawa: Caledon Institute of Social Policy.

Bezanson, K. 2006. *Gender, the State and Social Reproduction: Household Insecurity in Neo-Liberal Times*. Toronto: University of Toronto Press.

Bezanson, K., and M. Luxton, eds. 2006. *Social Reproduction: Feminist Political Economy Challenges Neo-Liberalism*. Montreal and Kingston: McGill-Queen's University Press.

Brown, W. 2006. "American Nightmare: Neoliberalism, Neoconservatism and De-Democratization." *Political Theory* 34, no. 6: 690–714.

Cameron, B. 2006. "Social Reproduction and Canadian Federalism." In *Social Reproduction: Feminist Political Economy Challenges Neo-Liberalism*, edited by K. Bezanson and M. Luxton, 45–74.

Canada. Department of Finance. 2008. *The Budget Speech 2008: Responsible Leadership*. 26 February. Cat. No. F1–23/2008–1E. Ottawa: Department of Finance Canada.

– Special Committee on Social Services. 1943. *A Report on Social Security for Canada*. Ottawa: House of Commons.

Canadian Centre for Policy Alternatives (CCPA). 2009. *Federal Budget 2009*. Ottawa: CCPA.

Chase, S. 2008. "Small Change for Tighter Times." Toronto, *Globe and Mail*, 27 February. Online edition. Retrieved 27 February at www.theglobeandmail.com/servlet/story/RTGAM.20080227.wbudget27/BNStory/budget2008

Conservative Party of Canada. 2005. *A New $1,200 Choice in Child Care Allowance for Pre-School Kids*. 5 December 2005. Retrieved 3 March 2008 from www.conservative.ca/EN/1091/33693

Cossman, B., and J. Fudge. 2002. *Privatization, Law and the Challenge to Feminism*. Toronto: University of Toronto Press.

Canadian Research Institute for the Advancement of Women (CRIAW). 2006. *New Federal Policies Affecting Women's Equality: Reality Check.* Ottawa: CRIAW.

Curry, B. 2007. *Environment Trumps Economy, Poll Suggests.* Toronto, *Globe and Mail,* 29 January. Online edition: www.theglobeandmail. com. Accessed 12 December 2007.

Drury, S. 2004. "The Making of a Straussian." *The Philosophers* 25.

El Akkad, O. 2008. *Tax-Credit Crackdown on Films Puts Spotlight on Evangelical Community.* Toronto, *Globe and Mail,* 4 March. Online edition: www.theglobeandmail.com. Accessed 4 March 2008.

Finch, J., and J. Mason. 1993. *Negotiating Family Responsibilities.* London and New York: Tavistock/Routledge.

Flanagan, T. 1995. *Waiting for the Wave: The Reform Party and Preston Manning.* Toronto: Stoddart.

– 2007. *Harper's Team.* Montreal and Kingston: McGill-Queen's University Press.

Friedman, M. 1964. *Capitalism and Freedom.* Chicago: University of Chicago Press.

Friendly, M., and J. Beach. 2005. *Early Childhood Education and Care in Canada.* Toronto: Childcare Resource and Research Unit.

Gairdner, W., ed. 1998. *After Liberalism: Essays in Search of Freedom, Virtue, and Order.* Toronto: Stoddart.

Galloway, G. 2007. "Few Companies Keen to Provide Daycare." Toronto, *Globe and Mail,* 27 October. Accessed 27 October 2007 at www.theglobe andmail.com.

– 2000. "Separation, Alberta-Style: It Is Time to Seek a New Relationship with Canada." Toronto, *National Post,* 8 December, A18.

Harper, S. 2002. "Now Is the Time for Social Conservatives to Move Forward, Not Retrench." *The Report Newsmagazine,* 21 January, 17.

– 2003. *Rediscovering the Right Agenda.* Speech to the Civitas meeting. 25 April, Toronto. Retrieved 12 February 2008 from ww.ccicinc.org

– 2008 [1997]. *Speech to the Council for National Policy.* June 1997. Text retrieved March 2008 at ttp://www.ctv.ca/servlet/ArticleNews/story/ CTVNews/20051213/elxn_harper_speech_text_051214/20051214/

Harper, S., and T. Flanagan. 1998. "Conservative Politics in Canada: Past, Present, and Future." In *After Liberalism: Essays in Search of Freedom, Virtue, and Order,* edited by W. Gairdner,168–193.

Harper, S., T. Flanagan, T. Morton, R. Knopff, A. Crooks, and K. Boessenkool. 2001. "Open Letter to Ralph Klein." Toronto, *National Post,* 26 January, A14.

Hayek, F.A. von. 1963. *Individualism and Economic Order*. Chicago: University of Chicago Press.

Johnson, W. 2006. *Stephen Harper and the Future of Canada*. Toronto: McClelland and Stewart.

Laxer, J. 2006. "Is Harper Not for Turning?" *Toronto Star*, 20 January, A21.

Leblanc, D. 2009. "Liberals Gain Stream as Economy Sputters." Toronto, *Globe and Mail*, 20 January. Retrieved 20 January 2009 at http://www.theglobeandmail.com/servlet/story/RTGAM.20090120.wpoll21/BNStory/politics/home

Lewis, J., and S. Giullari. 2005. "The Adult Worker Model, Gender Equality and Care: The Search for New Policy Principles and the Possibilities and Problems of a Capabilities Approach." *Economy and Society* 34, no.1: 76–104.

Luxton, M. 2006. "Friends, Neighbours and Community: A Case Study of the Role of Informal Caregiving in Social Reproduction." In *Social Reproduction: Feminist Political Economy Challenges Neo-Liberalism*, edited by K. Bezanson and M. Luxton, 263–95.

MacDonald, M. 2008. "Stephen Harper and the Theo-Cons: The Rising Clout of Canada's Religious Right." *The Walrus*, 12 February. Available at: www.walrusmagazine.com/print/2006.10–politics-religion-stephen-harper-and-the-theocons/ Retrieved 12 February 2008.

McKeen, W. 2004. *Money in Their Own Name: The Feminist Voice in Poverty Debate in Canada, 1970–1995*. Toronto: University of Toronto Press.

McKeen, W., and A. Porter. 2003. Politics and Transformation: Welfare State Restructuring in Canada. In *Changing Canada: Political Economy as Transformation*, edited by L. Vosko and W. Clement, 109–34. Montreal and Kingston: McGill-Queen's University Press.

Myles, J., and P. Pierson. 1997. "Friedman's Revenge: The Reform of 'Liberal' Welfare States in Canada and the United States." *Politics and Society* 25, no.4: 443–72.

Pierson, P. 1996. "The New Politics of the Welfare State." *World Politics* 48:143–79.

– 2001. *The New Politics of the Welfare State*. New York: Oxford University Press.

Prince, M.J. 1999. "From Health and Welfare to Stealth and Farewell: Federal Social Policy, 1980–2000." In *How Ottawa Spends 1999–2000*, edited by L.A. Pal, 151–96. Toronto: Oxford University Press.

Rice, J.J. 1995. "Redesigning Welfare: The Abandonment of a National Commitment." In *How Ottawa Spends: A More Democratic Canada?*, edited by S.D. Phillips, 185–208. Ottawa: Carleton University Press.

Rice, J.J., and M.J. Prince. 2000. *Changing Politics of Canadian Social Policy*. Toronto: University of Toronto Press.

Simpson, J. 2001. *Message to Stephen Harper: Don't Do It!* Toronto, *Globe and Mail*, 20 July, A13.

Staples, S., and B. Robinson. 2007. *More Than the Cold War: Canada's Military Spending 2007–08*. Foreign Policy Series. Toronto: Canadian Centre for Policy Alternatives.

Statistics Canada. 2007. "Marriages." *The Daily*, 17 January 2007. Ottawa: Statistics Canada.

Ursel, J. 1992. *Private Lives, Public Policy: 100 Years of State Intervention in the Family*. Toronto: Women's Press.

CHAPTER SIX

Adão e Silva, Pedro. 2002. O modelo de welfare da Europa do Sul: Reflexões sobre a utilidade do conceito. *Sociologia, Problemas e Prácticas* 38: 25–59.

Banco de Portugal. 2007. Indicadores de conjuntura, accessed online at www.bportugal.pt on February 8, 2007.

Burton, Mark and Carolyn Kagan. 2006. Decoding *Valuing People*. *Disability & Society* 21(4): 299–313.

Capucha, Luís, Miguel Cabrita, Ana Salvado, Maria Álvares, Ana Lúcia Paulino, Susana Santos, and Rita Mendes. 2004. *Os Impactos do Fundo Social Europeu na Reabilitação Profissional de Pessoas com Deficiência em Portugal*. Vila Nova de Gaia: Centro de Reabilitação Profissional de Gaia.

Carvalho da Silva, Manuel. 2000. Um olhar sobre a evolução da Europa Social. *Sociologia, Problemas e Práticas* 32, 55–68.

Chouinard, Vera and Valorie Crooks. 2005. 'Because they have all the power and I have none': State restructuring of income and employment supports and disabled women's lives in Ontario. *Disability & Society* 20(1): 19–32.

Comissão para a a Análise da Situação Orçamental. 2005. Relatório da Comissão para a a Análise da Situação Orçamental, accessed online at www.portugal.gov.pt on May 30, 2005.

Conselho de Ministros. 2003. Plano nacional para a inclusão social. Resolução do Conselho de Ministros n° 192/2003, *Diário da República*, Série I-B, n°295.

Devlin, Richard and Dianne Pothier 2006. Introduction: Toward a critical theory of de-citizenship. In *Critical disability theory: Essays in philosophy, politics, policy and law,* ed. Dianne Pothier and Richard Devlin 1–22. Vancouver: UBC Press.

Drake, Robert F. 2000. Disabled people, New Labour, benefits and work. *Critical Social Policy* 20(4): 421–439.

Fraser, Nancy. 2005a. Mapping the feminist imagination: From redistribution, to recognition to representation. *Constellations,* 12(3): 295–306.

Fraser, Nancy. 2005b. Reframing justice in a globalizing world. *New Left Review* 36(Nov-Dec): 69–88.

Galvin, Rose. 2006. A genealogy of the disabled identity in relation to work and sexuality. *Disability & Society* 21(5): 499–512.

Grover, Chris and Linda Piggott. 2005. Disabled people, the reserve army of labour and welfare reform. *Disability & Society* 20(7): 705–717.

Hantrais, Linda. 2000. Social policy in the European Union (2nd edition). New York: St. Martin's Press.

Jones, Melinda and Lee-Ann B. Marks. 1999. Law and the social construction of disability. In Disability, divers-ability and legal change, eds. Melinda Jones and Lee-Ann B. Marks 3–24. The Hague and Boston: Kluwer Law International.

Kallianes, Virginia and Phyllis Rubenfeld. 1997. Disabled women and reproductive rights. *Disability & Society* 12(2): 203–221.

Kittay, Eva F. with Bruce Jennings and Angela A. Wasunna. 2005. Dependency, difference and the global ethics of longterm care. *The Journal of Political Philosophy,* 13(4): 443–469.

Leibfried, Stephen and Herbert Obinger. 2001. Welfare state futures: An introduction. In *Welfare state futures,* ed. Stephen Leibfried 1–13. Cambridge: University Press.

Leiria, Paulo. 2000. Enquadramento Geral. In *A reforma da segurança social – Contributos para reflexão,* ed. Pedro Telhado Pereira. Oeiras: Celta Editora.

Marques, Fernando. 1997. *Evolução e Problemas da Segurança Social em Portugal no após-25 de Abril.* Lisboa: Edições Cosmos.

Martins, Bruno S. 2007. Trilhos que tardam: As agendas perdidas na deficiência? *Cadernos Sociedade e Trabalho,* 8: 197–211.

Masuda, Shirley. 1998. *The impact of block funding on women with disabilities.* Ottawa: Status of Women Canada, http://www.swc-cfc.gc.ca/.

Morris, Jenny. 1995. Creating a space for absent voices: Disabled women's experience of receiving assistance with daily living activities. *Feminist Review,* 51(Autumn): 68–93.

Parker, Sarah and Betina Cass. 2005. New paradigms of disability in social security law and policy in Australia: Implications for participation. *Disability Studies Quarterly,* 25(4), http://www.dsq-sds.org.ezproxy.library.yorku.ca/.

Rioux, Marcia and Christopher Riddle. Forthcoming. Values in disability policy and law. In *Critical Perspectives on Human Rights and Disability Law*, ed. Lee Ann Basser, Melinda Jones, & Marcia Rioux. Netherlands: Martinus Nijhoff Publishers.

Rioux, Marcia and Fraser Valentine. 2006. Does theory matter? Exploring the nexus between disability, human rights, and public policy. In *Critical disability theory: Essays in philosophy, politics, policy and law*, ed. Dianne Pothier and Richard Devlin 47–69.Vancouver: UBC Press.

Rodrigues, Eduardo V. 2000. O Estado-Providência e os processos de exclusão social: Considerações teóricas e estatísticas em torno do caso português. *Sociologia*, 10, 173–200.

Roulstone, Alan. 2000. Disability, dependence and the New Deal for disabled people. *Disability & Society* 15(3): 427–443.

Russel, Martha. 2002. What disability civil rights cannot do: Employment and political economy. *Disability & Society* 17(2): 117–135.

Segurança Social. 2001.*Sistema de Solidariedade e Segurança Social*. Accessed online at www.seg_social.pt on 27 August 2005.

Segurança Social. 2005. *A nova Lei de Bases do Sistema de Segurança Social – Lei nº32/2002 de 20 de Dezembro*. Accessed online at www.seg_social.pt on 27 August 2005.

Sousa, Jerónimo, José Luís Casanova, Paulo Pedroso, Andreia Mota, António Teixeira Gomes, Filipa Seiceira, Sérgio Fabela, and Tatiana Alves. 2007. *Elementos de caracterização das pessoas com deficiências e incapacidades em Portugal*. Vila Nova de Gaia: CRPG – Centro de Reabilitação Profissional de Gaia.

Sousa Santos, Boaventura, Manuel Bento, Maldonado Gonelha, and Alfredo Bruto da Costa. 1998. *Uma visão solidária da reforma da segurança social*. Lisboa: União das Mutualidades Portuguesas e Centro de Estudos Sociais da Faculdade de Economia da Universidade de Coimbra.

Titchkosky, Tania. 2003. Governing embodiment: Technologies of constituting citizens with disabilities. *Canadian Journal of Sociology* 28(4): 517–542.

United Nations. 1993. The Standard Rules on the Equalization of Opportunities for Persons with Disabilities. Adopted by the United Nations General Assembly, forty-eighth session, resolution 48/96, annex, of 20 December 1993.

Veiga, Carlos, Jaime Sousa, Natália Nunes and Sérgio Fabela. 2004. *Contributos para um modelo de análise dos impactos do Fundo Social Europeu no domínio das pessoas com deficiência*. Vila Nova de Gaia: Centro de Reabilitação Profissional de Gaia.

Wareing, David and Christopher Newell. 2002. Responsible choice: The choice between no choice. *Disability & Society* 17 (4): 419–434.

Wilton, Robert D. 2006. Working at the margins: Disabled people and the growth of precarious employment. In *Critical disability theory: Essays in philosophy, politics, policy and law,* ed. Dianne Pothier and Richard Devlin 129–150.Vancouver: UBC Press.

Young, Iris M. 1998. Polity and group difference: A critique of the ideal of universal citizenship. In *The citizenship debates: A reader,* ed. Cershon Shafir 263–290. Minneapolis: The Minnesota University Press. Unshaken

CHAPTER SEVEN

Armstrong, H., P. Armstrong, et al. 1997. *Medical Alert: New Work Organizations in Health Care.* Toronto: Garamond Press.

Armstrong, P. and H. Armstrong. 2002. *Wasting Away: The Undermining of Canadian Health Care.* 2d ed. Oxford: Oxford Unversity Press.

Armstrong, P., H. Armstrong, et al. 2000. *Heal Thyself: Managing Health Care Reform.* Toronto: Garamond Press.

Baird, D. 1986. *The Story of Firefighting in Canada.* Erin, ON: The Boston Mills Press.

Bakker, I. 1997. "Identity, Interests and Ideology: The Gendered Terrain of Global Restructuring." In *Globalization, Democratization and Multilateralism.* edited by S. Gill,127–139. Tokyo, New York, Paris: United Nations University Press.

Barrows, D., and H.I. Macdonald. 2000. *The New Public Management: International Developments.* Toronto: Captus Press.

Bledsoe, B. 2007. "Should EMS Be Part of Public Safety? Another Perspective." *Journal of Emergency Medical Services* (2 August 2007), available at http://www.jems.com/news_and_articles/columns/Bledsoe/Should_EMS_Be_ a_Part_of_Public_Safety.html

Bossarte, R. M., and M. Larner. 2004. "Gender and Organizational Change: Integration, Culture and the Fire Service." Retrieved 20 August 2006, from www.nd.edu/soc~2/workpap.

Brodie, J. 2007. "Reforming Social Justice in Neoliberal Times." *Studies in Social Justice* 1, no. 2: 93–107.

Brown, W. (1995). *Finding the Man in the State. States of Injury: Power and Freedom in Late Modernity.* Princeton, NJ: Princeton University Press.

Burstyn, V. (1999). *The Rites of Men: Manhood, Politics and the Culture of Sport.* Toronto: University of Toronto Press.

Chetkovich, C. 1997. *Real Heat: Gender and Race in the Urban Fire Service*. Brunswick, NJ: Rutgers University Press.

Cochrane Times.12 October 2006. "Roles of Fire Service Have Changed." Retrieved 1 Nov. 2006 from www.firefightingnews.com/printerfriendly.cfm?articleID=19130.

Dear, M.J., and J.R. Wolch. 1987. *Landscapes of Despair: From Deinstitutionalization to homelessness*. Princeton, NJ: Princeton University Press.

Fine, M.D. 2007. *A Caring Society? Care and the Dimlemmas of Human Service in the 21rst Century*. Hampshire, UK, and New York: Palgrave Macmillan.

Glasbeek, A. 2006. "My Wife Has Endured a Torrent of Abuse": Gender, Safety, and the Anti-Squeegee Discourses in Toronto 1998–2000." *Windsor Yearbook of Access to Justice* 24: 55–76.

Gordon, S., P. Benner, et al. 1996. Introduction. In *Caregiving: Readings in Knowledge, Practice, Ethics and Politics*. Edited by S. Gordon, P. Benner and N. Noddings, vii-xv. Philadelphia: University of Pennsylvania Press.

Gordon, T. 2005. "Political Economy of Law-and-Order Policing." *Studies in Political Economy* 75 (Spring): 53–78.

Hochschild, A. H. 1979. "Emotion Work, feeling rules and social structure." American Journal of Sociology 85(3):551–75.

Hubbard, P. 2004. "Revenge and Injustice in the Neoliberal City: Uncovering Masculinist Agendas." *Antipode* 36, no.4: 665–86.

International Association of Firefighters AFL-CIO, C. 2001. "The Critical Need for Public Prehospital Care in Canada: Utilizing the Efficiencies of a Fire-Based EMS System." Submission to the Romanow Commission on the Future of Health Care in Canada.

Kimmel, M. (1990). "After Fifteen Years: The Impact of the Sociology of Masculinity on the Masculinity Of Sociology." *Men, Masculinities and Social Theory*. Edited by J. Hearn and D. H. J. Morgan, 93–123. London: Unwin Hyman.

Lasky, R. 2006. *Pride and Ownership: A Firefighter's Love of the Job*. Tulsa, Oklahoma: Pennwell.

Leger-Marketing. 2005. *Professional Barometer*. Montreal: Leger Marketing/Gallup International.

Mosher, J.E. 2000. "Managing the Disentitlements of Women: Glorified Markets, the Idealized Family and the Undeserving Other." In *Restructuring Caring Labour: Discourse, State Practice and Everyday Life*. Edited by S. Neysmith,30–51. Toronto: Oxford University Press.

Ontario Fire Marshall. 2007. *Standard Incident Report Review Revised SIR Codes*. Toronto: Office of the Ontario Fire Marshall.

Ross, J. 2000. "Emergency Medical Services: Groaning While Growing." *Canadian Journal of Emergency Medicine* 2, no. 1: 35.

Scott, C., and K.K. Myers. 2005. "The Socialization of Emotion: Learning Emotion Management at the Fire Station." *Journal of Applied Communication Research* 33, no. 1: 67–92.

Sky, L. 2003. *Crisis Call*. Toronto: Skyworks.

Smeby Jr, L.C. 2005. *Fire and Emergency Services Administration: Management and Leadership Practices*. Boston: Jones and Barlett.

Smith, N. 1996. *The New Urban Frontier: Gentrification and the Revanchist City*. London: Routledge.

Stiehm, J.H. 1982. "The Protected, The Protector, The Defender." *Women's Studies International Forum* 5, nos. 3,4: 367–76.

Tanner, C., P.Benner, et al. 1996. "The Phenomenology of the Patient." In *Caregiving: Readings in Practice, Ethics and Politics*. Edited by S. Gordon, P. Benner, and N. Noddings, 203–19. Philadelphia: University of Pennsylvania Press.

Toronto. 2005. *Toronto Fire Services Annual Report 2005*. Toronto: City of Toronto.

– 2006. *Fire Services Division Annual Report 2006*. Toronto: City of Toronto.

Yarnal, C.M., L. Dowler, et al. 2004. "Don't Let the Bastards See You Sweat: Masculinity,Public and Private Space, and the Volunteer Firehouse." *Environment and Planning A* 36: 685–99.

Young, I.M. 2003. "The Logic of Masculinist Protection: Reflections on the Current Security State." *Signs* 29, no. 1: 1–25.

CHAPTER EIGHT

Armstrong, Pat, and Hugh Armstrong. 1994. *The Double Ghetto: Canadian Women and Their Segregated Work*. 3d ed. Toronto: McClelland and Stewart.

Barrett, Michele, and Mary McIntosh. 1982. *The Anti-Social Family*. London: Verso.

Bezanson, Kate. 2006. *Gender, the State, and Social Reproduction: Household Insecurity in Neo-liberal Times*. Toronto: University of Toronto Press.

Brodie, Janine. 1996. *Women and Canadian Public Policy*. Toronto: Harcourt Brace.

Cohen, Marjorie. 1997. "What Women Should Know about Economic Fundamentalism." *Atlantis. A Women's Studies Journal* 21, no. 2 (Spring/Summer): 97–107.

Day, Shelagh, and Gwen Brodsky. 1998. *Women and the Equality Deficit: The Impact of Restructuring Canada's Social Programs.* Ottawa: Status of Women.

Drolet, Marie. 1999. *The Persistent Gap: New Evidence on the Canadian Gender Wage Gap.* Income Statistics Division, Statistics Canada, Catalogue No. 75F0002MIE99008. Ottawa: Minister of Industry.

Galabuzi, Grace-Edward. 2006. *Canada's Economic Apartheid: The Social Exclusion of Racialized Groups in the New Century.* Toronto: Canadian Scholars' Press.

Gill, Stephen, and Isabella Bakker, eds. 2003. *Power, Production and Social Reproduction: Human In/Security in the Global Political Economy.* Basingstoke, Hampshire: Palgrave Macmillan.

Harvey, David. 2005. *A Brief History of Neoliberalism.* Oxford: Oxford University Press.

Lloyd, Genevieve. 1984. *Man of Reason: "Male" and "Female" in Western Philosophy.* Minneapolis: University of Minnesota Press.

Luxton, Meg. 2001. "Family Responsibilities: The Politics of Love and Care." 32[d] Annual Sorokin Lecture, University of Saskatchewan, Saskatoon.

Luxton, Meg, ed. 1997. Feminism and Families: Critical Policies and Changing Practices. Halifax: Fernwood.

Luxton, Meg, and Ester Reiter. 1997. "Double, Double, Toil and Trouble ... Women's Experience of Work and Family in Canada, 1980–1995." In *Women and the Canadian Welfare State: Challenges and Change, edited by* Patricia Evans and Gerda Wekerle, *197–221.* Toronto: University of Toronto Press.

Luxton, Meg, and June Corman. 2001. *Getting By in Hard Times: Gendered Labour at Home and on the Job.* Toronto: University of Toronto Press.

– 2005. "Families at Work: Making a Living." In *Canadian Families: Diversity, Challenge and Change,* edited by Nancy Mandell and Ann Duffy, 346–72. Toronto: Thompson.

Luxton, Meg, and Bonnie Fox. 2009. "Conceptualizing Family." In *Family Patterns and Gender Bonds* (3d ed.), edited by Bonnie Fox, 3–20. Toronto: Oxford University Press.

Maroney, Heather Jon, and Meg Luxton. 1997. "Gender at Work: Canadian Feminist Political Economy since 1988." In *Understanding Canada: Building on the New Canadian Political Economy,* edited by Wallace Clement, 85–117. Montreal and Kingston: McGill-Queens University Press.

National Council of Welfare. 1999. *Poverty Profile: A Report by the National Council of Welfare 1997.* Ottawa: National Council of Welfare.

National Union of Public and General Employees. "Newfoundland offers to negotiate pay equity settlement." http://www.nupge.ca/news_2005/no7deo5a.htm (posted 7 December 2005; viewed on 24 March 2009.

Phillipps, Lisa. 2002. "Tax Law and Social Reproduction: The Gender of Fiscal Policy in and Age of Privatization." In *Privatization, Law, and the Challenge to Feminism,* edited by Brenda Cosman and Judy Fudge, 41–85. Toronto: University of Toronto.

Statistics Canada. 2000. *Women in Canada 2000: A Gender-Based Statistical Report* Ottawa: Minister of Industry.

Strathern, Marilyn. 1992. *After Nature: English Kinship in the Late Twentieth Century* Cambridge: Cambridge University Press.

Thatcher, Margaret. 1987. "Interview." *Women's Own* (31 October).

Townsen, Monica. 2000. "Women in Canada Remain Among 'Poorest of the Poor.'" *The CCPA Monitor* 7, no. 1. The Canadian Centre for Policy Alternatives, May.

Vosko, Leah. 2000. *Temporary Work: The Gendered Rise of a Precarious Employment Relationship.* Toronto: University of Toronto Press.

Wallis, Maria, and Sui-Ming Kwok. 2008. *Daily Struggles: The Deepening Racialization and Feminization of Poverty in Canada* Toronto: Canadian Scholars' Press.

Yalnizian, Armine. 1998. *The Growing Gap: A Report on Growing Inequality Between the Rich and the Poor in Canada.* Toronto: The Centre for Social Justice.

CHAPTER NINE

Ali, T. 2003. *The Clash of Fundamentalisms: Crusades, Jihads and Modernity.* London: Versa.

Armstrong, Pat, and Hugh Armstrong. 2005. "Public and Private: Implications for Care Work." *Sociological Review* 53, series 2: 167–87.

Armstrong, Pat, Hugh Armstrong, and M. Patricia Connelly. 1997. "Privatization." *Studies in Political Economy* 53 (Summer):1–5.

Armstrong, Pat. 1997. "The Welfare State as History." In *The Welfare State in Canada*, edited by Raymond Blake, Penny Bryden, and J. Frank Strain, 52–71. Concord ON: Irwin.

Armstrong, Pat, and Hugh Armstrong. 1978. *The Double Ghetto: Canadian Women and Their Segregated Work.* Toronto: McClelland and Stewart.

Armstrong, Pat, Carol Amaratunga, Jocelyne Bernier, Karen Grant, Ann Pederson, and Kay Willson, eds. 2002. *Exposing Privatization: Women and Health Care Reform.* Aurora, ON: Garamond.

Armstrong, Pat, and Kate Laxer. 2006. "Precarious Work, Privatization, and the Health Care Industry: The Case of Ancillary Workers." In *Precarious Employment: Understanding Labour Market Insecurity in Canada*, edited by Leah Vosko, 115–38. Montreal: McGill-Queen's University Press.

Baines, Donna. 2004. "Caring for Nothing: Work Organization and Unwaged Labour in Social Services." *Work, Employment and Society* 18, no. 2: 267–95.

Bernstein, Stephanie, Katherine Lippel, Eric Tucker, and Leah Vosko. 2006. "Precarious Employment and the Laws Flaws: Identifying Regulatory Failure and Securing Effective Protection for Workers" In *Precarious Employment: Understanding Labour Market Insecurity in Canada*, edited by Leah Vosko, 203–20.

Canada. 2002. *Building on Values: Report of the Commission on the Future of Health Care in Canada* (Romanow Report). Ottawa: Commission on the Future of Health Care in Canada.

Canadian Broadcasting Corporation (CBC). 1999. Henry Mintzberg in Conversation. "Ideas." Toronto: CBC.

Canadian Institute of Health Information. 2005. Canada's Health Care Providers." 2005 Chartbook. Ottawa: Canadian Institute of Health Information, available at http://secure.cihi.ca/cihiweb/dispPage.jsp?cw_page=PG_409_E&cw_topic=409&cw_rel=AR_35_E

Chaoulli v. Quebec (Attorney General), 2005 SCC 35, [2005] 1 S.C.R. 791 Date: 9 June 2005. http://csc.lexum.umontreal.ca/en/2005/2005scc35/2005scc35.html

Cohen, Marjorie Griffin, and Marcy Cohen. 2004. *A Return to Wage Discrimination: Pay Equity Losses Through Privatization in Health Care*. Vancouver: Canadian Centre for Policy Alternatives.

Contenta, Sandro, Jim Rankin, Betsy Powell, and Patty Winsa. 2008. "Why Getting Tough on Crime Is Toughest on the Taxpayer." *Toronto Star*, 19 July, A1, A14.

Evans, Robert. 1993. "Health Care Reform: The Issue from Hell." *Policy Options* (July-August): 35–41.

Exworthy, Mark, and Susan Halford. 1999. *Professionals and the New Managerialism in the Public Sector*. Philadelphia: Open University Press.

Fox, Bonnie, ed. 1980. *Hidden in the Household*. Toronto: The Women's Press.

Grant, Karen R. C.Amaratunga, P.Armstrong, M.Boscoe, A. Pederson, K.Willson, eds. 2004. *Caring For/Caring About: Women, Homecare and Unpaid Caregiving*. Aurora, ON: Garamond.

Guberman, Nancy. 2004. "Designing Home and Community Care for the Future: Who Needs to Care?" In *Caring For/Caring About: Women, Homecare and Unpaid Caregiving*, edited by Karen Grant et al., 75–90.

Hamilton, Roberta. 1978. *The Liberation of Women*. London: Allen and Unwin.

Health Services and Support–Facilities Subsector Bargaining Assn. v. British Columbia, 2007 SCC 27, [2007] 2 S.C.R. 391 Date: 8 June 2007.

Klein, Naomi. 2007. *The Shock Doctrine. The Rise of Disaster Capitalism*. Toronto: Knopf Canada.

Lilly, Meredith B., Audrey Laporte, Peter C. Coyte. 2007. "Labor Market Work and Home Care's Unpaid Caregivers: A Systematic Review of Labor Force Participation Rates, Predictors of Labor Market Withdrawal, and Hours of Work. *The Milbank Quarterly* 85(4): 641–90.

Luxton, Meg. 1980. *More than a Labour of Love: Three Generations of Women's Work in the Home*. Toronto: The Women's Press.

Marsh, Leonard. 1975. *Report on Social Security for Canada 1943*. Toronto: University of Toronto Press.

Martin, Brendon. 1993. *In the Public Interest? Privatization and Public Sector Reform*. London: Zed Books.

Mimoto, H., and P. Cross. 1991. *The Growth of the Federal Debt*. Canadian Economic Observer (June): 1–17.

Mintzberg, Henry. 1979. *The Structuring of Organizations (1979)*. New York: Prentice-Hall.

Morton, Peggy. 1972. "Women's Work Is Never Done." In *Women Unite: An Anthology of the Canadian Women's Movement*, 46–68. Toronto: Canadian Women's Educational Press.

National Forum on Health. 1997. *Building on the Legacy Volume 2*. Ontario: Minister of Public Works and Government Services.

Ontario Health Coalition. 2004. "Over $100 Million Wasted in Secretive P3 Hospital Deal." Media release. 6 August. http://www.web.net/ ohc/ 040806.htm 4.5k 24/Apr/2006. Downloaded 16 July 2008.

Osberg, Lars. 2008. *A Quarter Century of Economic Inequality in Canada 1981–2006*. Ottawa: Canadian Centre for Policy Alternatives.

Osborne, David, and Ted Gaebler. 1993. *Reinventing Government: How the Entrepreneurial Spirit Is Transforming the Public Sector*. New York: Penguin.

Pollock, A., J. Shaoul, and N. Vickers. 2002. "Private Finance and 'Value for Money' in NHS Hospitals: A Policy in Search of a Rationale." *British Medical Journal* 324(18 May):1,205–9.

Royal Commission on Health Services (Hall Commission). 1964. *Report*. Ottawa: Queen's Printer.

Seccombe, Wally. 1974. "The Housewife and Her Labour under Capitalism." *New Left Review* (January/February):3–24.

Shapiro, Evelyn. 1997. *The Cost of Privatization: A Case Study of Home Care in Manitoba*. Ottawa: Canadian Centre for Policy Alternatives.

Stein, Janice Gross. 2001. *The Cult of Efficiency.* Toronto: Anansi.

Stiglitz, Joseph. 2008. "A Global Lesson in Market Failure." Toronto, *Globe and Mail*, 7 July, A17.

Taylor, Malcolm. 1987. *Health Insurance and Canadian Public Policy.* Montreal: McGill-Queen's University Press.

Toronto Star. 2008. "Ottawa Invests $25M in Ethanol Plant." 19 July, A19.

Tucker, Eric. 2006. "Will the Vicious Circle of Precariousness Be Unbroken? The Exclusion of Ontario Farm Workers from the Occupational Health and Safety Act." In *Precarious Employment: Understanding Labour Market Insecurity in Canada*, edited by Leah Vosko, 277–98.

Ursel, Jane. 1992. *Private Lives. Public Policy.* Toronto: The Women's Press.

Vosko, Leah, ed. 2006. *Precarious Employment: Understanding Labour Market Insecurity in Canada.* Montreal: McGill-Queen's University Press.

Index

fire services: cost reduction, 138–9;
   health care provision, 136–8;
   socioeconomic conditions, 147
Flanagan, T., 94–5
Foucault, M.: liberalism study, 41;
   and power and resistance, 134
freedom: social, 9–10; of young
   people, 28
Friedman, M., 7, 11, 29, 93
fundamentalism: market, 184; religious, 35, 95–6, 200

gender: and disability, 113–15;
   health care provision, 149–50;
   inequality in the labour force, 74,
   169; and racism, 72; regimes,
   12–16
genocide, racialization and, 16
globalization: defined, 23; fear of
   uncompetitiveness, 36; just regulation of, 4
governance: debt and deficit reduction, 108; quality of, 12
governments: accountability, 198,
   199; Conservative, 92–3; support
   to private corporations, 192–3
Group of Twenty (G20), and
   market principles, 5

Hall Royal Commission on Health
   Services, 191
Harper, Stephen: intellectual approach of, 91–8, 108; social reproduction, 107
Harris, Mike, and restructuring, 76,
   167, 171
Harvey, D., 29, 35, 76, 166
Hayek, F.A. von, 7–12, 29, 93–4
health care: allocation to fire services, 143; Canadian Charter of

Rights and Freedoms challenge,
   195; chronic care reform, 136–7,
   143–8; deinstitutionalization,
   141–7; firefighter's record keeping, 152; loss of rights, 193;
   privatization, 24, 192, 194;
   responsibility, perceptions of,
   171–4, 179; state withdrawal
   from, 160
housing, privatization, 24
human capital: development of, 42;
   and global trade, 53

identity: created through market
   exchanges, 58; personal and societal, 176–7
immigrants, and low incomes, 78
immigration, 34, 47–8, 52–7, 83–5,
   186
inclusiveness, 132–3
income: support, changes to, 137;
   and women's sustenance, 109
individual, individualism: choice,
   personal, 174–7; commodification, inherent limits of, 36;
   cultural change, 27; employment
   standards, 83–5; entitlement, 51;
   freedom, 7–8, 10, 19, 41–3; gender regimes,12–16; risk management, 38–9; self-reliance and the
   workplace, 77; social relations, 11
inequality: class, racialized, 169;
   public and private, boundaries of,
   186, 189; racialized, 77–8;
   wealth and chance, 160. See also
   equality, equity, inequity
inequity: labour market, 12; 2008
   crisis, 10; Universal Child Care
   Benefit, 100–1. See also equality,
   equity, inequality